GLOBAL CHILDHOODS

019

For Mabel and Olive
For Tim

GLOBAL CHILDHOODS

~ *ISSUES AND DEBATES* ~

KATE CREGAN AND *DENISE CUTHBERT*

Los Angeles | London | New Delhi
Singapore | Washington DC

Los Angeles | London | New Delhi
Singapore | Washington DC

SAGE Publications Ltd
1 Oliver's Yard
55 City Road
London EC1Y 1SP

SAGE Publications Inc.
2455 Teller Road
Thousand Oaks, California 91320

SAGE Publications India Pvt Ltd
B 1/I 1 Mohan Cooperative Industrial Area
Mathura Road
New Delhi 110 044

SAGE Publications Asia-Pacific Pte Ltd
3 Church Street
#10-04 Samsung Hub
Singapore 049483

Editor: Chris Rojek
Editorial assistant: Gemma Shields
Production editor: Katherine Haw
Copyeditor: Mary Dalton
Proofreader: Rosemary Morlin
Indexer: Kay Dreyfus
Marketing manager: Michael Ainsley
Cover design: Lisa Harper
Typeset by: C&M Digitals (P) Ltd, Chennai, India
Printed in India at Replika Press Pvt Ltd

© Kate Cregan and Denise Cuthbert 2014

First published 2014

Library of Congress Control Number: 2014930432

British Library Cataloguing in Publication data

A catalogue record for this book is available from the British Library

ISBN 978-1-4462-0899-1
ISBN 978-1-4462-0900-4 (pbk)

MIX
Paper from
responsible sources
FSC® C016779

At SAGE we take sustainability seriously. Most of our products are printed in the UK using FSC papers and boards. When we print overseas we ensure sustainable papers are used as measured by the Egmont grading system. We undertake an annual audit to monitor our sustainability.

CONTENTS

ABOUT THE AUTHORS

Kate Cregan is the author of *Sociology of the Body* (2006), *The Theatre of the Body* (2009) and *Key Concepts in Body and Society* (2012). The majority of her writing and research is on understandings of embodiment across time, space and cultures, with particular reference to medical interpretations of the body, medical technologies and the representation of the body in images. She has two allied research interests, in ethics (human, social and research) and how the praxis of becoming a writer informs the process of becoming a researcher. She has extensive experience teaching and researching in the humanities and social sciences, including teaching ethics to medical students. Currently, she is co-ordinator and senior lecturer of the interdisciplinary Graduate Researchers in Print (GRiP) programs in the Faculty of Arts, Monash University and is a Visiting Fellow in the School of Graduate Research at RMIT University.

Denise Cuthbert has published extensively on children and children's issues in the fields of adoption, child removal and child placement. With Marian Quartly and Shurlee Swain, she is the co-author of *The Market in Babies: Stories of Adoption in Australia* (2013); and with Ceridwen Spark edited *Other People's Children: Adoption in Australia* (2009). Her research has investigated Indigenous child removal, intercountry adoption, adoption policy and practice, the management of children in disasters, and child abuse in Malaysia. It appears in leading journals including *Social Policy and Society, International Social Welfare, Australian Journal of Politics and History, Journal of Historical Sociology* and many others. Currently she is the Dean of the School of Graduate Research at RMIT University. Related to this role, she maintains an active research and publication program in higher education policy, pedagogy and practice.

ACKNOWLEDGEMENTS

The authors' primary thanks go to the editor, Chris Rojek, and to the editorial assistants who saw this book through from beginning to end: Jai Seaman, Martine Jonsrud and Gemma Shields. They would also like to thank the people who, directly or indirectly, supported the completion of the manuscript. Special thanks are owed to Kay Dreyfus who offered expert assistance in pulling the final manuscript together.

Kate's sincere thanks are extended to the 2010 students of *Global Childhoods*; all those at *Mixed Business* (especially Lauren, Tom, Lauren, Erin and Ash); John Waugh; Camille and Rebecca Robinson; and of course her co-author Denise Cuthbert, all of whom actively sustained her through the long process of writing the book. In particular, Kate acknowledges the extraordinary generosity, friendship and support of Professor Tomi Kushner of the University of California, Berkeley and Professor Doris Schroder of UCLAN, respectively editor-in-chief and section editor of the *Cambridge Quarterly of Healthcare Ethics*, the journal in which Kate first worked through ideas that appear in their final form in Chapter 9.

Denise wishes to acknowledge Professor Daine Alcorn, formerly Deputy Vice Chancellor Research and Innovation at RMIT for her support for the research and writing of this book. Thanks are also extended to her excellent colleagues in the School of Graduate Research at RMIT for generously making allowances for her to write which on occasion added extra work and responsibilities to their loads. Denise's ideas on children and childhood were challenged and informed through several research collaborations: first, with Professors Marian Quartly and Shurlee Swain who were co-investigators on the Australian Research Council funded History of Adoption in Australia project; second, with Ceridwen Spark and Patricia Fronek; and thirdly, with Yarina Ahmad, whose doctoral work on child abuse in Malaysia informs the Malaysian case study in Chapter 3, and Sara Niner. Ideas developed in this book owe much to this earlier work and these wonderful colleagues. Thanks are also owed to her co-author, Kate Cregan; and, finally, Tim North for his love, support and willingness to pick up the slack while the book was being completed.

The authors and publishers would like to express their thanks for the following permissions:

Cregan, K. (2013) '"Who Do You Think You Are?": Childhood and Identity in Australian Healthcare Ethics', *Cambridge Quarterly of Healthcare Ethics*, 22 (3): 232–37. Copyright © 2013 Cambridge University Press. Reprinted with permission.

Cregan, K. (2014) 'Sex Definitions and Gender Practices: An Update from Australia', *Cambridge Quarterly of Healthcare Ethics*, 23 (3): in press. Copyright © 2014 Cambridge University Press. Reprinted with permission.

LIST OF ABBREVIATIONS AND ACRONYMS

ACERWC	African Committee of Experts on the Rights and Welfare of the Child
ACRWC	African Charter on the Rights and Welfare of the Child
ADF	Australian Defence Force
AI	Artificial Insemination
AIHW	Australian Institute for Health and Welfare
ARTs	Assisted Reproductive Technologies
ASPCA	American Society for the Prevention of Cruelty to Animals
BMIs	Body Mass Indices
CAAFAG	Children Associated with Armed Forces or Armed Groups
CHH	Child Headed Households
DDR	Disarmament, Demobilisation and Reintegration
ECCE	early childhood care and education
FGM	Female Genital Mutilation
GD	Gender Dysphoria
GDRC	Geneva Declaration on the Rights of the Child
GID	Gender Identity Disorder
HIC	High-Income Country
HIV/AIDS	Human Immunodeficiency Virus/ Acquired Immunodeficiency Syndrome
HREOC	Human Rights and Equal Opportunity Commission (Australia)
ICA	Inter-country Adoption
ICRC	International Committee of the Red Cross
ILO	International Labour Organization
IVF	In Vitro Fertilisation
LIC	Low-Income Country
MDGs	Millennial Development Goals
MIC	Middle-Income Country
NYSPCA	New York Society for the Prevention of Cruelty to Animals
NYSPCC	New York Society for the Protection of Cruelty to Children
OECD	Organisation for Economic Development and Co-operation
PID	preimplantation diagnostic screening
PTSD	Post-Traumatic Stress Disorder
RSPCA	Royal Society for the Protection of Cruelty to Animals
SCAN	Suspected Child Abuse and Neglect (Malaysia)
STIs	Sexually Transmitted Infections
UHMs	Unaccompanied Humanitarian Minors
UN	United Nations
UNCRC	United Nations Convention on the Rights of the Child

UNDRC   United Nations Declaration on the Rights of the Child
UNHCR   United Nations High Commissioner for Refugees
UNICEF   United Nations International Children's Emergency Fund
UNUDHR   United Nations Universal Declaration of Human Rights
WB   World Bank
WHO   World Health Organization

Part One

KEY IDEAS AND THEORETICAL APPROACHES IN THE STUDY OF CHILDREN AND CHILDHOOD

1

KNOWING CHILDREN: THEORY AND METHOD IN THE STUDY OF CHILDHOOD

- Policies and practices aimed at 'protecting the best interests' and 'the rights of the child' are premised on Global Northern ideas of children and childhood.

- The Global Northern understanding of children and childhood is strongly influenced by theories of children as adults in 'development', which permeates a range of fields of intellectual endeavour (e.g. education, law, medicine).

- That approach is increasingly subject to analysis and criticism, based on the theoretical approaches that see children as partaking in a process of socialization (e.g. sociology, anthropology, politics).

- As a result of the intensification of various globalizing forces, those ideas are becoming dominant around the world, although they remain unevenly adopted and openly contested, both by national systems and in local practices.

INTRODUCTION

Anyone who has seen the globally syndicated genealogical documentary programme *Who Do You Think You Are?* (Wall to Wall and BBC 1, 2004–present) will have some familiarity with just how much childhood can depend on economic, social, political and geographic context. The popularity of tracing family ancestry in the Global North, which has grown exponentially over the past 30 years or so, necessarily begins with returning to the subject's origins and from there traces back through the births (and deaths) of forebears. It is, in essence, a project that can only be achieved by searching through successive lifespans and therefore successive childhoods.

What is a child? On one level the answer to this question may appear blindingly simple.

1. A child is a young human being.

2. A child is in the stage of life known as childhood.

3. A child is *not* an adult.

These intuitive answers seem to be straightforward truth statements. But are the key terms used in our discussion, child and childhood, so easily delineated and defined by seeing them paired with obverse terms, adult and adulthood? What about adolescents and teenagers: are they necessarily children? Are they uniformly *not* adults? When applied to the lived realities of specific people, do these responses even begin to answer our primary question?

A cursory glance at relatively recent history swiftly yields the answer, no. From the 1920s onwards, children and childhood came to be understood and approached in developed, modern societies in ways that were utterly foreign prior to, and for the majority of the world's population at, that time. This was the result of militation for reform in the treatment of children over the nineteenth century that slowly led to the events, proclamations and declarations that culminated in the UN Convention on the Rights of the Child (UNCRC 1989). The UNCRC, at which we shall look in some detail in Chapter 3 of this book, is the keystone in contemporary constructions of childhood and the demarcation of the child as a specific form of human being (Bhabha, 2006) on a global scale.

In the spirit of genealogical television, we begin our historical contextualization of 'the child' with examples from the British and Australian experience of the lives of three specific children living just prior to the 1920s – Bob Ingham, Nell Duffy and Lance Davey – a time when child reform movements were gaining significant strength internationally but before they were codified by the League of Nations in the Geneva Declaration of the Rights of the Child (1924). Each of these narratives illustrates an aspect of our point about the historically contingent nature of contemporary views of childhood, at that turning point in the construction of the Global Northern child.

By 1915, aged 15, Robert (Bob) Ingham was sailing the Mediterranean, indentured in the British Merchant Navy as it regularly supplied the Royal Navy during the First World War.[1] Bob had left his home near Stroud in Gloucestershire, where his widowed mother and younger siblings remained. In later life, Bob claimed that he 'jumped ship' in Melbourne around 1921, and went 'bush', and indeed his Merchant Navy record does not give a discharge date. In 1927 he married Agnes (Anne) Duffy, the younger sister of Nell Duffy. Nell Duffy and Lance Davey were the grandparents of Kate Cregan, one of the authors of this book.

As had been the case for several centuries in the UK, sending a son to sea was a recognized way of ensuring that he acquired further skills or practical training, had secure employment that kept him fed and sheltered, and enabled him to contribute to the family income. An apprenticeship in the Merchant Navy was a recognized path to a career at sea in what was, at that time, a thriving industry. As its name implied, the Merchant Navy was unlike the Royal Navy in being based on trade rather than warfare. The Merchant Navy was not as socially prestigious as the Royal Navy, but it was a job with potential prospects.[2] A youth's wages and rank might reflect his 'junior' status and inexperience, but he would be expected to behave, to all intents and purposes, as an adult (Heywood, 2001).

Ellen (Nell) Duffy was unusual for a girl growing up in a large family in the Australian bush in the second decade of the twentieth century – outback of the mining town Broken Hill, NSW – in still being in school at the age of 14. Nell's sister Edith, two years older, was already married and had had a daughter at the age of 15. Amenities in the family home were few and utilities non-existent: there was no plumbing, electricity, gas, bathroom, laundry or toilet. All the washing was done by hand, outside, and a wood stove was the only means of cooking and heating water. Washing and cooking were labour intensive core tasks and were exclusively viewed as women's work (Roberts, 1985). When in 1916 Nell's mother gave birth to Jack, her tenth and last live birth (of 12 full-term pregnancies, eight of whom survived into adulthood), Nell left school. Summoned from the classroom by her younger brother Carl, Nell was expected to take over her mother's household duties and the baby's care during her mother's month of 'lying in'. By the time Nell was called home from school in 1916, candles, soap, shoes and cloth could be bought in Broken Hill but in addition to cooking and hand-washing, knitting, sewing, milking, and butter- and cheese-making remained common domestic duties. With her elder sister married, her one older brother in work and eight younger siblings to care for, it was both a practical and logical choice for Nell to start work in the home.

Lance Davey was 16 in April 1917 when he took part in an armed robbery in Footscray – a working-class suburb of greater Melbourne – in the company of another young man. Lance had left school (having achieved the 'qualifying certificate') and was employed as an 'electrical improver' in a small city engineering company, Hoey and Bowen's, where he had met his accomplice, Walter Gleeson (*Advertiser*, 8 September 1917: 3). Lance had turned 17 by the time he was apprehended in September 1917, and although his legal counsel argued he should be tried in the Children's Court because he was 'under seventeen' at the time of the offence, Mr Brown of the Criminal Prosecution Service and the presiding magistrate disagreed (*Advertiser*, 1 September 1917: 2). Founded in 1906, the Children's Court of Victoria was a recent, and professedly enlightened, innovation for the specialized handling of legal cases involving those 16 and younger, whether as malefactors or in cases to determine guardianship. However, the fact remained that those who had reached the age of 17 were considered mature and rational enough to be fully culpable for their actions and to be tried, sentenced and imprisoned as adults (Carrington and Pereira, 2009).

Accordingly Lance was charged, tried and found guilty as an adult before the Supreme Court of Victoria and sentenced to three months' imprisonment, suspended on his 'entering into bonds to be of good behaviour for three years' (*Argus*, 19 September 1917: 11). Had the sentence not been suspended, it is highly likely Lance would have been sent to the formidable Pentridge Prison. Gleeson, the owner of the gun, had already served three months in prison for the hold-up (*Weekly News*, 8 September 1917: 2), and subsequently received six months 'with hard labour' for related thefts from Hoey and Bowen (*Advertiser*, 1 September: 3).

The histories of these three young people from Kate Cregan's family are replicated by the experiences of their contemporaries in the first decades of the twentieth century, or at least by those of similar socio-economic backgrounds. In the context of contemporary understandings of childhood – with compulsory schooling, restrictions on employment for people under 17 and legal frameworks in line with the UNCRC that assume not-yet-fully-developed responsibility for those under 18 – these narratives may seem to reveal conditions of childhood and youth that are exploitative and unjust. And yet, none of these young people considered these events, nor the expectations placed on them, nor their treatment to be unusual. None of these three young people could vote until they turned 21[3] and when in paid employment received lower than adult wages: but, in practice, they were functioning as responsible (or irresponsible) citizens long before that age.[4] Further, their experiences were, at the time, relatively enlightened. As we shall see in Chapter 3 in relation to child labour reform in the nineteenth century, the fact that these young people had been in school until 13 or more was a very different state of affairs from their own parents' or grandparents' generations.

In the early twentieth century, most young people in the Global North over the age of 14 were expected to be in full-time work, whether paid or in the home, unless they were of a class that could afford to keep them idle or in schooling long enough to become professionals. As we shall see in Chapter 5, children were on street-corners in the largest cities in the USA, selling newspapers and organizing against their employers when required (Gillespie, 2013). From other US examples we can also see that children in agricultural families were expected to contribute to the family's economic enterprises:

> Remembering her own childhood in Massachusetts in the years 1806 to 1823, Elizabeth Buffum Chace recalled: 'In this house, besides the ordinary housework of those days, various manufactures were carried on: candle making, soap making, butter and cheese making, spinning, weaving, dyeing and of course all the knitting and sewing, the dressmaking and tailoring and probably the shoe making and the millinery of the large household were performed within its limits – and the children, whether native or adopted, began very early to do their share.' (Lovell, 1937: 4, cited in Stern et al., 1975)

From these brief and very specific examples we can begin to map an approach to exploring rather than simply answering our primary question, and to canvassing the meanings of what it is to be a child and what constitutes childhood. Already we can see a vision of children and childhood radically different from dominant contemporary ideas, having perhaps more in common with some of the lived realities of children in developing and under-developed countries that we shall encounter in the case studies in Part Two. The task of Part One, therefore, is to analyse and contextualize those dominant notions as historically and politically informed.

What we demonstrate throughout *Global Childhoods* is that the dominant approaches to children and childhood embedded in UNCRC owe at least as much to the history of knowledge in Western Europe as they do to contemporary, or historical, issues affecting children. The study and interpretation of efforts to militate for better treatment of children, and the policies formulated around children and childhood are all embedded in more generalized social and political upheavals of the nineteenth and twentieth centuries. As we will show, the understanding and regulation of the embodied lives of children has mutated along with wider epistemological shifts (Elias, 2000; Foucault, 1991; Ariès, 1962) and just which fields of knowledge are considered appropriate in the upward shaping of children has changed over time.

GLOBAL CHILDHOODS

In Western Europe, religion provided the guiding hand for much of the ethical and moral considerations around children and childhood until at least the end of the seventeenth century. Religious dogma pervaded common cultural expectations of appropriate social and filial relations ('honour thy mother and father both') whether one had access to formal education or not. The offspring of the wealthy and rising classes received these tenets as promulgated in early educational theory and administered in early educational practices (Erasmus, 1530; Castiglione, 1528; Luke, 1989). As Western European nations set about seeding their empires around the globe, they also began the long and ongoing process of globalizing Global Northern culture and knowledge (see, for example, Said, 1978; Schiebinger, 1993) through such processes as education. Children, and understandings of childhood, therefore were amongst the earliest objects of colonization and cultural domination (Fass, 2007). Such processes have been slow and uneven, yet global childhoods shaped in the image of Global Northern childhoods have been in formation for centuries.

As state structures became more secular across Europe from the eighteenth century onwards, many religiously informed attitudes towards the upbringing of children, their proper treatment and their role in society remained in place, but appeared in less spiritual and increasingly 'liberal' guises (Locke, 1690, 1693; Rousseau, 1762; Piaget 1972). Or, rather, the agreed moral and ethical precepts that were once the exclusive domain of faith persisted but became absorbed and naturalized into less spiritual, more scientific practice. As we shall see in more detail in Chapter 2, the notions of children and childhood with which we are familiar in Global Northern cultures today emerged out of these secular inheritors of spiritual assumptions and approaches. The child was presented through a range of relevant expert knowledge systems that over centuries have hardened into realms of professionalism (Foucault 1975, 1988, 1991). In particular, the professional realms of law, medicine and education have been paramount in defining, delimiting and regulating children both at the centre and the periphery of colonial empires. By the late nineteenth century, psychology and sociology also began to play a significant part in the theorization of childhood.

In late- or post-modernity, the theoretical questions posed in these various disciplinary fields (education, law, medicine, psychology, sociology) are accepted as 'legitimate', and are dominant in the formation of knowledge concerning children and childhood. Around the globe, laws both define and defend the division between adult and child. For example, those defined as children under the law are not necessarily held accountable for their actions to the same degree as those recognized as adults, and are often incarcerated in separate institutions. Medicine has specialities and sub-specialities devoted to the care of children, from gametes onwards. Reproductive medicine, foetal medicine, paediatrics, child and adolescent health and all their sub-specialities are focused on the body of the (legally defined) child. Education is upheld as a universal right of children and conceived of as a primary means of 'training up' children into adulthood. Psychology is committed to an understanding of children as the natural precursor to adults in 'development': malleable, vulnerable and also in need of specialist treatment according to the stage of development. Sociology looks at both the local and the global socio-political and environmental determinants that affect children and childhoods as objects in themselves. As we shall see in our case studies in Part Two, just how evenly these principles are applied, within and across cultures, is less clear-cut.

Each of these authoritative fields' construction of 'the child' in the Global North has been disseminated within the slow and uneven processes of globalization during the European imperial colonization of Asia, the Americas, Africa and Australasia. This process intensified in and across the twentieth century, as children and childhood increasingly became specific objects of concern on a global scale in the activities of non-government social reformers, in the deliberations of the League of Nations and subsequently at the United Nations. The fact that geopolitical power was centred in the Global North over the course of much of the twentieth century – and that proceedings, policies and conventions in those global bodies were, as a result, infused with Global Northern 'world views' – has led to the domination of particular understandings of children and childhood that have often been at odds with the realities of children's day-to-day lives in local settings in developing and under-developed nations of the Global South.

With these factors in mind, *Global Childhoods* begins by approaching the dominant discourses around children and childhood that stem from the Global North; and then offers case studies of examples where universalizing views have been shown to be flawed or inapplicable. Part One provides a critical analysis of the ways in which childhood studies have arisen in the Global North, unravelling the inter-penetrating constructions and interpretations of children and childhood. We begin, in this chapter, with an exposition on the key theoretical frameworks that suffuse professional discourses on childhood. In Chapter 2, we step back to repeat our initial question, 'What is a child?', by looking at the historical construction of the notion of the Global Northern child, and how that has shifted and changed over time. Chapter 3 addresses approaches to children as objects of global and national concern, as evidenced in policy and legal efforts. These arguments are extended into Chapter 4, which concentrates on the formulation and global implementation of the United Nations Convention of the Rights of the Child (UN 1989).

Part Two then looks at the interplay of these Global Northern assumptions about what it is to be a child in a series of case studies from developed, developing and under-developed nations. In each instance we can see where the terms of the UNCRC, its Optional Protocols (UN 2000b, 2000c) and related policies are challenged, and local circumstances adapt and contest the central assumptions of a universalizing notion of children and childhood. These case studies begin with the analysis of the places and spaces that are central in discussions of childhood, that is, home, school and work (Chapter 5). Chapter 6 analyses approaches to children in 'disasters', taking child soldiers and children orphaned in disasters as examples where aid delivery imports notions of childhood that are problematic. Children as victims of state persecution and forced migration form the basis of discussion in Chapter 7, and the ambiguities in the economics of children, how children are 'valued' is the focus of Chapter 8. Finally, the future of children and childhood is discussed in Chapter 9, using examples from debates in reproductive medicine and bioethics.

THEORIZING CHILDHOOD

Before moving on to contest the universalizability of the taken-for-granted notion of children and childhood, we will begin by unpacking the theoretical underpinnings and the basic assumptions comprehended in the debates and issues affecting children around the globe. As we noted above, the dominant globalizing understanding of children and childhood is a temporal and spatial product, and a focus, of a number of professions: law, medicine and education (over many centuries), and more recently psychology and sociology. Relatedly, the theoretical debates these professions engage in focus on two broad strands of theorization in relation to children and childhood: the child in the process of 'development' and the child in the process of 'socialization'. In the remainder of this chapter we outline key ethical, epistemological and methodological questions in the specialized study of childhood. We do so by highlighting the tensions and contradictions that are inherent in the disjuncture between these two approaches in Euro-centred childhood studies which are most closely identified with two academic disciplines: psychology and sociology.

While the roots of each of these two fields may be seen to reach back much further than their acceptance as scholarly fields (see Chapter 2), they came to prominence as academic disciplines in the late-nineteenth and early-twentieth centuries. Each is concerned to explain why human beings behave or act as they do, and how humans conceive of themselves (form an identity), but from radically different ideological premises. One is concerned with humans primarily as individuals, the other with humans primarily as members of a group.

Psychology, in its concentration on the psyche of the individual, characterizes childhood as a period of development. As such, children are conceived of as a natural category, proto-adults, and what happens during the early life stages is proposed as having ongoing effects into adulthood. The developmental child can be broadly characterized as irrational, untrained, irresponsible and ignorant, but at the same time s/he is deserving of care, protection and guidance (primarily from the family) in coming into being as an adult human being. Sociology, by contrast, looks at children as parts of a larger whole – society. While also characterizing childhood as a period of growth and maturation of a (social) being in the making – the qualities of which can affect the formation of the adult – the frame of those influences is social rather than individual, and depends on wider input and interactions from the social 'group' and the economic, social and political context. In this, a child is a social construction. Developmentalism and socialization, or what might be termed the nature (innate individualism) versus nurture (social determinism) debate on children, starts to appear in its earliest form in the 1670s, as we shall see from some of the examples given in Chapter 2. Here, we are more concerned with their current application.

What developmentalism and socialization have in common is a concern with issues of identity. They are also each focused on children as non-adults. Where the developmental and socialization approaches differ is in the degree to which they interpret a child as: not yet capable of rational decision-making; in need of education (whether formal or informal); less physically skilled and less intellectually able than an adult; primarily concerned with taking part in activities of learning and playing; not to be involved in work until at least 15, or to take on economic (or other 'adult') responsibility. Where those differences originate is in the disparate understanding of the child and childhood.

DEVELOPMENTALISM

The term developmentalism is used to characterize the broad understanding of the individual child's or youth's mind (and body) as something that is in the process of being formed: that is, as an individual or identity in the process of 'becoming'. Further, this theoretical approach proposes that the processes and progress of that formation can be positively or negatively affected. Developmentalism is, today, most closely associated with the work of the French educational psychologist Piaget (1972), although as we will see in the following chapter, it has antecedents in the writing of John Locke (1690) and J. J. Rousseau (1762). It is a theoretical approach that arose out of both psychological and educational theory. The historical dominance of the latter field in the management of children in the Global North has facilitated the depth of the acceptance of its premises in the treatment of children across fields.

Psychology, as based in the Cartesian mind/body split, prioritizes the intellect over the body while also being concerned with the physical effects of mentalities, both in childhood and long after in adulthood. Sigmund Freud's proposition of the psychosexual phases of infancy and early childhood, which need to be successfully negotiated or resolved to reach fully formed adulthood and avoid the development of pathologies, is a key and culturally weighty example of such thinking. Subsequent psychoanalysts like Jung, Lacan and Kristeva – to name but a few – have their own adaptations of these foundational and formational phases of the child's psyche.

The development of the child, as a proto-adult, is also marked out on the body. Just as doctors became preoccupied (some, eugenically obsessed) with measuring aspects of the adult human body in the late-nineteenth century (Schiebinger, 1993), so too did the developing child's body become a site of observation. The measurement of height and weight against age was an innovation that came out of the public health movement (Foucault, 1975), intended to define the ideal stages of growth in a healthy individual. Developmentalism is then not only related to education and psychology, it has direct links to biomedical and/or bio-psychosocial approaches to the human body (and mind). It is a theoretical grounding found in contemporary epidemiology and public health initiatives as promoted by both governments and medical bodies. Age and weight charts, recommendations on the appropriate ages and stages for developing particular capacities (language, gross and fine motor skills) are all part of the developmentalist approach to children, which inevitably centres on managing a child's body. So, within developmentalism there is a strong emphasis on the child as an object of physical observation and surveillance (Foucault, 1975)

In this way of understanding children, the child is a material object, something to be measured, compared, controlled and actively formed. Examples of this approach to children and youth can be found not only in the practices of paediatricians and infant-health workers, but also in campaigns about the negative effects of alcohol on the brains of teenagers; research into young people's incapacity to effectively use rational judgement; their propensity to indulge in risk-taking behaviour; or their capacity to maintain attention in a classroom at particular ages. The developmental child is rarely an agent and far more likely to be seen as a vulnerable innocent in need of protection.

These endeavours have become embedded in educational curricula, with children increasingly monitored for developmentally framed physical parameters and capacities in schools. This is particularly the case in the earliest years of teaching children. The developmental child is involved in education and play – or play as education – and not exposed to pursuits or pressures that belong to the adult world. A developmental child is an individual project in the process of 'becoming' an adult. There is little room for agency in this construction of childhood. The developmental child is by and large a passive object, raw material waiting to be moulded into a later human being, which he or she is on the path to becoming. Developmental assumptions have been embedded in educational and medical constructions of the child over centuries. They are also to be found in legal discourse affecting children.

We will go into much greater depth on the following point in Chapter 4, but it is worth noting here that there are developmental assumptions infused throughout the pre-eminent and globally dominant policy document aimed at the legal protection of children: the United Nations Convention on the Rights of the Child (UNCRC). The language of the UNCRC implies a developmental approach, even if not, according to Daiute, taken to the logical extension of enabling greater empowerment of and change for children within the Convention itself (Daiute, 2008). For example, the phrase 'evolving capacities of the child' implies a process of maturation which allows the various bodies that implement the UNCRC at a national level to confirm children's rights as 'embedded in nations' rights'. However, those in power do not necessarily represent everyone.

Whether 'evil', 'innocent', 'immanent', 'naturally developing' or 'unconscious' (James, Jenks and Prout, 1998), the developmental child is deep-rooted in Global Northern culture and pervasive as a model applied through educational, psychological, medical and legal discourse. In turn, the effects of that dominance are felt throughout the Global South in its permeation of various waves of colonialism, through UN charters, and through international aid. But the developmental model of the child is also contested. Social and political theories of children and childhood stand in opposition to and critically analyse the developmental construction of the child.

SOCIALIZATION

Socialization is a term that comprehends a broad and influential understanding of the creation of society as a whole. It is a basic element in the formation of the 'self' or of identity, and goes back to the work of early sociologists such James (1890), Cooley (1902) and G.H. Mead (1934). Cooley's notion of the looking-glass self and Mead's propositions around self-awareness and self-image each grounded early notions of identity in sociology. Socialization is the process by which we come to form our understanding of ourselves, our identity, through our interactions with others. In that process individuals have agency. We identify with and respond to the approval or disapproval of the group. While, in its earliest expressions, this theorization of identity took into account the formation of selfhood within childhood, it was essentially more concerned with the end-product: the adult. So, like psychology and education, early socialization theory was more concerned with the child as an agent in the process of 'becoming'.

More recently, socialization has been used as an approach to the conceptualization of children, which comes out of sociological and liberal political theory. While, in its earliest form, socialization focused on children not as important social agents in and of themselves, but rather as a stage or stages in the formation of the 'real' social agent, the emphasis began to change in the 1980s. It would be fair to say that Leena Alanen was one of the earliest sociologists, and certainly now one of the best known, to promote programmatically 'Rethinking childhood' (1988) and the socialization of children within sociology and other social sciences. Shortly after the publication of her ground-breaking article, she co-founded the journal *Childhood*, and remains a central figure in the field. Her approach concentrates on the child's or youth's ability to control and to act consciously: to be social actors or agents in their own right. The child's ability to self-determine is uppermost from this point of view.

Not unlike Luther's provocation for the Reformation of Catholicism, James and Prout's (1990) allied agenda took the shape of a set of six theses for a revolution in approaches to children and childhood. The most pertinent of these propositions for our purposes are the first four: that childhood is a social construction; that it is a variable of social analysis; that children's social relationships and culture are 'worthy of study in their own right'; and that children are and must be seen as active (not passive) subjects (James and Prout, 1990: 8). This is no longer a 'becoming' child; this is a 'being' child. Subsequent strands of debate in this field, following on debates on adult subjectivity (Lee 2001, cited in Hallden, 2005), have included discussions of the child as both 'being and becoming' (Hallden, 2005). Rather than just concentrating on a child as either in a state of 'becoming' a social agent (Qvortrup et al., 1994) or in a state of 'being' 'worthy of study' in his or her own right (James and Prout, 1990), children (and adults) are each in a state of 'being and becoming'. That is, children have an experiential reality 'in the moment' of childhood that is a valid site of agency (and object of study) and they are also aware of and can articulate their experience as a state of progression to a future self.

Examples of agency or self-determination in children (in a developed country) might include being able to make representations for themselves in the public sphere (legal actions, medical procedures, political campaigns, youth parliaments, etc.) or to enjoy balancing education and play (which includes all forms of extra-curricular pursuits). In developing or under-developed countries, that agentic self-determination may involve a child's need to find a balance between being responsible for contributing to the family unit by undertaking paid labour and the pursuit of an education (see Chapter 8). In countries that are experiencing social and political unrest, this may even extend to children taking part in war: that is, putting their bodies on the line in theatres of armed conflict (Chapter 6).

We can look to the treatment of children for life-threatening or terminal illnesses for a confronting example of child agency from the Global North. A news story, ostensibly about the opening of a new waiting room in a cancer clinic's children's ward, was broadcast on a Melbourne television station under the heading, 'Normality for Cancer Patients'.[5] At base, however, the report concerned an aspect of childhood that we prefer not to talk about in the Global North, because it is no longer a familiar or quotidian experience. (In under-developed countries with high infant mortality rates, such as Afghanistan and Papua New Guinea, people are more likely to witness personally that children may, and do, die.) This particular piece was reported as a 'good news' story, because donations had made possible the inclusion of the latest video-games and other technological diversions for those waiting, some for chemotherapy, in a brightly coloured and cheerful space.

Doctors have for some time been educated to consider their patients' point of view and build a consultative doctor–patient relationship (rather than a paternalistic one). However, in nearly all instances people under the age of 16 have to rely on parental consent when they are in need of medical treatment. The sense of normality in the opening of the waiting room in this cancer ward equated to suppressing and ignoring the reality of the situation of these children by retreating into a fantasy world of 'children as innocents at play'. The assumption implicit in the attempt to normalize this life-threatening situation is that children are not capable of processing such serious information as their impending death.

One research study of terminally ill children in hospital (Bluebond-Langer, 1978 cited in Ryan, 2008: 572–4) makes clear how the reactions of adults and professionals around the children ignored or suppressed their agency in the dying process. In consultations and in daily treatments, the (uncomfortable) adult professionals preferred instead to divert conversation away from the eventuality and practicalities of dying. While the doctors were approaching their patients from a developmental perspective, the children were in fact perfectly aware of their situation and were capable of displaying sophisticated agency. Ryan (2008: 573) even gives an example: a child rejected the physician's attempt to cajole him with a question about what he would be 'when he grew up', 'with the heated response, "I'm not going to be anything"'. Ryan notes, however, that the majority 'accommodated a "mutual pretense"'. In this particular example we see the practical tension between a professional with embedded developmental assumptions and the reality of the child (under the age of 12) as a social agent capable of understanding his or her own state of 'being and becoming'.

As the field of 'childhood studies' has grown since Alanen, James, Jenks, Prout, Qvortrup and others shifted the discourse on childhood from 'becoming', to 'being', and to 'being *and* becoming', other strands of social theory have been highly influential in approaches to the study of children and childhood. One in particular is Bourdieu's concept of habitus, because habitus and hexis (embodiment) are formed through what Hallden calls 'being and becoming'. The applicability of habitus in the conceptualization of childhood will become more obvious when we turn to our case studies, particularly in the discussion of the places of childhood (Chapter 5). What the notion of habitus may offer us for the moment is a way to conceptualize and accommodate more interplay between developmentalism and socialization, rather than a stark and uncompromising binary opposition.

Since the time that the work of Alanen and other sociologists of childhood first began to appear (see Wyness, 2006), similar endeavours have been underway in anthropology, which has brought to the discussion a wide body of evidence of the cultural specificity of most of the Global Northern UNCRC ideas of childhood. Lancy (2008) and Montgomery (2009) are but two of an increasing number of anthropologists questioning the effects of the normalization of a culturally and historically contingent notion of childhood on societies with different understandings, as we will see in Part 2 of *Global Childhoods*.

GLOBAL CHILDHOODS

We have canvassed examples from law, medicine, education, psychology and sociology that contain aspects of both developmental and socialization approaches to children and childhood. These meta-theoretical debates are played out in the research literature on children in each of these professional fields, to a greater or lesser extent. This is at least in part because the histories of these disciplines are interpenetrating.

Psychology (including educational psychology) and sociology were groundbreaking and influential academic disciplines that were gaining credibility in the last years of the nineteenth and the early decades of the twentieth century. As such, they played into the legal frameworks regarding children that were formulated after the First World War, particularly the deliberations of the League of Nations. Almost contemporaneously, Norbert Elias,[6] who was to become an extremely influential sociologist from the middle of the twentieth century, was working on his (Western

European) social history of civilization in the medieval period through to the twentieth century, which drew heavily on theories of the education of children and the regulation of their embodied actions. This work had a second spring after the Second World War, at which point Ariès and the *Annales* School started to look at history in a different way, including the history of the family. In these movements, children were predominantly seen as subordinate; they still are. But these academic areas had the authority of delimitation to frame newer ways of looking at the categories of 'child' and 'childhood'. In doing so, childhood gained gradations and stages.

On the developmentalism continuum teenagers and youths are objects of control, but they are also accorded capacities younger children such as infants and pre-adolescents are not. Legally, youths are expected to have the rational capacities to avoid breaking the law and at the same time they are 'minors' and not accorded full standing under the law. Youths are therefore subject to higher penalties for breaking the law but treated more leniently as not yet capable of fully responsible decision-making. With respect to bodies, this has practical applications in the ways youth are treated by legal bodies or peace-keepers when they have been participants in armed conflicts. Such youths are also the subject of social anxiety and moral panics, as members of gangs or as child soldiers (see Chapter 6). On the other hand, from the point of view of socialization, 'being' youths may also be seen as capable of self-determination. They may have the right to 'choice' in the management of their own bodies (medically), in how they use their bodies (sexually) and in where they place their bodies (in protests). The bodies of youths are causes of concern for their likelihood to put themselves at risk of physical harm (train-surfing, joy-riding, extreme sports). The bodies of youths are also the key focus of concern over eating disorders, which is an extension of the concerns over healthy development.

This counter-posing of the developmental and socialized notions of children and childhood also brings into question the universal applicability of documents such as the UNCRC. In a long, dense and excellent summary of the formation and subsequent criticisms of the UNCRC, Harris-Short (2001) acknowledges and demonstrates the culturally informed (Global Northern) bases of the Universal Declaration of Human Rights (UNUDHR), the precursor to and intimately allied with the UNCRC. The main arguments that have been used to justify its universality have been both ethnocentric and morally imperialistic, or at least still based in notions of rights inherent in an individual 'self' (which is not the basis of all states/nations' conceptions of citizens).

Rights-based discourse on children, as found in the UNCRC, and welfare-focused scholarship and policy on children are consistently at odds in their framing of children as rights-bearing individuals on the one hand, and 'objects of concern' in need of special care and protection. Who knows best about the conditions of children and childhood? Can children be 'objects of concern' (to researchers, policy-makers, educators, etc.) and subjects in their own right? What are the contradictions between conceptions of children as rights-bearing individuals, and as immanent subjects in need of protection? Is it possible – or even desirable – to produce knowledge about children with their involvement as subjects with agency? What does child-centred methodology look like? And how can knowledge about children be produced with their involvement as agents and subjects, and not merely as 'objects of concern'?

This book is intended to give a broad overview of how contemporary approaches to childhood were formed by framing answers to these questions. We aim to show how the dominant ideas that are embedded in everyday practices and policies towards children, and the prevailing disciplinary methods applied in those policies and practices, are not easily universalized to all children, across time, place and culture. In her study of inter-country adoption in the Americas, historian Karen Dubinsky remarks that childhood is an invention of the West (Dubinsky, 2010: 16). We outline a narrative which shows that, concomitant with the invention of a particular idea of childhood in Western Europe (Chapter 2), nineteenth-century European imperialist and twentieth-century economic development agendas imposed this invention on the rest of the world (Chapters 3 and 4). That imposition commenced in the early-modern period (1500–1800), through colonizing activity, particularly missionary activity in imperial territories in the Americas, Asia, Africa and Australasia and continued in the aid and development initiatives of the twentieth century.

In these endeavours the children of the world – or those who could be reached – were quite systematically 'remade' as Christians, taught European languages, put into European clothes, educated to European norms and standards, told that their cultures and practices were primitive and that their future lay in transforming themselves through 'civilization' and modernization. To this end, many children were forcibly removed from their families and communities for (what they were told was) their betterment and advancement. The efforts of these early missionaries pre-dated the particular conception of childhood that emerged slowly and unevenly from the end of the eighteenth century and the rise of industrialization, and which obtains in policy documents today.

While this missionary work continued into the twentieth century, this century of World Wars (both 'hot' and Cold) elevated the project of consolidating childhood to a secular and civil mission of governments, inter-governmental bodies, and non-government organizations (some of which had origins in missionary enterprises). While shifting from a largely religious to a secular framework, the childhood project remained firmly rooted in Global Northern conceptions of childhood – which have also mutated over the course of the century.

The twentieth century saw an intensification of the management of childhood as an increasingly professionalized, medicalized, and psychologized domain. Parents and families were no longer simply entrusted with the raising of children. Raising children became a state-monitored and regulated activity with regimes related to education, health and other activities mandated by law, and with associated monitoring for compliance. As the century progressed, national governments themselves became subject, through their ratification of international conventions, to monitoring by global bodies with respect to their treatment of children. Dealing with children became the preserve of the expert; one which has been increasingly observed and even policed in the contemporary period. For example, police checks – or working with children checks – are now required in many

Global Northern jurisdictions in order to teach, coach children's football teams, or participate in other activities involving children.

As the twentieth century progressed, the scope of the global childhood project also expanded and transformed. First the League of Nations, then the United Nations, accompanied by a plethora of national and transnational child-focused bodies too numerous to list, proliferated to form a more or less coherent global children's movement which drove the childhood agenda across the world. The aims of this movement shifted and developed from the largely religious objective of salvation to the largely economic aspirations centred on development. By the middle of the twentieth century it had moved on again, to the multiple, integrated objectives encapsulated in the rights-based UNCRC of 1989. Notably, the UNCRC added civic and political dimensions to the understanding of children and childhood. The capacity to endorse and then enact this version of childhood became a key marker of modern nationhood in the 1990s, notwithstanding deep and unresolved tensions within the UNCRC itself, with respect to its simultaneous and potentially contradictory claims to universalism and to respect for cultural and other diversity in the lives of children.

As any book on childhood must recognize, the global child – as most fully imagined and articulated in the 1989 UNCRC – is an invention of the Global North in line with the invention of childhood itself. The global child as envisaged in the UNCRC, and a great deal of developmental activity associated with the so-called Global Children's Movement, is directed to advancing the interests and assuring the rights of a normative version of the child. While making some concessions to differences between children, the Convention implicitly assumes throughout and explicitly states in the preamble, that the end goal of childhood is the formation of an adult citizen competent and capable of living individually and contributing productively to a Western-style liberal democracy.

One of the achievements of the twentieth century's focus on childhood, as documented in this book, is to formulate the category of childhood as a privileged, special period of development and in doing so to establish this category as a global norm. The success of this endeavour has brought mixed blessings to the children of the world. While many now enjoy material conditions which they otherwise would not, many others do not. Through our exploration of the history and governance of children and childhood, fleshed out by case studies of children's lived realities and an analysis of the international policies that affect them, we aim to bring into sharper relief the critical issues and debates that are entailed in the construction of *Global Childhoods*.

NOTES

1 Parts of this narrative are based on oral testimony and, as with any oral history, there may be aspects where memory has reshaped details, but the key points are supported by archival records.
2 See Jane Austen's depictions of both of adults and young boys sent to sea, based on her own brothers' careers in the Royal Navy, on officers being drawn from the 'gentlemanly' and 'noble' classes.

3 Over the first decade of the twentieth century Australian women were enfranchised. The Federal Whitlam Labor government lowered the voting age from 21 to 18 in 1973, so in fact even young men who at 19 or 20 became eligible to be drafted into the Vietnam War between 1964 and 1972, could not vote.

4 Shamefully, Indigenous Australians were treated in the same manner no matter what their age, able to serve in wars but unable uniformly to vote in Federal elections until 1962 (AEC, 2006) and for many their wages were withheld and controlled (until 1972), or inequitable and lower, in some cases until 1986 (Kidd, 2006).

5 'Normality for cancer patients: The Peter MacCallum Cancer Centre has a funky new waiting room', Seven Nightly News (Channel Seven, Melbourne, Friday, 16 April 2010. http://search.informit.com.au.ezproxy.lib.monash.edu.au/documentSummary;dn=TEV20101504268; res=TVNEWS.

6 Elias had been studying to be a doctor before becoming an ambulance-man in the First World War but decided to pursue a doctorate in sociology after the end of the war.

Further reading

Alanen, L. (1988) 'Rethinking childhood', *Acta Sociologica*, 31 (1): 53–67.

Fass, P. (2007) *Children of a New World: Essays in Society, Culture and the World*. New York: New York University Press.

James, A., Jenks, C. and Prout, A. (1998) *Theorizing Childhood*. Cambridge: Polity.

Lancy, D.F. (2008) *The Anthropology of Childhood: Cherubs, Chattels, Changelings*. Cambridge: Cambridge University Press.

Montgomery, H. (2009) *An Introduction to Childhood: Anthropological Perspectives on Children's Lives*. Chichester: Wiley.

Qvortrup, J., Bardy, M., Sgritta, G. and Wintersberger, H. (eds) (1994) *Childhood Matters: Social Theory, Practice and Politics*. Aldershot: Avebury Press.

Uprichard, E. (2008) 'Children as "being and becomings": Children, childhood and temporality', *Children & Society*, 22: 303–13.

Wyness, M. (2006) *Childhood and Society: An Introduction to the Sociology of Childhood*. New York: Palgrave.

2

WHAT IS A CHILD?: MAKING MEANING OF CHILDREN AND CHILDHOOD

- Definitions of and activities considered appropriate to children and childhood have varied over time. In other words, childhood has a history.

- The dominant idea of childhood in the Global North is the outcome of wider effects of modernity in Western Europe and the social, cultural and political changes it engendered from the late seventeenth to the twentieth century.

- The ways in which that dominant idea was popularized were largely through educational texts, initially sacred but increasingly secular over time, aimed at training up children into adults.

- Critical analysis of the Global Northern history of childhood allows us to assess what it might mean to apply the dominant construction of the child in the absence of the material conditions of modernity that have shaped them (economic, social, political, etc.).

INTRODUCTION

We begin this chapter by repeating our primary question – What is a child? – as the first step in problematizing children and childhood. It should already be clear that any answer to that question will not only be epistemological (dependent on the knowledge system in which the question is posed), it is just as much a temporal and spatial inquiry (dependent on when and where the question is asked). Here, we contextualize the dominant definitions of children and childhood in terms of their historical antecedents in the Global North, specifically in the ways that they have been framed in Western European culture. We do so because it is this geographically and temporally specific, and relatively recent, view of children and childhood that is at the heart of the dominant conceptions that have shaped policy and law around children over the twentieth century (as within the UN Convention on the Rights of the Child).

We argue that ideas about what it is to be a child and what constitutes childhood are dependent on social, political and historical context. As we shall see in more detail in later chapters, within a century – almost within living memory – particular concepts of childhood have been legally formalized, a process that began in developed, Global Northern countries in the 1920s but has since spread globally (Chapter 4). This has come about partly through political reforms and global socio-political movements intent on law reform initially aimed at child protection, and beyond that at the advancement of children through a child's rights framework. Another part of the impetus for this formal re-evaluation has come as a result of shifts in educational theoretical models, influenced by bio-psychosocial models of identity and embodiment. These in turn have influenced, and been influenced by, medical responses to children and childhood, and to relatively recent sociological analyses.

Most importantly for our purposes in the writing of *Global Childhoods*, our aim is to question whether what has been so successful in the globally and geopolitically dominant theorizing on children and childhood is universally applicable. That is to say, just as these definitions can be seen to be historically contingent, we need to be aware of how they may continue to be contingent on socio-cultural grounds. A child protectionist might disagree with such a suggestion, whereas a children's rights activist might not: the reality is complex and cannot be answered in simple or polarized answers. To reiterate, the historical examples we look at here are from industrially developed countries of nations in the Global North, and from them we will see that there is a lack of universality or universalizability of current understandings of children and childhood with respect to the past. Further, what a child is, or what childhood means, remains constituted differently in other contexts. In taking this approach, we pick up on the formative shifts in the analytical approaches introduced in Chapter 1, specifically developmentalism and socialization.

CENTURIES OF (WESTERN EUROPEAN) CHILDHOOD

The credit (or blame) is generally given to French social historian Philippe Ariès for being the first to claim, in *Centuries of Childhood: A Social History of Family Life* (1962), that childhood as we think of it in contemporary modern societies is a social and cultural invention. Ariès argues that the contemporary concept of childhood in Western Europe has gradually taken shape over the past five centuries, and more particularly since the late eighteenth century. Ariès's basic argument on childhood (to the mid-twentieth century) is that it is a construct of bourgeois sentimentality and arose as part of early-modern and modern identity formation amongst the rising middle classes. He claims that childhood and the differentiations we would understand – between infant, child, adolescent, youth, adult and aged infirmity – only came into being in the seventeenth and eight-eenth centuries.

Basing his thesis on the analysis of representations in art and in educational man-uals, Ariès argues that this evolution of childhood is observable through shifts in the age- and social strata-appropriate positioning of games, clothing and education. Norbert Elias (2000) mounted comparable arguments in relation to the agency of manners, promulgated by Desiderius Erasmus (1466–1536) in his advice to a young prince, as disseminating wider 'civilizing processes' through the embodied regula-tion of social classes.

> If a serviette is given, lay it on your left shoulder or arm. If you are seated with people of rank, take off your hat and see that your hair is well combed. Your goblet and knife, duly cleansed, should be on the right, your bread on the left. Some people put their hands in the dishes the moment they have sat down. Wolves do that. … If you are offered something liquid, taste it and return the spoon, but first wipe it on your serviette. (Erasmus, *De civilitate morum puerilium* 1530, cited in Elias, 2000: 76–7)

Similarly, Ariès plots the movement of the bodily control and regulation of chil-dren as a point of increasingly specific differentiation of the child (as non-adult) from the adult. Thus, the evolution of the idea of childhood took hold, in part, through bodily techniques: age-specific clothing such as skirts for small boys before they could wear breeches (knee length pants); sports or pastimes intended to train up a body to a specific physique and ideal of health; and, education that entailed physical requirements (sitting still) and involved physical correction when behavioural requirements were not met (corporal punishment). On the latter point, with regard to education, we see parallel arguments in Elias in his disquisitions on Ersamus's advice to his young prince.

Using medieval and early-modern illustrations (largely from France, Germany and Italy) in support of his thesis, Ariès argues that the major physical differen-tiations between life-stages at that time were, respectively: between the infant in the cradle, the neophyte-adult, and the aged and the bed-ridden (imbecilic) infirm, who have returned to an infant-like state. The illustrations from the four-teenth through to the sixteenth centuries that he analyses track life-stages through embodied changes but do not include a period that is recognizable as 'childhood'. First came infancy, followed by a remarkably extended youth or prime of life, and eventually old age.

This line of argument has antecedents in the literary trope of the 'ages of man', which has existed in poetry since Hesiod (f.750–650 BCE) and Ovid (43 BCE–17 CE). This division of the lifespan is perpetuated in Jacques's lines in Act II, Scene vii of Shakespeare's *As You Like It*, and as such retains some currency in English-speaking communities where Shakespearean tropes permeate the language. Three of Shakespeare's seven ages describe adult occupations (lover, soldier and judge) and two represent old age ('the lean and slipper'd pantaloon' of retirement, and dementia's 'second childishness and mere oblivion, sans teeth, sans eyes, sans taste, sans everything'). Only two refer to life prior to adulthood: 'the infant, /mewling and puking in the nurse's arms. / Then the whining schoolboy, with his satchel / And shining morning face, creeping like snail / Unwillingly to school' (Shakespeare, *c*.1599). The former falls into the broad social realm of 'home' and the latter is clearly placed in 'school', with the emphasis firmly on the 'school*boy*'. Only exceptional females, like Elizabeth I, were highly educated: although a few girls had briefly accessed the system of charitably funded grammar schools, such as Shakespeare is believed to have attended, all were excluded by the end of the sixteenth century (Fraser, 1984: 152–3). Once 'school' is over, by 14 at most for the few privileged able to attend in the first place, a life of 'work' begins. What the seven stages do not spell out (but both Ariès and Elias do) is that the age at which the majority of children entered the world of work was as low as seven. Indeed, the apprentice boy actors playing the younger female parts when Jacques's lines were first spoken, some of whom might have started in one of the children's companies, would have been well aware of this (Gurr 1987, 2009).

As Ariès describes it (1962: 26), the contemporary idea of adolescence – an extended period in which one becomes a social being – did not exist. Rather, '[t]he idea of childhood was bound up with the idea of dependence: the words "sons", "varlets" and "boys" were also words in the vocabulary of feudal subordination'. So, conversely, a 'lad' or 'boy' could be in his twenties. (We can see that the latter term of subordination continued to be used well into the twentieth century, as applied pejoratively to adult African-American males.) More contentiously, Ariès argues (ibid.: 46–7) that because small children were considered more likely to die they were also in some way less important, or less emotion was invested in them: recognition of their subjectivity only came with the likelihood of survival. He claims the changes that led to the invention of a sentimentalized childhood are evident in the inclusion of infants in funerary monuments and family portraiture in the seventeenth century.

Ariès's thesis was taken up enthusiastically throughout the 1960s and 1970s by historians in France and beyond. In the decades since its publication it has been mobilized as a model for further research (e.g. Shorter, 1975; Stone, 1979) but also contested by a widening of the geographic or textual focus (e.g. Macfarlane, 1970, 1985; Ozment, 1999) and by insistence on deeper nuance (e.g. Pollock, 1983, 1987; Cressy, 1997; Ryan, 2008). Historian Lawrence Stone's *The Family, Sex and Marriage in England 1500–1800* (1977), which was similarly influential in British social history, followed a similar trajectory of the shaping effects of modernity on domestic life and, while not concentrated on children *per se*, includes children's place in the family and in society. Like Ariès, Stone found affective individualism to be at the heart of the metamorphoses in family life in modernity and therefore in parent–child relationships. The closed unit of parents and children (rather than wider social networks) thereby became the dominant construction of the family and children gradually became objects of affective, pastoral control (at least for the middle and upper classes).

Since the advent of second-wave feminism, feminist social historians (such as Fraser, 1984; Laurence, 1994) have been politically dedicated to including discussions of children in the histories of women, generally in terms of the effects of childbearing and rearing on women. In other words, the focus has been largely on the impact of repeated pregnancies on maternal and infant mortality, and on women's roles as the moral guardians of future citizens. The dynamic of treating children as 'womenandchildren' (Alanen, 1988) is not uncommon in writing across the disciplines from the 1970s, 1980s and 1990s. However, what is most noteworthy in the work of these feminist historians is their concentration on the relationships between mothers and infants, and their research on the shifting emphasis over the seventeenth and eighteenth centuries on how, and how much, infants should be cared for by the mother, and popular debates that were increasingly critical of middle-class mothers putting infants out to (lower-class) wet-nurses.

Relatedly, feminist historians have been amongst those who have criticized Ariès's evidence for his claims regarding the lack of attachment to infants prior to the eighteenth century (Pollock, 1983). We shall see below that it is demonstrably untrue that infants were considered unimportant, both from the evidence of literary sources and from legal statutes for the prosecution of crimes such as infanticide. It is also fair to say of Ariès's main evidentiary sources, that what appears in art or an educational manual is not necessarily good evidence of lived realities. Representations almost always serve other purposes than simply to reflect reality, and educational manuals might be said to hold up an ideal of childhood behaviour, rather than providing evidence of how children actually behaved. Finally, the over-stated claim that childhood itself is an invention is not sustainable. Across time, space and cultures there have been understandings of a differentiation between humans on the basis of stages of life: hence the prevalence (even ubiquity) of rites of passage to mark full membership in communities and societies at a given age, often at puberty. What has changed, and continues to differ, is how the phase called childhood or the type human being known as 'child' is demarcated and constructed; and, in line with this, how the meanings attached to childhood and the roles and values associated with children have also altered (see Chapter 8).

Ariès's contribution has nonetheless been inestimable and his general thesis stands: namely, that our contemporary understanding of childhood has evolved over time, as has our expectation of what is and is not appropriate in the treatment of children. Further, the research engendered by the endorsement or rebuttal of his claims has resulted in the foundation of a solid field of historical and sociological inquiry into children and childhood that ratifies the main point. That is, the dominant understanding that is grounded in the history, politics and culture of the Global North is the outcome of a process of change impelled by economic, social and political factors over time (see King, 2007, for a synthesis of historical accounts; Zelizer, 1985).

We can also agree that up until at least the seventeenth century in Western Europe (and its colonial dominions), seven was generally considered the age of rational capacities and it was from this age onwards that children might be sent into other households as apprentices or indentured servants, or into the military forces such as the navy (Heywood, 2001; Bishop, 1982). While some children might not have been apprenticed quite so young, perhaps being indentured to a guild or trade between ten and 13, once infancy and whatever schooling one was able to access were exceeded, one entered work (Heywood, 2001). For those of the lowest socio-economic demographics, of necessity, work began as early as one could prove oneself capable of and useful at performing a required task, boy or girl. But when work and home were often spatially inseparable – on a farm, in a large household, in a tradesman's dwelling – the entry into work might also be a slow process of small tasks and general assistance, leading to the acquisition of skills and responsibility over time. In the same way that wives were the unspoken working partners of guildsmen and tradesmen, so too were the children of the household contributors to the household activity and income.

Over the seventeenth century there were wider social, economic and political shifts in early modernity underway, in which the discourses around children and childhood were involved. Just as the wider forces of modernity were characterized by the reinterpretation of human consciousness and social and political life, so was attention on children refocused. The reconceptualization of human identity by thinkers such as Thomas Hobbes (1651), John Locke (1690) and René Descartes (1641) was part of a wider shift towards rational individualism. Such reasoning was largely directed at the adult, but implicit within it was the assumption that children's minds were in a process of development, and that they were adults/citizens/social beings in formation. The individual, and the developmental child, were both the product and object of investigations of the 'new' sciences.

The majority of that attention fell onto the educable child but also on infants (generally in relation to birthing and breast-feeding). Depending on class, work in general was not considered unusual for children and was to some extent comprehended in education, in terms of offering the acquisition of skills and training necessary for adult employment. For the remainder of this chapter we will give interpretations of a number of exemplary English texts that provide evidence of the construction of the Western European infant and child, from the seventeenth through to the early nineteenth century, and show that children *did exist* as a category of human being and that infants *were* valued. We give these examples not in order to generalize about how children lived, as Ariès did, but rather to emphasize how children were being discursively constructed, re-imagined, at very specific points of time and in very particular ways.

'MEWLING INFANTS' AND AFFECTIVE ATTACHMENT

In 1623, during the reign of James I (1603–1627), a notable legal act was introduced in Great Britain. It was reissued, after the Civil War and the demise of the Republican Government (1649–1660), during the reign of James I's grandson, Charles II (1660–1686) as *Anno vicesimo primo Jacobi Regis, 43 &c. an act to prevent the destroying and murthering of bastard children* (1680). The Act's stated aim was to monitor and control unmarried mothers, who were alleged to have been passing off acts of infanticide as still-births, and to punish those who did not comply with the requirement that the birth be witnessed, the most likely witness being a midwife or female relative.

Whereas many Lewd Women that have been delivered of Bastard Children, to avoid their shame and to escape punishment, do secretly bury or conceal the Death of their Children, and after, if the Child be found dead, the said Women do alledge that the said Child was born dead, whereas it falleth out some times (although hardly it is to be proved) that the said Child or Children were Murthered by the said Women their lewd Mothers, or by their assent or procurement. [...] In every such case the said Mother so offending shall suffer Death, as in the case of murther, except such Mother can make proof by one Witness at the least, that the Child (whose death by her so intended to be concealed) was born dead.

(*Anno vicesimo primo Jacobi Regis*, 1680)

The reality of birthing at the time was that both infant and maternal mortality was very high, whether witnessed or not (Fraser, 1984; Cressy, 1997). Two matters stand out: first, the Act is seemingly unconcerned, or perhaps inconsistent in its concern, that married women might also commit infanticide. Secondly, it is paradoxical that this level of concern is so high at a time when infants who died before baptism (chrysoms), legitimate or otherwise, were unceremoniously buried in the common grave pit.[1] Nevertheless, what we can infer from this act, and the evidence of successive governments' concern to promulgate it, is that infants *did* matter.

Early in seventeenth-century England infants mattered at the very least because unsupported infants were potential drains upon the charity of the parish and were objects of Poor Laws (Stone, 1979; Laurence, 1994). As we discuss in Chapter 7, the challenges of managing members of the population who were surplus to requirement and a drain on the state led, in England, to the mass deportation of criminals and the children of the poor to colonial outposts – a practice which persisted from the early-seventeenth through to the nineteenth and twentieth centuries.[2] Infants also mattered because, when legitimate, they provided a secure line of inheritance for property. Infants, in these terms, mattered as economic units and as objects through which females could be controlled: we say females because the age of consent for girls was 12 (Fraser, 1984: 9), albeit marriages of girls so young appear to have been more likely to occur among the elites than the masses (Stone, 1979: 40–45). However, there is also clear evidence, from literature, that they were valued in and of themselves. Ben Jonson (1975) wrote sonnets on the deaths of two of his children, 'On My First Daughter' (*c.*1593) and 'On My First Son' (1603). While these sonnets are highly crafted literary representations, they nevertheless speak of affective attachment to infants and children. The earlier sonnet on the death of his daughter Mary, at six months old, makes clear the sense of grief at her loss in her 'mother's tears'. The subject of the later poem, Jonson's 'loved boy', was seven at the time he died of plague, so no longer an infant. Nevertheless, while consciously artful in referencing a poem by Martial in its epigraph, Jonson's poem speaks of the affective impact of the loss of a child who had just reached the age of reason.

By 1708, when the unmarried Mary Ellenor was prosecuted under James I's Act for giving birth to an illegitimate male infant who was found dead in the privy (drop toilet) of St Olaves Silver St, the vitriol against her, the public condemnation of her actions, and the sense of protectiveness towards the infant are clear in the depositions against her (Cregan, 2009: 276–8). Much had changed since the first publication of the Act. Most obviously, apart from the revolution mid-century and the Great Fire in 1666, London's population had trebled to approximately 600,000 inhabitants: this had concrete economic, social and political effects on people's lives and levels of unease. There were general political concerns about the potential for civil unrest amongst the masses, which intensified with the outbreak of riots, such as those against the surgeons at Tyburn gallows in the late-seventeenth and early-eighteenth centuries (Linebaugh, 1975). Murderous mothers of bastard infants – like 'the Irish', 'Sailors', 'the poor' – were metonymic of greater anxieties engendered by urban modernity. When Mary Ellenor was tried, she represented only one woman of thousands prosecuted under the Act, who were seemingly 'out of control'. In the eighteenth century, the socio-political concern that focused on the preservation of infants saw a shift in the regulation of birthing, with the rise of the scientific man-midwife, particularly among women of higher classes (Cody, 2005). Yet, for most, female family members and midwives of necessity remained the norm as birth attendants into the twentieth century.

Infants were also the subject of debates that related to their physical care, such as swaddling and feeding (Pollock, 1983). Swaddling, a process of binding in strips of cloth, was a common practice across classes until it came under scientific (and political) attack during the eighteenth century. Doctors and political reformers (like J.J. Rousseau) advised that infants should be dressed in loose clothing to allow free movement and the development of healthy limbs. Similarly, in the eighteenth century, arguments against wet-nursing in favour of mothers feeding their own children began to appear. The wealthier the woman, the greater her capacity to choose whether to swaddle, or to put her infants into the arms of a wet-nurse. For the infants of the poor placed in foundling hospitals, wet-nursing was a necessity (Heywood, 2001).

From the fifteenth to the eighteenth century, upper-class women frequently gave their infants into the care of wet-nurses, who were often part of the household, to be breast-fed until the age of two. This might have been in order to enable the mothers' greater social and conjugal engagement, or to ensure the infant's survival, if the mother had died as a result of, or in, childbirth. Arguments against wet-nursing were at once supported by scientific rationale as to its dangers – largely based on denigrating the characters of poor wet-nurses – and appealed to ideas of affective attachment (Pollock, 1987). At the turn of the seventeenth century these practices – birthing attended by midwife or female relative, breast-feeding and swaddling – were near universal to procreative human beings, but arguments that stemmed from rationalist, scientific, and politically informed debates on the care and control of children led to change (Heywood, 2001).

In the increasingly industrialized cities of eighteenth-century Western Europe, people were numerous, urban poverty was rife and living conditions for the lower classes were appalling. The urban poor became a source of concern and subject to greater attention and regulation for fear of their power to create public disturbances (Linebaugh, 1975, 1992), as did their children. Foundling hospitals were set up with the stated intention to aid in the survival of children whose parents were unable or unwilling to keep them, although the effect of the institution was more often to contain and control the child (Heywood, 2001). Stone's affective infant of the eighteenth-century British bourgeoisie, therefore, had his or her obverse in the child of the urban poor, as seen in Hogarth's narrative prints of London's debauchery. Hogarth's mid-eighteenth-century satire, *Beer Street and Gin Lane* (1751), in its contrasting of the respective roads to health and depravity includes images of infants being dropped on their heads or fed gin by their drunken female carers in Gin Lane (Cody, 2005). These signs of early liberal urban and child reform debates do not so much show that infants mattered more than they had previously but that they had started to become part of the discourses of progressive modernity, of a wider social and political set of concerns.

As discussed in Chapter 8, a crucial development influencing political and social thinking on these questions was the publication in 1798 of Thomas Malthus's *Essay on the Principle of Population as it Affects the Future Improvement of Society*. Malthus posited an integral and dynamic relationship between population and the wealth of nations, which further focused attention on children as either a future workforce – for agriculture, commerce and industry – or as a potential drain on the wealth of the nation. More directly related to our current discussion, Malthus's work was highly influential on emerging attitudes to the role of education in shaping the children of the nation for productive roles.

THE EARLY MODERN CHILD: 'WHINING SCHOOLBOYS'

Something of an age of educational reform (primarily for boys), influenced by both religious and scientific thinking, was underway in Western Europe from the mid-seventeenth century. In Great Britain, where Catholicism had been muted in the sixteenth century and a Puritan had replaced a king in the mid-seventeenth century, religiously inspired books appeared, such as *A School of Nurture for Children: The duty of children in honouring their parents* (1656). Advice manuals like this, and those published in the century that followed, provide examples of tracts devoted to the upbringing and education of children, allowing us some insight into the mutable nature of children and childhood. To explore our point further we take two popular examples, Robert Russel's illustrated *A Little Book for Children* (1698), a piously aimed advice manual, and Robert Ainsworth's *The Most Natural and Easy Way of Institution* (1698), which offers a more rationalist-inspired approach. The comparison of two excerpts from these books is illustrative of mobile and competing constructions of children and childhood. If we begin with Robert Russel's text we can see immediately that a key issue is identifying and instilling moral sensibilities in a didactic religious format.

> Thirdly: A good Child is one that is very dutiful to his Parents, and is very careful to do what his Father and Mother bids him, knowing that in obeying them, he obeys God, Ephes. 6. 1.

Fourthly: A good Child is one that behaves himself well at Church, or at any place where the Word of God is preached, whilst wicked Children run out of the Church, and play about the Church-yard all the Sermon time: this poor Child sits still all the Sermon time, and hearkens what the Minister saith, and labours to get part of the Sermon to repeat to his Father and Mother when he comes Home. (Russel, 1698: 10–11)

[...]

A bad Child ... when his Master comes to call him forth, he cannot say his lesson ... after he has left school, he loiters and plays about streets, so that it is dark night when he comes home; and if his Mother chide him, then he has a lie to tell, and some excuse to make to hide his fault ... and if his Father and Mother leave him at home, and shut him in a doors, then all the time that they are gone, he plays and rudes among his Brothers and Sisters, so that when his Father and Mother comes home from Church, there lies the stools and chairs flung about House, and every thing is out of order. (Russel, 1698: 13–14)

This is clearly an example of religiously inspired writings on the upbringing of children. Such texts stress that it is spiritual instruction that is of utmost importance, primarily in following the biblical tenets of filial obedience and the injunction to 'honour thy father and mother'. Learning involves schooling that is based on memorizing lessons, but the most important lessons come from imbibing ideas of proper behaviour, obedience and respect, from one's minister and one's parents. At the same time, children are considered capable of, but not necessarily inclined to, self-rule. So, proper learning also involves the kinds of self-control that we find in Ariès's discussion of childhood. This also has much in common with Elias's interpretation of Erasmus's expectations of his young pupil (Elias, 2000): a 'good child' *does not play* when 'he' should be attending to a lesson or returning to his home.

What is perhaps most striking to the contemporary reader is the unconcern with which Russel writes of parents shutting their children into the home, unsupervised and unattended, while they attend to their own spiritual lives. Here we have an expectation that the school-age child will be responsible and mature – at a time when grammar schooling, if accessed at all, was highly unlikely to extend past the age of 12. The child under discussion is therefore pre-pubescent and yet held to account for his or her actions. There is a sense that this vision of a child is backward-looking, that it is embedded in prior traditions of religious dominance more suited to the early seventeenth century and earlier modernity.

Robert Ainsworth's approach is strikingly different, not least in the language in which it is expressed:

The reasons of the slow proficiency and careless institution of our Children are such as with the Parents, or Master, is chargeable with. First, the Parents, who don't ordinarily take care to have their Children taught to read, till they are so habituated to vice and idleness, that their teacher must have as much labour to bring 'em into love with their book, as otherwise would have taught 'em to read ... No doubt, as soon as they can speak, they may be taught to read either by Father or Mother, with ease and pleasure, without ever imposing it as a task upon 'em. The ingenious Mr Locke tells us of a person of great quality and worth, who by pasting the six vowels [including Y] on the six sides of a die, and the remaining 18 consonants on the sides of three other dice, has played his son into spelling and reading with the greatest eagerness imaginable ... If they do take care to send 'em to school, perhaps 'tis to some Woman who never knew any thing of orthography, though she may make shift to read her prayers, or murder a gazette, confounding one period with another, which she must needs do, having never been acquainted with the Rules of Pointing [punctuation]. Hence it comes to pass that *vulgar people*, who only have learned to read and write at this rate, commit such horrible blunders in spelling, and making no points, are at the hazard of having no one, that writes true, to understand what they mean. (Ainsworth, 1698)

Although these two books were published in the same year, the difference in the attitude to the schooling and the construction of children found in the writing of Robert Ainsworth, reflected in the mode of address to the reader, is obvious. Ainsworth is an admirer of John Locke, the empiricist philosopher and social contract theorist who was part of an intellectual revolution that rejected prior forms of knowledge formation in favour of scientific method. Locke argued that human consciousness begins as a *tabula rasa*: in other words, *children* begin as blank slates upon which adult identity is written. According to this view, parents are responsible for making the correct decisions in seeing that blank slate filled. The process begins with parental intervention but it is increasingly assumed that the management of children's education will be outside the family and home, as part of scientific, progressive educational interventions.

Here, children are held far less responsible for any lack of application or attending to their lessons. Ainsworth argues for the active teaching of children, by their parents, from the earliest ages. Poor outcomes are the result of poor decisions on the part of parents and/or schoolmasters who do not ensure children are taught appropriately. Embedded is a political argument against female teachers, as incapable or ignorant and implicitly lower class, which plays into a larger debate begun by women like Bathsua Makin (Makin, 1673) and Mary Astell (Astell, 1694, 1697), who argued for the systematic education of girls. Many writers have shown the links between the rise of science and the binary pairings which oppose and yet link respectively such terms as Man/Woman, Science/Nature, rational/irrational: as men became allied with rational science, women were relegated to associations with nature and irrationality (Lloyd, 1984; Schiebinger, 1993). In striking contrast to Russel's condemnation of 'ruding', Ainsworth, appealing to Locke's authority, considers 'play' to be an appropriate method of learning, as is demonstrated by a member of the upper classes in the ingenious game with the dice. Such an attitude is immediately recognizable in relation to contemporary understandings of what is appropriate to the life of the child.

Play is linked to learning, but it is not yet characterized as the main occupation of children. Rather it is a means of bringing children into rational functionality and of avoiding 'vice and idleness'. Education (literacy) is a primary method of writing upon that blank slate of childhood consciousness and needs to be done early. This attitude is still apparent towards the middle of the eighteenth century. If we look again to Hogarth, we find in *Industry and Idleness* (1747) satirical representations of later stages in the lives of children: the 'idle' young apprentice who neglects his education and his trade, going to ruin and the gallows, is contrasted with his industrious counterpart. In *Marriage à la Mode* (1743) we find a pox-ridden and seemingly pre-pubescent female prostitute at the side of her nobleman paramour, as a quack is consulted regarding syphilis. Failure to divert the (very) young from vice and idleness sets the character of the youth and adult.

Finally, the mention of Locke is pertinent to our earlier point about those wider forces affecting social, political and cultural mores in which the discourse around children and childhood is embedded. Not only is the metonymic use of Locke's name indicative of the long, slow and uneven movement away from the dominance of religion and doctrinal belief towards the sciences and empirical evidence, it invokes associations intimately related to the rise of liberal political theory and the discourse on rights: of man, of woman and, eventually, of child.

THE MODERN CHILD: 'NOBLE SAVAGE'

As we turn to the eighteenth century, and particularly to liberal dialogues on what it is to be human and to assert right and agency, Jean-Jacques Rousseau (1712–1778) provides the clearest and most targeted construction of children and childhood.

> Nature intends that children shall be children before they are men. If we insist on reversing this order we shall have fruit early indeed, but unripe and taste-less, and liable to early decay; we shall have young savants and old children. Childhood has its own methods of seeing, thinking, feeling. … With children use force, with men, reason; such is the natural order of things. (Rousseau, *Emile*, 1762)

Here we have the child as an entity in and of itself, a necessary stage in the progressive development of the individual. Rousseau's conception of children as unformed, pre-rational, not-yet-men in need of forceful management, is not so far removed from his ideas of the 'noble savage'. The noble savage is revered on the one hand, and condemned on the other, for 'his' lack of rational capacities. The difference with (male urban) children is that they will grow into fully formed rational individuals, given time and the right educational environment. Children are creatures who can, and need, to be brought to reason out of their innocent savagery, in the bosom of the (bourgeois) family.

Rousseau clearly conceives of childhood as a stage on the way to and a state separate from adulthood, and asserts that this is as it should be. Children are constructed as decidedly pre-rational creatures upon whom the exercise of force (punishment) is warranted. There is also a sense that children need to be kept in their state of natural ignorance and only enlightened as befits their stage of development, a view that reflects the (romanticized) notion that children need to be protected from the world. This is almost completely the opposite of the views expressed by Erasmus, whose clear intention was to induct children into the world.

Like Ainsworth, Rousseau is writing about, not to, children. Erasmus and Russel, on the other hand, assume that the child can be spoken to directly. While their texts are didactic in tone, the intended audience is regarded as capable of rationally apprehending the advice given. Erasmus does not doubt his pupil's capacities to live up to a level of sociability, merely his knowledge of the finer points of how to do so. We must remember that the passage from Erasmus was written in a period when the greatest division in the life course occurred at the age of seven; infancy was of little interest to the moralist, he is concerned with the stage of rational capacity (at which time, in what was then predominantly Roman Catholic Europe, one was admitted to the sacraments of Holy Communion and Penance). In this vision of the child, maturity and self-control was a primary expectation from a young age.

We stated above that ideals are not always reliable indicators of reality. The changes in rhetoric, specifically in relation to expectations of children's behaviour, are nevertheless illustrative of the differences in what was projected upon actual children in different periods. The examples we have given offer insights into the kinds of regulation considered appropriate for children from noble and/or bourgeois families, spanning the early-modern through to the industrialized modern period in Europe. The last extract in particular represents the thoughts of a highly influential writer on the social and moral education of children whose impact spanned the period from early modernity to industrializing modernity.

The writings of Erasmus, Locke and Rousseau reached beyond their initial intended readership and primary languages, to become influential in approaches to upbringing and to ideas about children and childhood across Europe. As such they can be taken as generalizable, although not universalizable, to the dominant attitudes to children over the modern period. Erasmus's educational program was not necessarily only available to the openly intended pupil, the child of the nobility or the elite; the recipient could equally be an adult of a (slightly) lower social class, literate in Latin, who aspired to the manners and knowledge of the upper classes. Rousseau, on the other hand, was specifically proffering advice on the upbringing of children and wrote in the vernacular (French).

From this small sample we can already see stark contrasts in the expectations, the perceived abilities and presumed capacities of children with profound implications for the lives of children and the meaning and values ascribed to childhood. As Norbert Elias has argued, in the medieval and early-modern period in Europe, literacy belonged largely to the nobility, so it is the social rules they formulated for their children – to which the classes closest to them also aspired and which slowly trickled down through the classes – that survive in print from those times.

Children in other (lower) classes were far less likely to receive education until at least the seventeenth century, but the popularity of Erasmus meant that over time his writings were translated not only into one but into many European vernacular languages.

What we can also see is that over 400 years, a period of radical social and political upheaval that saw major revolutions in social formations across Europe, there are concurrent mutations in the understanding of childhood and the expectations placed upon children, beginning with the social elites. In keeping with Ariès's thesis, there is also an emphasis on the greater demarcation and periodization of childhood over time.

CONTESTING THE MEANING OF CHILDHOOD

What Ariès started has flowed outward to many disciplines beyond history and is particularly important in understanding the cultural specificity of ideas of childhood, such as those upheld in the United Nations (UN) Convention on the Rights of the Child (1989) and in the International Labour Organization's (ILO) Convention on the Worst Forms of Child Labour (1999), as will be seen in Chapters 3 and 4. In such documents the UN explicitly and implicitly promotes an idea of childhood as a time of innocence and vulnerability, which we have argued is an historically and culturally contingent construction that is not necessarily appropriate or helpful in situations where people under the age of 18 can be shown to be agents in control of their lives. The young in Europe were once considered to have the ability to take all that life offered or required of them from a much earlier age than we are inclined to think of as possible now, much as children in developing countries might be active and productive contributors to the family economy today.

In approaching a more complex notion of global childhoods we have begun with a general and historicizing overview of ideas of childhood that, to a greater or lesser extent, influence the way children are understood in contemporary societies in the Global North. Central to this overview is the consideration that childhood is a constructed and highly managed stage of life, to which increasingly expert knowledges across various field are applied (as in the education of children). Indeed, the category of child and the boundaries of childhood 'always already' exist specifically in relation to the category of adult.

In the thought of Rousseau and Locke, we begin to see evidence of a break in understanding on which both developmental and socialization theories of childhood – albeit a long way off – are grounded. In Rousseau, in particular, we can discern an approach to children that is developmental: children are authentic (Romantic) natural creatures in the process of formation. Infants are born with innate capacities ready to be shaped, like lumps of clay. Socialization, on the other hand, assumes that children have the capacity to be social actors, participants in their own construction. This is closer to Locke's suggestion that children may be brought to learning through play, or through habituating regimes. There is also evidence of a movement towards the modern family – what is commonly called the nuclear family – and away from traditional forms of family that send children away to other households to be socialized, apprenticed and educated at ages as young as seven. Instead, institutions (rather than the home) to which children may still be sent away become the places that define childhood and control children, involving increasingly 'scientific' interventions into the process of shaping and disciplining children's minds and bodies to make them fit for productive economic lives. Locke's and Rousseau's descriptions of children and childhood are more recognizable because these elite views have slowly become accepted as 'natural' and 'common sense' across society in developed countries of the Global North.

There has been significant change across time and place to create the contemporary dominant Global Northern childhood. Children have mutated from being assets to sentimental objects, from physically trained social actors to psychologically developed individuals. These Western or Global Northern conceptions of childhood are what Lancy (2008) and Montgomery (2009) have criticized as being insufficient to deal with wider experiences of childhood. In the Global North, individuality is the primary understanding of subjectivity, and rights-bearing individuals are the product of centuries of the politics of liberalism and modernity (Giddens, 1991). However, armed with the knowledge of the historical contingency of the dominant idea of childhood we have the capacity to re-assess the effect of applying that notion in other places or cultural settings.

Thus far, we have dealt with the history of childhood in terms of infancy, which was largely circumscribed within the domestic sphere, and the child as educable, whether at home, at church or in schools. For the most part, the child at work was uncontested and unremarkable until the late eighteenth century. It was not until the nineteenth century that the conditions of children in the midst of intense industrialization and heightened modernity inspired militant child reform movements. We will leave a discussion of the understanding of children in relation to child labour reform for the following chapter.

NOTES

1   The unbaptized, excommunicated and those who had committed violence upon themselves were forbidden the ceremonial rites of burial. *The Book of Common Prayer* [...] *of the Church of England* (1662), p. 216.
2   The transportation of British criminals to the colonial Americas began in the early-seventeenth century and, famously, to Australia from 1788 until 1868, although slowing dramatically after 1840 (see Ekirch, 1990; Hughes, 1987). British colonial child migration began in 1618 (to Virginia), but was systematic from 1860 to the mid-1970s (see the interactive timeline, http://otoweb.cloudapp.net/timeline/, which includes images of original documents, accessed 9 October 2013).

Further reading

Ariès, P. (1962) *Centuries of Childhood: A Social History of Family Life.* Tr. Robert Baldick. New York: Alfred A. Knopf.

Cody, L.F. (2005) *Birthing the Nation: Sex, Science and the Conception of Eighteenth-Century Britons.* Oxford: Oxford University Press.

Heywood, C. (2001) *A History of Childhood: Children and Childhood in the West from Medieval to Modern Times.* Cambridge: Polity.

King, M.L. (2007) 'Concepts of childhood: What we know and where we might go', *Renaissance Quarterly*, 60: 371–407.

Laurence, A. (1994) *Women in England, 1500–1760: A Social History.* London: Phoenix.

Pollock, L. (1987) *Lasting Relationships: Parents and Children Over Three Centuries.* Hanover, NH: University Press of New England.

Stone, L. (1979) *The Family, Sex and Marriage in England, 1500–1800* (abridged edition). Harmondsworth: Penguin.

3

GLOBAL CHILDHOODS: CHILDREN AS OBJECTS OF NATIONAL AND GLOBAL CONCERN

- The twentieth century has been called the 'century of the child' and saw the emergence of children as the focus of national and international policy concern with numerous international treaties and agreements focused on children formulated in the course of the twentieth century.

- Modernizing nations articulated legislative and policy frameworks around children in line with modern standards of child development, education and protection and in order to ensure compliance with international obligations under treaties and conventions, including the UNCRC.

- The care of children within families came under scrutiny by the state, while the standard of care provided by nations for their children came under scrutiny by the international community.

- Despite advances in the conditions of childhood in many parts of the world, children and childhood remain objects of concern, and even anxiety.

- The late twentieth and early twenty-first centuries have seen the emergence of accounts of the 'death of childhood' suggesting that not only children themselves but the condition of childhood are imperilled by late modernity.

INTRODUCTION

In 1900 the Swedish educator Ellen Key nominated the new century as the 'century of the child' (Key, 1900), advocating a focus on children and their rights as the final stage in the perfection of humanity. Her treatise on children *Barnets århundrade* (1900) was rapidly translated into other European languages and into Japanese, appearing in English in 1909 under the title *The Century of the Child* (Trans. Franzos, 1909; see also Lengborn, 1993). In retrospect it may be seen that Key's pronouncement of the coming century as one in which humanity must address the condition of childhood, anticipated (and might have contributed to) the concerted legal, welfare, political and development activity directed to advancing the interests, protecting the welfare and finally enshrining the rights of children in that century. Key's work also presaged corresponding attention to children over the course of the century which led to the development of particular disciplinary specialities devoted to children (for example child psychology) and also elevated knowledge about children and childhood to the status of expert professional knowledge, as we suggest in Chapter 2. As the century progressed it was no longer sufficient to rely on common sense or past practice in dealing with children. Governments, courts and parents came to rely on child experts and professionals in childhood matters.

Key's book assisted in elevating the issue of childhood onto the world stage through its wide translation. While European in its values and assumptions (like much development in policy and legislation in the century she prefigures), Key's book is universalizing in its claims and aspirations; it participates in the emerging internationalism that marked this period of history. Her concerns go beyond the children of any one country to encompass the children of the world. The universalism of Key's claims struck chords with emerging internationalist political and philanthropic movements at the turn of the twentieth century which would give rise to international legal frameworks for the advancement of children and their welfare through the establishment of the League of Nations and the United Nations. While the care, education and welfare of children remained the responsibility of national governments, as the century progressed a range of international instruments was applied to encourage, guide and sometimes coerce nations to adopt global standards. The emergence of the global child and the idea of childhood which underpins these standards were the products of the increased internationalization of politics and law surrounding children and childhood that developed in the course of the twentieth century.

In 2000, following the adoption of the Convention on the Rights of the Child (UNCRC) in 1989 and a century after the publication of Key's book, the General Assembly of the United Nations met for its Millennial Sessions (UN, 2000a) at which a resolution was adopted that led to the Millennial Development Goals (MDGs). The purpose of the MDGs is to focus development activities towards the eradication of poverty and the encouragement of significant increases in key development indicators – several of which are focused on infants and children – by 2015. In addition to the UNCRC and the MDGs, the intervening century saw a plethora of governmental and intergovernmental initiatives, and non-governmental child-focused activism and research.

A list of key initiatives includes the establishment of international philanthropic organizations focused on child welfare including the Save the Children Fund in 1919, UNICEF in 1946 and World Vision in 1950; major child rights documents from the League of Nations (1924) and the UN (1959, 1989); the adoption of two key Hague Conference Conventions on children, one on international abductions (1980) and the second on inter-country adoption (1993); and conventions from the International Labour Organization (ILO, 1973, 1999) on child labour. Following the ground-breaking research by Dr Henry Kempe (Kempe et al., 1962; Kempe and Kempe, 1978) which brought battered baby syndrome to the attention of authorities, child abuse became another global issue of concern with the First International Congress on Child Abuse and Neglect held in Geneva in 1976, which in turn led to the founding of the International Society for the Prevention of Child Abuse and Neglect. Children in war received attention with the major report by Graça Machel (1996) which prompted an Optional Protocol supplementing the UNCRC on children in war (UN, 2000c). A further protocol (UN, 2000b) also addressed the prevention of child trafficking and child sexual exploitation and included international co-operation on global paedophilia networks and child sex tourism; they focused attention on the plight of the girl child through the UN and its agencies including UNICEF through actions on equity in the education of girls, child marriage and female genital mutilation (FGM) (UNICEF, 2013). Rising global concern with the welfare of children has also resulted in governmental inquiries into systematic child abuse in countries including Ireland and Australia, especially sexual abuse, in institutions devoted to the care of children, including church-run facilities.[1] Organizations focused on children and programmes devoted to children in general or particular groups of children encompassed, for example, child refugees, child workers, abused children, trafficked children, orphans or unsupported children, girl children, disabled children, or children with HIV/AIDS. These groups proliferated in the course of the twentieth century in what may be seen to be the activation of the optimistic, progressivist and modernist vision articulated by Key and others at the beginning of the century.

In this chapter we take a broad look at these developments. Implicit in our discussion is the question of the degree to which the increased internationalization and then globalization of standards of childhood from the Global North have actually benefited children themselves. We conclude with some very contemporary observations on emerging concerns emanating largely from the affluent countries in the Global North but now increasingly in evidence in rapidly developing economies including China and Malaysia. That is, fears that through technologization, sexualization, commodification and other features of contemporary life, childhood and children are actually imperilled, and imperilled by some of the very advantages and protections which developed economies have sought to bestow on them.

CHILDHOOD ON THE WORLD STAGE

International child-focused political activity did not arise in a vacuum. There are significant intellectual, social and political antecedents for the emergence of the concept of childhood that came to dominate international thinking and practice related to children in the twentieth century. Similarly, there is a number of factors which provided the impetus for this emerging concept of children to assume its place as a political issue of international concern and to internationalize the politics of childhood. For the purposes of our discussion in this chapter, we tease out only a few of them. They are, first, the rise of internationalist movements to address social reform issues, including labour issues, women's issues (particularly votes for women) and, gaining momentum after the end of the First World War, pacifism and world peace. Related to this, we look briefly at the rise of international feminist maternalist movements which aided in the promotion of children's issues on the international political agenda. Finally, we make reference to the long history of Christian missionary involvement in the education and 'advancement' of children in colonial and other non-Western territories, which offered a set of methodologies for intervention in the lives of children in many parts of the world and contributed to the idea that social change and development were best addressed through children. This historical survey encompasses the establishment of key agencies: Save the Children Fund in 1919 and UNICEF in 1946.

INTERNATIONALIST SOCIAL MOVEMENTS

The rise of internationalist social and political movements occurred from the mid- to late nineteenth century and intensified in the early decades of the twentieth century. Examples of international coalitions or movements include the anti-slavery movement in the early nineteenth century and the internationalization of the labour movement towards 1900. The development of internationalism was linked to the growing sense of membership of a world community amongst particular groups across the UK, Europe and the USA, which came to shape intergovernmental relations in the twentieth century and led to the formation of the League of Nations in 1920. Internationalism fostered international perspectives on social issues, and assisted in the development of a 'world' outlook (as distinct from one bounded only by the nation or in some cases empire). This world outlook found expression in other developments, such as the wave of World Fairs or International Exhibitions which swept Europe and the United States from the middle of the nineteenth century – as exemplified best by the Great Exhibition held in London in 1851 and a similar event in Paris in 1889. Notably, the rally song of socialists across the world, 'The Internationale' (1871), dates from this period. Arguably, the shifting awareness and the framing of people and issues within a world context provided some of the pre-conditions for the later development of a sense of globalism which, when accompanied by rapid technological advances from the middle of the twentieth century, gave rise to the phenomenon of globalization as we understand it today.

SAVE THE CHILDREN FUND (1919)

In the aftermath of both World Wars (1914–18, 1939–45), organizations focused on the welfare of children emerged to address the dislocation of tens of thousands of children across Europe. Their intention was to provide relief to children facing famine and poverty as a result of wartime blockades and as communities struggled to return to productivity in the post-war reconstruction phases. The Save the Children Fund, for example, had its origins in the UK in 1919 after the conclusion of the First World War. The Fund focused initially on addressing the starvation of German children due to blockades which persisted after the Armistice (Hailey, 1999; Sellick, 2001) and prevented food supplies reaching sections of the German population. Founded by sisters, Eglantyne Jebb and Dorothy Buxton, the Save the Children Fund embodied an internationalist approach to the welfare of children and is an early sign of the emergence of the concept of the world's child – to whom all nations, irrespective of politics and other considerations, owe obligations of care and protection. This conception of the child as deserving the protection of all humanity emerged more clearly into view with the League of Nations' Geneva Declaration of the Rights of the Child (GDRC) in 1924, in which it is stated that the child is owed the best that (an undifferentiated) mankind can offer it.

Jebb and Buxton faced opposition within Britain to their efforts to direct aid to the children of former enemies, but through framing concern for children as universal – indivisible along lines of nation, race or politics – they secured sufficient consensus for their cause. Children were held to be exempt from geopolitical considerations and deserving of assistance irrespective of nationality. Branches of the organization were established in other parts of Britain, in Scandinavia and elsewhere. The universalist child-centred agenda of the Save the Children Fund struck a chord with early-twentieth-century thinking on co-operation between nations with respect to children and was incorporated in part into the work of the League of Nations, established in 1920, where it found a sympathetic forum in a body committed to the pursuit of disarmament and peace between nations. A set of five principles drafted by Jebb was adopted with minimal change in the League's 1924 Declaration on the Rights of the Child (GDRC), which we discuss in more detail in Chapter 4.

INTERNATIONAL ANTI-CRUELTY MOVEMENTS

The foundation of the Save the Children Fund and the foregrounding of children's issues also owe much to the nineteenth-century welfare reformers who addressed child labour laws and child poverty, and to contemporaneous movements to counter cruelty to children. There was a comparative disregard for children relative to animals (Scott and Swain, 2002); the movement for the protection of children from cruelty was subsequent to and modelled on the movement against animal cruelty. The movement to prevent cruelty to animals, which agitated for legislation and the prosecution of individuals found to be in breach of anti-cruelty laws, developed from the Humane Society movement (originally founded as the Society for the Recovery of Persons Apparently Drowned in England in 1774). The campaign to prevent animal cruelty readily spread across England, with local societies forming in most major cities, and in Ireland in 1840. The English society was established in 1824 and received Royal patronage in 1840 whereby it became the Royal Society for the Protection of Cruelty to Animals (RSPCA).

Reflecting the increasing internationalization of social issues in the period, the movement to prevent cruelty to animals crossed the Atlantic and took root in the USA, where societies were established in New York in 1866, Pittsburgh in 1867 and San Francisco in 1868. Other comparable organizations focused on preventing

cruelty to animals and assuming the name of Humane Societies also sprang up
in many US cities. The Humane Society of Detroit, for example, was established
in 1877. The movement also spread to Canada with societies established first in
Montreal in 1869 and Ontario in 1873. In Australasia, societies were established in
all Australian colonies between 1871 and 1892, with the Society for the Prevention
of Cruelty to Animals in the colony (which became a state at Federation in 1901) of
Victoria being the first. A New Zealand society was established 1882. The humane
treatment of all animals – including labouring animals – was taken as a marker of an
advanced civilization and legislation was developed which made animal mistreatment and cruelty criminal offences in many jurisdictions in the English-speaking
world.

In 1874 in New York, Etta Wheeler sought intervention in the case of the sustained cruel treatment of a child and, facing rebuffs from several charitable organizations, finally turned to the animal charity, the American Society for the Prevention
of Cruelty to Animals (ASPCA), established eight years earlier in 1866. In agreeing
to take up the case of the abused child, called Mary Ellen, the founder of the animal
charity, Henry Bergh, resolved to establish an organization focused on child cruelty
and its prevention and secured the financial support of philanthropist John D. Wright.
The New York Society for the Prevention of Cruelty to Children (NYSPCC),
the first organization of its kind devoted to child protection, was established with
Wright's support in 1874 and incorporated in 1875 (NYSPCC, 2000). The NYSPCC
arose directly from the New York society founded to protect animals from cruelty
(NYSPCA), based on the RSPCA. The objective of the NYSPCC was:

> to rescue little children from the cruelty and demoralization which neglect,
> abandonment and improper treatment engender; to aid by all lawful means
> in the enforcement of the laws intended for their protection and benefit; to
> secure by like means the prompt conviction and punishment of all persons
> violating such laws and especially such persons as cruelly ill-treat and shame-
> fully neglect such little children of whom they claim the care, custody or
> control. (NYSPCC, 2000)

The NYSPCC was emulated in other cities across the USA, England and Australia.
It provided a model for child protection which persisted into the twentieth century
when a number of factors, including the professionalization of social work and the
emergence of the concept of child abuse as distinct from child cruelty, generated
the need for different approaches to child protection (Kempe et al., 1962; Scott and
Swain, 2002).

INTERNATIONALISM, PACIFISM, MATERNALIST FEMINISM AND CHILD WELFARE

Other influences can be seen in the philosophical underpinnings of the Save
the Children Fund and the emergence of children's issues onto an international

stage. These include the emergent movements of internationalism and pacifism, which were bolstered in the aftermath of the First World War, the horrors of which convinced many in the international community that it must be the 'war to end all wars'. The principles of pacifism, which balanced uneasily against the interests of national sovereignty, were influential in the formation in 1920 of the League of Nations, a forerunner to the United Nations. The League was committed to the maintenance of peace between nations by providing a forum for the collective diplomatic settling of international disputes that might otherwise lead to war.

Pacifism has a long history in Europe. The Renaissance scholar Desiderius Erasmus advocated against war in his *The Praise of Folly* (1509) and *The Complaint of Peace* (1517), and pacifist principles and the abhorrence of war (except in rare circumstances) were espoused by several nonconformist Protestant sects, including the Quakers and the Amish. A more secular pacifist movement developed in the nineteenth century, originally in response to the loss of life in the Napoleonic Wars (1803–15), with the formation of a number Peace Societies in Britain, Europe and also the USA. Similar organizations emerged again towards the end of the nineteenth century and in the first decades of the twentieth century, particularly in response to the First World War. A commitment to the well-being of children became intertwined with pacifist politics in the later period. This is especially evident in the work of the US activist Jane Addams, whose own activism and writings combine concerns with women and children with a commitment to pacifism. Addams was awarded the Nobel Peace Prize in 1935.

In addition to the influence of international pacifism, the incipient international focus on children exemplified by the foundation of Save the Children drew on and embodied several strands of early feminist activism that were both international and maternalist in orientation. The activism of the sisters Jebb and Buxton with respect to the welfare of children is aligned with similar maternalist-feminist activism focused on the welfare of children in the UK, the USA, Australia and New Zealand. As noted above, the feminist agenda at this time included issues such as the vote for women, which were controversial because they challenged received notions of the appropriate place and roles of women (that is, not active in the public sphere). Women voicing public concern on issues related to the welfare of children and the family, on the other hand, was considered more appropriate to their gendered roles and responsibilities for domestic matters, including the care of children (Brooklyn, 2012).

FROM SALVATION TO DEVELOPMENT: MISSIONARY LEGACIES AND THE TWENTIETH-CENTURY FOCUS ON THE CHILD

The concerns for children arising from industrialization in Europe and North America, and the rise of internationalist social justice movements, many focused on women and children, account for some influences elevating the welfare of children onto the international political stage. But the internationalization of children's issues also drew on much longer traditions, such as the activity of religious missionaries and, to varying degrees, colonial authorities in colonial and imperial territories. Even in territories beyond Europe that were not formally colonized, such as China and Japan, missionaries found plenty of work to do. Christian missionaries were active in China from the mid-nineteenth century through to 1949 (Davin, 1992; Welch, 2005).

Missionaries took up the issue of children and their welfare, in particular, with the provision of health care, education and other activities such as preparation for domestic service and other forms of menial labour, all of which were linked to religious conversion. Further, through their periodical publications, missionary societies were able to open Europeans' eyes to aspects of the lives of children in remote territories. Thus the activities of missionaries directly and indirectly informed the emerging internationalist movements of the world beyond Euro-America, opening the eyes of many in Europe and the USA to the conditions faced by those living in other parts of the world and contributing to a world-wide perspective on social issues. With de-colonization in the period following the Second World War and other geopolitical shocks, such as the establishment of the People's Republic of China in 1949, some missionary organizations re-branded themselves and shifted their emphases from redemption to development. World Vision is one such organization, which moved from China to the war zone of Korea and readily established itself within a new child-focused framework of aid and development (Hailey, 1999).

Missionary intervention in the lives of Indigenous children around the world had complex and mixed outcomes, prompting ongoing debate amongst historians and post-colonial scholars. There is no doubt that missionary projects concentrated on improving health saved many lives. Education on the other hand was bundled with religious conversion and served as a vehicle for that conversion. Education delivered in European languages offered advantages such as employment in colonial administrations and enterprises for very able students; however, it simultaneously undermined, to the point of destruction in many cases, traditional cultures and communities. As discussed in Chapter 7, missionary and later state interventions in the lives of Indigenous children in Canada, the United States and Australia, resulted in many being forcibly removed from their families and communities for schooling and other less enlightened purposes (Choo, 1997; HREOC, 1997; Jacobs, 2009).

The educational component of missionary work has been described as an instrument of colonial oppression, since missionary education served expressly to educate 'native' children to assume their 'proper' place in the colonial hierarchy and disconnected them from their cultural traditions (Achebe, 1958; Mackenzie, 1993). Education is considered by others as providing the pre-conditions for the empowerment of Indigenous peoples (Mackenzie, 1993), particularly with respect to the struggles for independence from colonial domination. In many cases independence movements have been led by individuals who had received their education from missionaries or in colonial schools and furthered their learning in the universities of colonial powers in Europe. Ho Chi Minh, Mahatma Gandhi and Lee Kuan Yew, all of whom used the master's tools to dismantle the master's house, are cited as compelling examples of the empowerment gained through European education.

Much missionary activity focused specifically on children was motivated by a combination of a desire to assist the most vulnerable members of the community and recognition that children might be the most receptive to the religious and other education being provided, as this excerpt from a Tongoland missionary's report, published in the Zambezi Mission Record in 1909 explains:

> It is, as we have often said in these pages, the children upon whom the missionary places his chief hope; but even these he cannot gain without some sort of school [...] The native school is a means to the end.

(cited in Mackenzie, 1993: 57)

In this way, the mission school was seen as indispensable to the proselytization of Indigenous populations.

As documented by scholars including Welch (2005), Davin (1992) and others, missionary work with children (or with women and children) was regularly the focus of women missionaries, both lay women and orders of nuns who worked in colonial and other territories across the Pacific (Taylor, 2008), Asia, Africa and Latin America. The work of some women in colonial settings resulted in actions to address what they perceived to be the degrading treatment of women and children in many traditional societies. For some European women, the local women's conditions struck chords and intersected with the concerns of women's movements in Europe and America – primarily the Women's Suffrage movement – that aimed to address the legal, political and other inequalities experienced by women in their own countries.

The work of Antoinette Burton (1991) and Barbara Ramusack (1990) with respect to early British maternal feminists, and Bridget Brooklyn (2012) with respect to the early women's movement in Australia, has shown that internationalism was a characteristic of these early-twentieth-century women's movements. This internationalization was in part a response to the recalcitrance women reformers faced from their own governments, and partly an expression of an emerging awareness of the commonality of issues facing women and their children across the world. A comparable international outlook and a conviction that women around the world constituted a 'sisterhood' characterized the US maternalist movement in the early decades of the twentieth century. British feminists with different political orientations rallied around the cause of 'votes for women' and through their publications increasingly reached out to women across the world, including European and Indigenous women in colonized nations. While many British feminists assumed racial and cultural superiority to their 'brown' or 'yellow' sisters, the women's movement became increasingly internationalized in focus and orientation. For example, the situation of Indian women and girls became a focal point for British feminist activism (Ramusack, 1990). This internationalization of social issues gained pace in the early twentieth century when the rise of the internationalist pacifist movement, in direct response to the horrors of the First World War, intersected with concerns for children's welfare.

UNITED NATIONS INTERNATIONAL CHILDREN'S EMERGENCY FUND (UNICEF) (1946)

The League of Nations was dissolved in 1946. The League's commitment to peace between nations and its mechanisms for the resolution of disputes had failed. However, international commitment to the welfare of children did survive through this war, with actions undertaken by non-government organizations to expatriate children from war zones and provide relief for children in distress. Examples of interventions undertaken by both charitable organizations and individuals to assist children displaced by war include actions to rescue Jewish children and children suffering privation through lack of food due to the war.

With the cessation of hostilities, the world's nations again formed a union, the United Nations (UN), established in October 1945. With the end of the war, several nationalist independence movements in former colonial territories gained momentum – including India, Indonesia, the territories of French Indo-China (Vietnam, Laos and Cambodia), Malaya, and former colonies on the African continent. A number of these newly formed nations joined the United Nations in the first decade of its operation, opening the UN to concerns that extended beyond Europe but not wholly shifting its Eurocentric thinking. In 1946, the UN founded UNICEF, the United Nations International Children's Emergency Fund, which was established with the immediate objective of assisting the welfare, resettlement and support of tens of thousands of children displaced in Europe (UNICEF, 2003). Notably, as with the Save the Children Fund, whose efforts were first directed at the plight of German children starving as the result of blockades after the First World War, the founding director of UNICEF insisted that the children of 'ex-enemies' should receive relief along with the children of Allied countries. While a principled and commendable stance, this insistence reveals much about the power base of the United Nations.

In 1953, eight years after the conclusion of the Second World War, the need for emergency intervention on behalf of European children affected by the war was deemed to have passed, but the plight of children in other parts of the world persuaded the UN of the continued need for a re-branded UNICEF. The word 'emergency' was dropped from the organization's name and it turned its attention to the problems facing children in the developing world, in particular the newly independent de-colonized nations in Africa, South Asia and South-East Asia. Within the world economic development agenda that took shape in the post-war years, special assistance to children was re-framed as a regular part of UN business, no longer or not only a response to emergencies. As discussed in Chapter 4, the UN increasingly sought to impose standards on all member states for the care, education and welfare of children and, from 1989, their political and other rights, through its Declaration on the Rights of the Child (UNDRC)

(UN, 1959) and its more ambitious Convention on the Rights of the Child (UNCRC) (UN,1989).

THE CHILD AS OBJECT OF NATIONAL CONCERN

As the historian Karen Dubinsky notes (2010: 17), 'Politicians kiss babies for a reason: children make great symbols for the nation's political aspirations'. In this section, we explore the notion that the status of modern nations on the world stage is dependent to an increased degree on their treatment of children, for which they must give account. The status of the nation's children and the nation's capacity to comply with agreed international standards on the health, development, education and protection of children have become, over the course of the second half of the twentieth century to the present, an object of concerted concern, regular monitoring and detailed statistical reporting.

The increasing emphasis on children and childhood as political issues resulted in the nation-state engaging in more elaborate levels of legislation and policy development around children and childhood from the middle of the nineteenth century. Legislation was aimed at limiting and prescribing the actions of adults with respect to children and imposing increasing obligations on parents and employers of children to comply with legislated standards of child care. Starting from the wave of legislative reforms regulating child labour in the UK in the middle of the nineteenth century, and in response to growing awareness of the specific welfare and developmental needs of children, the modern nation-state increasingly regulated such areas of childhood as education and health, the latter especially through the introduction of vaccination programmes to eradicate the deadly and disabling diseases of childhood (such as polio and rubella). During the course of the twentieth century, child welfare, once the preserve of church and philanthropic organizations, became part of the bureaucracy of the modern state. Parents, other professionals and the judiciary increasingly came to rely on the professional expertise of social workers and child psychologists in settling matters of children's residence and welfare (Kunzel, 1993; Scott and Swain, 2002). Development was uneven, even within a nation like the USA, due to a federated political organization (shared by Australia and Canada) that gave states the authority in children's matters and resulted in large variations in legislated standards. A child in Alabama is regulated by different standards with respect to compulsory education, labour laws and age of consent (or majority) than is a child in New York or Boston.

By the early twentieth century, most children (and their parents) in the Global North were subject to laws requiring mandatory school attendance up to a given age, vaccinations and periodic health and development checks (as parenting came under scientific regulation). Tighter controls were introduced to regulate the labour and employment of children, and increased protections through the raising of the age of consent for children with respect to sexual activity and marriage. It is important to note that moves to institute compulsory education met with resistance on both philosophical and material grounds (Zelizer, 1985). Many families resented the intrusion of the state in their lives and its imposition of legal requirements on parents and saw these as an erosion of the autonomy of the family or, more properly, the authority of the father (Folbre, 1983). Other families struggled with the extended period of economic dependence imposed by mandated school attendance.

The period from the mid-nineteenth century to the early twentieth century may be characterized as one which saw increasing state concern with, and control over, the regulation of children and childhood, which meant necessarily greater degrees of regulation over those dealing directly with children: that is, parents, teachers and employers. While fathers might have resented the curtailing of their absolute authority over their families, the feminist Carol Smart (1989) observes that regimes of control and protection of children emerging from the mid-nineteenth century became instruments which simultaneously placed women as mothers under increased surveillance and control.

STATUS OF CHILDREN AND THE STATUS OF THE NATION

With childhood firmly installed as a global policy issue, the process which saw nations develop systems of control and regulation over children (and those dealing with them) was extended and complemented by international systems of control and regulation, through an increasing number of international treaties, conventions and protocols, by which the actions of nations with respect to the care, development and protection of the children within their borders were subject to increasing scrutiny, surveillance and, at times, sanctions. Organizations such as the UN's World Health Organization (WHO) and UNICEF, the International Committee of the Red Cross (ICRC), the Organisation for Economic Development and Co-operation (OECD), the World Bank (WB) and many others have significant research infrastructures which enable detailed data collection, analysis and reporting on the status of children in a given country. The international apparatus of the concern for children and their optimal development now includes data on rates of participation in schooling and level of schooling attained; infant and child mortality; child labour, family and household incomes; children's nutrition and in some cases body mass indices (BMIs); rates of birth registration; children's involvement in the criminal justice systems; and the trafficking of children within and across national borders. These data collection and reporting regimes are also instruments by which the performance of nations with respect to children is measured and compared – such as the MDG national scorecards (Center for Global Development, 2010).

Such international surveillance on occasion causes acute embarrassment for developed nations, including Australia, by bringing to light the conditions of some children in the nation. For example, in 2012 on the occasion of reporting on the progress in the implementation of the principles of the UNCRC, the Australian delegation to the UN faced robust interrogation on the conditions faced by most of the nation's Indigenous children whose outcomes fall below world averages on all key indicators, including health and education. The delegation was also questioned about Australia's systematic contravention of the human rights of child asylum seekers through its policy of mandatory detention, and the conditions and treatment faced by the many thousands of Australian children in various out-of-home care arrangements (UNICEF, 2012a).

To a large extent, a nation's capacity to provide world-standard care, development opportunities and protection for all of its children has become a significant marker of the modernity and development of that nation. Thus, further refining and emphasizing of the important link between the future of the nation and the future of its children, the capacity of the modern nation to take its place on the world stage and acquire the status of a 'developed' nation, is tied to the treatment it provides to its children and various child-related indicators, which are open to scrutiny by the international community.

The intertwined stories of the journey to national modernity and the fate of the nation's children are illustrated in the post-independence history of Malaysia. This South-East Asian nation achieved independence from British rule in 1957. Following a decade of political and inter-ethnic turmoil known as the Malaysian emergency (1950–60), after which emergency measures and severe restrictions on civil liberties remained in place, Malaysia settled to strong, centralized government focused on economic development. The aspirations of the Malaysian state are articulated in national planning instruments – the Malaysia Plans – which have been released every five years since 1966 and set the agenda for national development for the coming five-year development cycle.

In their attention to the situation of children in Malaysia, the Plans reveal the growing emphasis on children as human capital for the future (Ahmad, 2013: 20ff.) and Malaysia's response to its obligations, as a modernizing nation, to international treaties and agreements on children's issues. In seeking rapid economic development, successive national governments in Malaysia have attempted to balance their enthusiastic embrace of modernization and industrialization with adherence to Islam and (selective) respect for traditional ways of life (Stivens, 1998c). The Malay people were chastised by their British colonial overlords for their lack of discipline and work ethic, and their over-indulgence of their children and undisciplined child-rearing practices (ibid.). Since the mid-1960s, Malaysia has been intent on modernizing both childhood and family in the interests of economic development. However, this process is not without tensions in the context of the conservative Muslim majority of the population (Stivens, 1998a).

The first five Malaysia Plans, which cover the period from 1966 to 1990, reflect the status and concerns of Malaysia as a Low-Income Country (LIC). The plans are focused on the establishment of basic infrastructure; with respect to children, they are directed to primary education and basic health care, including dental care. In 1992, Malaysia moved from LIC to Middle-Income Country (MIC) status, in the World Bank's classificatory system. In 1991, a year before achieving MIC status, the Malaysian government announced its ambitions to achieve High-Income Country (HIC) status by 2020 in the major policy statement *Vision 2020* (bin Mohamad, 1991a, 1991b).

Thus, within the lifespans of many contemporary Malaysians, the nation has moved from an agricultural economy – with much of its population living traditional lives in networks of rural villages (kampongs) servicing rubber, sugar and palm oil plantations and other agriculture – to the third largest economy in South-East Asia, with its population increasingly based in large, modern and industrialized cities (Stivens, 1998a, 1998b). Malaysia, which withstood the ravages of the Asian Economic Crisis of the late 1990s relatively well, has been upheld as an exemplar of economic development and its achievements with respect to the condition of childhood are especially commended by commentators.

However, this rapid modernization and development have come with costs. Malaysia has achieved impressive outcomes on key development indicators, such as the Millennial Development Goals (MDGs) and other measures. For example, it has achieved near universal participation in primary education and impressive growth in participation at higher levels of education (Economic Planning Unit, Prime Minister's Department, Malaysia and UN Country Team Malaysia, 2010; Centre for Global Development, 2010). However, the conditions endured by some of the nation's children – in particular children of ethnic minorities and female children – remain causes for grave concern (UNICEF, 2010, 2012b; Child Rights Coalition Malaysia, 2012). Some of these concerns include the low rates of child birth registration in rural Malaysia that lead to statelessness (UNICEF 2010, 2012b); the openness of Malaysia's border to child traffickers (with unregistered children being particularly vulnerable); the ambiguities presented by a dual legal system in which Sharia religious law (known as Syriah law in Malaysia) operates alongside a civil system derived from the English model; the persistence of child marriages in rural and remote areas (UNICEF 2010, 2012b); dramatic increases in rates of reported child abuse (Ahmad, 2013); and high rates of teenage pregnancy and associated infanticide, infant abandonment or 'baby dumping' as it is popularly known in Malaysia (Niner et al., 2013a, 2013b).

Commenting on the social problems of child marriage and baby dumping, progressive commentators attribute them to the repressive moral codes in Malaysia which lead to persistent gender oppression and harsh Sharia law penalties for Muslims found guilty of sexual immorality. The impact of this repressive religious law is exacerbated by inadequate education on sex and reproduction, and lack of access to contraception (Niner et al., 2013). By contrast, conservative commentators attribute the social problems to the decline in traditional Malay or Malaysian values, the falling moral standards of Malaysian youth and the negative impact of modernization (Stivens, 1998a, 1998b; Niner et al., 2013). Addressing these concerns has proved a near intractable challenge for the Malaysian government, which is caught between the imperatives of modernization and a need to appease its Muslim majority population (Niner et al., 2013a, 2013b).

Accordingly, in the sixth and more explicitly in the seventh Malaysia Plans (1990–1995 and 1996–2000 respectively), there is evidence of the Malaysian government attempting to address issues relating to children, youth and families, which are a consequence of rapid development and modernization. Along with a sustained focus on health and education, the Seventh Malaysia Plan 1996–2000 announced measures directed at community development, providing social and other safety nets for children and young people who have been disconnected from extended families in the large cities, introducing parenting support and training programmes to stem the rising tide of child abuse and neglect, and setting up enhanced regimes for child protection such as the establishment of Suspected Child Abuse and Neglect (SCAN) teams at public hospitals (Ahmad, 2013).

While Malaysia ratified the UNCRC in 1995, it was not until the Eighth Malaysia Plan (2000–05) that the Malaysian government attempted to grapple with the more challenging requirements of the UNCRC with respect to the child's rights to prevention from harm and, less effectively, with the rights of children to participate in decisions affecting them. The steps taken to modernize the regulation of children's matters by the Malaysian state can be traced through progressive law reform, with the replacement of the Children's and Young Persons Act (1949), which dates from the colonial period, with the Child Protection Act (1991), which in turn was followed by the Child Act (2001) subsequent to ratification of the UNCRC (Ahmad, 2013: 2; see also Ariffin, 1995: 356).

Nonetheless, tensions remain between Malaysia's ambitions to achieve developed country status (and all that this entails) and its desire to keep at bay what many in the country see as the negative implications of modernization and development. The framing of many social problems as the consequence of the negative influences of Western culture or 'Westoxification' (Niner et al., 2013) is a feature of conservative public discourse in Malaysia. However, some traditional cultural practices, such as child marriage, place Malaysia at odds with its obligations under the UNCRC. Similarly, while research indicates that some child abuse in Malaysia (as in other modernizing Asian societies such as Singapore) may be related to the breakdown of extended family structures and the pressures placed on parents functioning with limited support in nuclearized family units, there is also ample evidence that the extended family structures of kampong life lead to the abuse of many children. Such abuse includes the physical chastisement of children by use of the cane and the sexual abuse of girl children in particular by male relatives living in close proximity (Niner et al., 2013). Further, as discussed briefly below, as a result of both the rapid rise of the middle class and increased consumer power in Malaysia, Malaysian children are now counted amongst the most obese in Asia. Within a generation, Malaysia and its children have moved from the perils of poverty and under-development to the different, but equally real, perils of affluence and development.

FROM CHILDREN IN CRISIS TO THE CRISIS IN CHILDHOOD

Running parallel with the focus of the international community on the implementation of the UNCRC, and more recently the achievement of the MDGs by the target year of 2015, is the emergence of a series of other concerns regarding the current state and future of childhood. These largely emanate from the Global North, but are in evidence also in some rapidly developing nations, such as Malaysia (Niner et al., 2013; Stivens, 1988a, 1998b). In the context of the developing world, concerns for children arise from evidence of poverty, lack of access to education, the need to work, or economic and cultural pressures to enter forced marriages, all of which are

deemed to rob children of their innate right to childhood and force children inap-
propriately into *un*childlike roles.

In the Global North and rapidly developing countries beyond, another set of
apprehensions arises from the conditions of material affluence in which many (but
not all) children live. These include anxiety about the impact of technology on the
lives of children; the precocious sexualization of children through age-inappropriate
clothing, popular culture and merchandise; the progressive sequestering and inactiv-
ity of children inside the home due to fears of dangers outside the home; and children's preoccupation with technologized entertainment. The latter was first signalled
by the mass consumption of television, then video games, then internet games, and
now social networking sites with their attendant dangers of cyber-stalking, on-line
paedophiles, and bullying to the point of suicide. Commonly disquietude is framed
in terms of children being rendered *unchildlike*.

CHILD 'GLOBESITY' AND ENDANGERED CHILDHOOD

Access to nutritious food is an issue which highlights the differentiated risks facing
children in developed as distinct from developing countries. Assuring the right of all
children to adequate nutrition to achieve normal growth and development remains
a key goal, as reflected in both the UNCRC and the MDGs. Access to adequate
food and nutrition is seen as having an axiomatic relationship to the realization of
children's rights more generally (Jones, 2005), and the persistence of hunger and
malnutrition for many children has influenced a veering of focus of the global
children's movement from the rights-based agenda of the late 1990s to the wider
development and well-being approach which appears to have emerged in the first
decade of the this century, as outlined in Chapter 4.

What is of great interest in the emergence of the well-being approach is that it
addresses the state of children in both the Global North and South, recognizing
that both development and under-development may be the sites for poor outcomes
for children. The aid and development approaches, which preceded the move to
children's rights and the rights-based approach itself, tend to focus on and potentially demonize nations and communities whose care for children fails to meet
accepted global norms (Nieuwenhuys, 1998; Pupavac, 2001). By distinction, child
well-being measures are being applied to children in a variety of settings and have
the capacity to break down the North–South dichotomy with respect to children's
policy. For example, in 2007, UNICEF undertook an analysis of child well-being
in affluent countries which indicates that child well-being (and its absence) may
exist in a variety of contexts; and while child well-being stands to be enhanced by
improved material conditions, many children in comfortable circumstances did not
present with strong well-being indicators (UNICEF, 2007a).

Childhood obesity first emerged as a public health issue in the developed or
affluent world, yet it is not a product of affluence *per se*. The groups of children
most affected by obesity in countries such as the USA, UK and Australia are the
children of the poor, whose diet disproportionately comprises relatively cheap,
calorific foods which are high in fats and sugars. Thus, there are populations of

children within affluent nations whose dietary intake is not compatible with normal development. This is not due to lack of food, but lack of access to the right kinds of food and poor eating habits. The result does not constitute malnutrition in the sense in which it is commonly understood as inadequate food intake or starvation, but malnutrition through intakes of food products which have high calorie load but little nutritional value.

The rising weight of children around the globe prompted the World Health Organization in 2012 to label child obesity as one of the most serious health challenges of the new century:

> Globally, an estimated 170 million children (aged < 18 years) are estimated to be overweight, and in some countries the number of overweight children has trebled since 1980. The high prevalence of overweight and obesity has serious health consequences [...] and not only cause premature mortality but also long-term morbidity. In addition, overweight and obesity in children are associated with significant reductions in quality of life and a greater risk of teasing, bullying and social isolation. Due to the rapid increase in obesity prevalence and the serious health consequences, obesity is commonly considered one of the most serious health challenges of the early 21st century. (WHO, 2012: 11)

The global dimensions of the problem have led to the coining of the term 'globesity' to describe it (Altman, 2012; Passi, 2013). For example, Malaysia, which is now classified as an upper MIC, is currently facing the 'double burden' syndrome (WHO, 2013), as explained by a public health researcher: 'While we are still grappling [with] the problem of under-nutrition, prevalence of obesity has clearly increased in the past decade [...] In fact, in countries like Malaysia, there are more overweight/obese children than underweight counterparts' (Sim, 2013). Similarly, in China, a country in which rapid economic growth has brought changes of diet and lifestyle to a rapidly expanding middle class, the number of children classified as obese has tripled in the period from 1986 to 2010 (Yu et al., 2012; Ji et al., 2013).

The WHO report from 2012 cited above gives just one indication of growing global concern about the weight of children. In both the UK and Australia concern has escalated to the point where serious debate has arisen in public health, medical and legal arenas. Discussion has concentrated on the question of whether obesity in children under 12 years should be considered an actionable matter of child neglect or abuse (Alexander et al., 2009; Varness et al., 2009; Voigt, 2012). The debate has spiked in England in the academic and popular press since 2007 (Cole and Kmietowicz, 2007; Grady, 2012), and emerged prominently in Australia in 2012 with reports of two child intervention cases in the state of Victoria that saw morbidly obese children removed from parents on the grounds of neglect (Lowe, 2012). Childhood obesity is framed as a problem for the children affected. Excessive weight represents grave health risks to the child and also renders them *unchildlike*, unable to participate in the normal activities of childhood and of a bulk not conformable to ideas of children's size. Such obesity is also framed as a threat to the future wealth of nations and the world: obese children who grow into obese adults are unlikely to be productive members of society but rather a drain on the public health budget. Leading Australian child health expert, Professor Fiona Stanley, named Australian of the Year in 2003 for her work in children's health, writes about the growing epidemic of childhood obesity as a pressing challenge facing Australia and other nations. Her framework for action on child obesity in Australia casts children's value in terms of human capital for the future (Stanley, 2005).

FROM CHILDREN AS OBJECT OF CONCERN TO FEARS FOR THE END OF CHILDHOOD

While the future of the nation might be endangered through the poor health of its children, its future human capital, there is also a strong sense that children might themselves be endangered by the conditions of contemporary life, as described above (Lynott and Logue, 1993; Kehily, 2010). Since the late twentieth century, a range of publications with titles evoking the end of childhood has appeared, addressed to both popular and academic audiences. These include laments on the death of childhood (Buckingham, 2000), the disappearance of childhood (Postman, 1982), children without childhood (Winn, 1983), toxic childhood (Palmer, 2006), and the hurried child who is forced by modern pressures to grow up too fast (Elkind, 1981). There is a sense of impending crisis for children and childhood in the contemporary Global North as revealed in Elkind's diagnosis that the concept of children which is 'so vital' to the traditional American way of life is threatened 'with extinction' in the society we have created (Elkind, 1981: 3). And, as we have seen, this crisis is now spreading beyond the North to rapidly developing nations: in Malaysia, for example, the effect of modernization on the nation's youth is likened to a 'social tsunami' (Niner et al., 2013a), which apocalyptically threatens to sweep away everything in its path.

What drives this combination of high anxiety and nostalgia with respect to the state of childhood? One part of the answer might lie in an observation made by Sharon Stephens in 1995, that there is, in late modernity, 'a growing consciousness of children at risk [and] a growing sense of children themselves as the risk' (Stephens 1995: 13). Stephens's observation points to the ambivalence about children and childhood that emerges persistently in considerations of children and their place in the world. It also points to the relationships between adults' concern for children and our concern for ourselves. If childhood is imperilled, so are we.

Grappling with these issues in national and international policy has occupied time, energy and resources over the course of the twentieth century to the present. National aspirations – and fears – are tied to the status and health of the children of the nation, and their educational outcomes, in complex ways. Surveying the achievements of the 'century of the child' and the first decades of the twenty-first century, we reflect critically that while national and global attention has been directed to children at levels unprecedented in human history, a truly child-focused approach to children and their lives seems still some way off.

NOTE

1   These include the Australian Royal Commission into Institutional Responses to Child Sexual Abuse which commenced hearings in 2012 and is due to finalize its report in 2014. The Victorian Parliamentary Inquiry into the Handling of Child Abuse by Religious and Other Organisations, also conducted in 2012–13, which handed down its two volume report, *Betrayal of Trust* (Family and Community Development Committee, 2013) in November 2103. In Ireland, the Commission into Child Abuse (the Ryan Commission) was announced in 2000 and commenced in 2006. It finalized its report in 2009, *Commission to Inquire into Child Abuse* (http://www.childabusecommission.ie/rpt/pdfs/).

Further reading

Geyer, M and Paulmann, J. (2001) *The Mechanics of Internationalism: Culture, Society, and Politics from the 1840s to the First World War*. Oxford: Oxford University Press.

Kehily, M.J. (2010) 'Childhood in crisis? Tracing the contours of "crisis" and its impact upon contemporary parenting practices', *Media, Culture & Society*, 32 (2): 171–85.

Koven. S. and Michel, S. (eds) (1993) *Mothers of a New World: Maternalist Politics and the Origins of Welfare States*. New York and London: Routledge.

Ladd-Taylor. M. (1994) *Mother-Work: Women, Child Welfare and the State, 1890–1930*. Urbana: University of Illinois Press.

Rush, E and La Nauze, A. (2006) *Corporate Paedophilia: Sexualisation of Children in Australia*. The Australia Institute, Discussion Paper 60 (http://www.tai.org.au/documents/dp_fulltext/DP90.pdf).

4

THE CONVENTION ON THE RIGHTS OF THE CHILD AND THE CONSTRUCTION OF THE NORMATIVE GLOBAL CHILD

- The UNCRC enshrines universal children's rights in international law.

- The UNCRC emerges from earlier welfare- or protection-based approaches to improving the lot of children but signals the dominance of a rights-based approach to children through the principle of participation.

- The adoption of the UNCRC institutionalizes at a global level an ambitious vision for childhood and children which has its roots in the Global North.

- Debates on the UNCRC highlight tensions between its claims to universalism and cultural relativism; its construction of a normative global child against which nations in the Global South are judged on their capacities to deliver; and the appropriateness and effectiveness of a rights-based approach to the advancement of children's interests and welfare.

- The adoption of the Millennial Development Goals by the UN in 2000, 11 years after adoption of the UNCRC, signals recognition of the limitations of a rights-based approach to children in a global context in which many communities still struggle with issues of basic survival, especially for infants and children.

INTRODUCTION

We have demonstrated that the construction of the normative global child – protected from harm, provided with the requisites for normal growth and development, restricted to the activities of formal schooling, play and recreation – emerged onto the world stage in the early twentieth century following several centuries of uneven intellectual, social and legal evolution. With the adoption by the United

Nations of the Convention on the Rights of the Child (UNCRC) in 1989, the conceptualization of the normative global child took a quantum leap with the articulation of childhood as a phase of life which not only required special provision and protection, but to which rights of the kind previously associated with adulthood applied. The elevation of the child to the status of a rights-bearing individual who, at the same time, retains exceptional status in that few responsibilities of children are articulated along with these rights is a triumph of late-twentieth century liberal individualist vision but has not been without controversy and criticism.

As discussed in this chapter, criticism of the UNCRC and reservations about its rights-based approach to advancing the interests of children come from many quarters and from a range of positions along the political, philosophical and ideological spectrum. Criticism encompasses opposition to the principle that children bear rights (or bear rights which may challenge the rights of adults, including their parents); this informs the non-ratification of the convention by both the USA and Somalia. There are also serious objections which are not opposed to children's rights *per se,* but remain sceptical about the degree to which endowing children with rights that many are unable to exercise without adult intervention — by reason of their age, capacities and access to resources — is the most useful way to advance the interests of children. Criticism of the UNCRC also includes objections to the claimed universalism of the rights it articulates which entails, in the eyes of many critics, the imposition of the culturally specific vision of childhood emanating from the Global North on all the children of the world.

In this chapter we examine the UNCRC and its rights-based approach to the legal recognition and treatment of children as distinct from earlier protective or welfare frameworks which first emerged in the nineteenth century and shaped both the League of Nations' and first United Nations' efforts to codify a set of principles advancing children's interests within the international community. We then provide an overview of the contents of the UNCRC highlighting its coverage of the principles of *provision, protection/prevention* and *participation* and its articulation of the principles of the child's 'best interests'. Finally, we consider some conceptual tensions within the document and in its application in different nations, focusing on the UNCRC's claim to universalism and the implications of this claim for the culturally and economically diverse lives of children across the globe. This discussion also draws on the African Charter on the Rights and Welfare of Children (1990), a document generated by the African Union, and on other critiques of the universalism of the UNCRC.

BACKGROUND TO THE UNCRC: FROM PROTECTION TO RIGHTS

The General Assembly of the United Nations adopted the Convention on the Rights of the Child (UNCRC) in 1989. This followed nearly a century of increasing international attention on children as outlined in Chapter 3 and nearly ten years of drafting and re-drafting, and difficult negotiations with member states.

The UNCRC stands as one of the most widely supported conventions of the UN – with, as already noted, only two member states, the USA and Somalia, yet to ratify. However, this wide support is compromised by a large number of reservations by over 40 signatory states expressing concerns, limited support, and interpretative caveats on the scope and operation of articles of the convention within those states (Schabas, 1996).

The UNCRC is the pre-eminent document on children's rights in the international landscape but is joined by several other similar documents dealing with specific subjects, including additional Optional Protocols to the UNCRC on the involvement of children in armed conflict and the sale, prostitution and involvement of children in pornography (UN, 2000b, 2000c). Other intergovernmental agencies and international organizations have also formulated treaties and conventions on matters pertaining to children, but these are generally specific in scope. Those developed after 1989 refer to the standards established in the UNCRC. Some notable examples of other conventions in the global childhood policy landscape include those of the International Labour Organization (ILO) on child labour (ILO, 1973, 1999); and two Hague Conventions on Private International Law, one pertaining to the abduction of children (Hague Convention, 1980), the second to inter-country adoption (Hague Convention, 1993). There are also alternative child rights conventions – most notably the African Charter on the Rights and Welfare of the Child (ACRWC, 1990) – which highlight deep reservations of some nations in the Global South about the emphases and cultural presumptions in the UNCRC.

As discussed in Chapters 1, 2 and 3, the modern and Global Northern view of childhood as a distinct period of human existence emerged slowly and unevenly over centuries. With the rise of large industrial cities across Europe and in North America, increased numbers of children engaged in work outside the family economies that predominated in earlier more agrarian-based societies. This is not to say that child labour was a product of industrialization – children have worked throughout history – but rather that industrialization brought about changes in the kinds of work children performed. Increasingly they worked outside family-based agrarian and cottage industries and away from their families. They were thus exposed to greater exploitation and abuse (although children have never been entirely protected from bad treatment within the family).

In the large industrial centres of England, such as Manchester and Birmingham, children often under the age of 10 were engaged in dangerous work in textile mills, glassworks, mines and many other industries. Deaths and serious injuries were commonplace as children suffered injuries and disease from industrial accidents and pollutants. Further, due to internal migration, increased numbers of children were left without extended family support as family members moved from the countryside to the large industrial centres where work could be found. Urbanization brought about changed conditions for many children; life in increasingly crowded cities made childhood, childhood labour and childhood poverty more visible than it had previously been, especially to those whose own children lived different lives and enjoyed protections not available to poor and working children.

This visibility was enhanced by the rise of print media – newspapers – whose production and distribution were aided by industrialization, including mechanized printing presses and, later, the development of railway systems that enabled wider and rapid dissemination of information. The plight of children in large industrial centres in England, Europe and in the USA, the situations of both those engaged in dangerous work in factories and other occupations and those living in poverty on the streets of large cities, became the focus of various philanthropic, charitable and law reform movements.

The first wave of legal reform related to children may be seen as a response to the situation of children in industrialized cities in the middle decades of the nineteenth century. Reform was paternalistic and protectionist in orientation. In this period, amongst the upper and middle classes, more sentimental views of children and childhood emerged that were not compatible with the harsh reality facing children in the working classes. Children of the more affluent classes increasingly had access to resources which spared them from the need to engage in work, and freed them to enjoy extended leisure and education, although extended formal education was more available to boys than to girls.

Social concern was directed to the problems of child poverty and child labour through the popular press, and by writers including Charles Dickens. This was evident most particularly in his *Oliver Twist,* which appeared initially as a serial from February 1837, and then as a novel in 1838. Dickens's portrayal of Oliver contrasts the emerging sentimental view of childhood as a period of innocence with the brutal conditions of an unsupported child exposed to the horrors of the workhouse (conditions similar to those Dickens had experienced as a child in a bootblacking warehouse while his father was imprisoned for debt), and criminal rings that recruited street children and inducted them into crime. Similar in its impact to the work of Dickens, Hans Christian Andersen's *Little Match Girl* (1845), which depicts the death of an impoverished girl who makes her living selling matches on the streets of Copenhagen, brought sentimental attention to the plight of poor and working children in Denmark. Books such as these brought the issues of child neglect and exploitation to the attention of middle-class readers amongst whom more sentimental views of childhood were firmly taking hold.

Early attempts to regulate child labour – in England, first in factories and later in mines – were strongly protective in nature. Cutting across the view that children, particularly those children who had no other means of support, were an exploitable source of labour, the emerging view that children were in need of special protection from the state persuaded legislatures to introduce measures to ensure the safety of children at work and that children below certain ages would not be employed at all. Arguably, while affording children much needed protection, this movement began the historical process of restricting children's economic independence in the Global North – a process which has continued to produce modern childhood, a phase of life which is almost entirely 'useless' (Zelizer, 1985) in economic terms and, apart from obligations to undertake formal schooling, frequently idle (Stern et al., 1975).

In line with ambivalent attitudes towards children as both under threat and constituting a threat to which we return at several points in this book, it may be noted that while many involved in early attempts to reform legislation to protect children more effectively were focused on children's welfare, this sentiment was often mixed with others. These included the view that street children, and children and youths who were not under the control of adults represented a present and potential threat to law, order and public safety in the rapidly growing cities of England and other industrializing countries in Europe and America. The child or young person who is not within the control of adults is 'out of place' (Wyness, 2006) and represents both endangerment and danger.

While one approach to the growing social problems represented by unsupported and unregulated children in England was law reform, another was deportation from England to other parts of the world, as we discuss in one of the case studies in Chapter 7. From the seventeenth to the twentieth centuries, thousands of poor children from England were transported to British colonies to provide cheap labour for colonists, and clear English streets of their worrying presence.

THE 1924 AND 1959 DECLARATIONS OF THE RIGHTS OF THE CHILD

A paternalistic view of the role of the state and parties, including parents (particularly fathers) in relation to children was reflected in law, education and other domains with oversight of, or responsibility for, children and was dominant well into the twentieth century. This paternalistic view was focused on welfare and almost by definition assumed that others – that is adults, those in responsibility and the state in cases in which the child had no parents or guardians – 'knew best' what was in the best interest of children. This approach to children's interests survives to the present but now sits uneasily alongside the children's rights approach to the advancement of children, as we outline in this chapter. Thus, while the document adopted by the League of Nations in 1924, the Geneva Declaration of the Rights of the Child (GDRC) (League of Nations, 1924) refers to the rights of the child, it remains embedded within the earlier protectionist or welfare framework. We have outlined already how this Declaration, adopted six years after the conclusion of the First World War, was in part a response to the horrors of that war. The GDRC comprises five articles, and is brief in comparison to both the 1959 Declaration and the 1989 Convention adopted by the UN – the latter extending to 54 articles.

However, the GDRC not only differs in its brevity from the later UNCRC but in the governing assumption that the child has little or no agency, and is the passive recipient of either good or bad treatment from adults, an assumption conveyed in the wording of the instrument in which the phrasing 'The child must [be provided with]…' is repeated in all five articles. Notwithstanding the use of the words 'rights of the child' in its title, the GDRC is better understood as an articulation of the special duties and responsibilities *owed* to children by adults, as expressed in this headnote which precedes the five articles:

> [M]en and women of all nations, recognizing that mankind owes to the Child the best that it has to give, declare and accept it as their duty that, beyond and above all considerations of race, nationality or creed:

1. The child must be given the means requisite for its normal development, both materially and spiritually;

2. The child that is hungry must be fed; the child that is sick must be nursed; the child that is backward must be helped; the delinquent child must be reclaimed; and the orphan and the waif must be sheltered and succoured;

3. The child must be the first to receive relief in times of distress;

4. The child must be put in a position to earn a livelihood, and must be protected against every form of exploitation;

5. The child must be brought up in the consciousness that its talents must be devoted to the service of fellow men. (GDRC, 1924)

Articles 1–3 deal with the obligation of adults to make available all that is necessary for the child to develop normally; this includes food, health care, 'upbringing' and discipline, shelter and support, and relief in times of crisis. Articles 4 and 5 turn attention from the child *per se* to the child as potential citizen, with calls for the child to be provided with the means to earn a livelihood (while being protected against exploitation) and for children to be raised in the consciousness that their talents must be devoted to the service of others. In this way, Articles 4 and 5 are concerned with provision for the child which will ensure the development of a productive and socially minded responsible adult. This focus on the child as future citizen reflects a long-standing tension between the *being* and the *becoming* of children in policy and practice related to children: that is, between their inherent worth as children and their value cast in terms of whether they will be productive citizens in the future (an issue to which we return throughout this book). While the GDRC is an advance in terms of its recognition of children as requiring special attention from adults in order to reach their full potential, it does not substantially challenge earlier views of children with respect to their capacities and agency. Children remain objects of the concern and actions of adults and are not understood to be subjects in their own right. Their value is framed heavily in terms of their future potential as productive members of society.

THE UN DECLARATION OF THE RIGHTS OF THE CHILD (1959)

The 1959 UN Declaration of the Rights of the Child (UNDRC) (UN, 1959) comprises ten principles. It elaborates in more detail on several of the articles of the 1924 GDRC and includes additional principles with respect to education (Principle 7), the child's rights to identity and citizenship (Principle 3); and what might be termed an emerging awareness of the humanity of children and their psycho-social needs. The latter include references to their need for love in addition to food and shelter (Principle 6); their need for play and recreation for normal development (Principle 7); recognition of the personal differences between children through reference to the personality of the child (Principle 6); and a principle which deals specifically with children with disabilities (Principle 5). In Principles 2 and 7, the 1959 UNDRC articulates the 'best interests' principle as being a paramount consideration for nations in the enactment of laws for the protection and advancement of children (Principle 2) and in the provision of education and guidance in the development of children (Principle 7).

It is illuminating to compare the 1924 and 1959 documents for what the comparison reveals about the shifts in views of childhood in the intervening 35 years. In Principle 4, the GDRC (1924) holds that '[t]he child must be put in a position to earn a livelihood, and must be protected against every form of exploitation'. This article, along with the provision in Principle 5 that the child 'must be brought up in the consciousness that its talents must be devoted to the service of fellow men', provide only oblique reference to the education of the child – the principle that children should have access to formal education is nowhere articulated in the GDRC. The statement that the child 'must be put in a position to earn a livelihood' can cover circumstances such as those in which a child learns from an early age the craft or occupation of a family member. For example, the shepherd's child who learns to tend the flock from childhood is 'put in a position to earn a livelihood' from shepherding later in life without the need of formal education of any kind. The same applies to a range of other occupations in which tutelage may be gained from within the family or wider community – carpet weaving and many other crafts, fishing, farming, and so forth. Traditionally, as we saw in Chapter 2, many apprentices started learning their trade – often living in the family of the master tradesmen – from as early as 10 or 12 years, with this training taking the place of formal schooling. Confirming that this article assumes that it is through work and not through formal education that many children will be 'put in a position to earn a livelihood', this article stipulates that the child must be protected against 'every form of exploitation' in response to the awareness of the vulnerability of the labouring child.

By contrast, the 1959 Declaration makes different assumptions about how children's interests with respect to their future capacities are best served – and this is through formal education, access to which is cast as an entitlement:

Principle 7

The child is entitled to receive education, which shall be free and compulsory, at least in the elementary stages. He shall be given an education which will promote his general culture and enable him, on a basis of equal opportunity, to develop his abilities, his individual judgment, and his sense of moral and social responsibility, and to become a useful member of society. (UNDRC)

This principle imposes a burden on the state in realizing children's access to education: the state must provide 'free and compulsory' education 'at least in the elementary stages'. This education, while aimed in part at the utilitarian objective of supporting the child to grow into a 'useful member of society', assumes benefits other than utility: in other words, the personal development of the child, culturally, morally and socially. The 35 years between the 1924 GDRC and this UNDRC of 1959 are marked by transformations in policy and practice on education, and the normalization of increased years of school attendance for more and more children, as distinct from informal learning which might take place in a variety of work-related settings. Framing education as a right of childhood reflects the broader view, across the Global North at least, that childhood is a time for learning and development, and not for work and labour. The capacity of nations to provide universal elementary education, along with the financial ability of families to support children through extended years of schooling during which children's economic contribution to the household is limited, are variable and contingent on the wealth of nations and of the families within them.

Also by contrast, the 1959 UNDRC offers an expanded provision on the prevention of exploitation of the child in which, notably, employment in work before an appropriate minimum age and certain forms of employment are held potentially to prejudice the health, education and normal development of the child.

Principle 9

The child shall be protected against all forms of neglect, cruelty and exploitation. He shall not be the subject of traffic, in any form. The child shall not be admitted to employment before an appropriate minimum age; he shall in no case be caused or permitted to engage in any occupation or employment which would prejudice his health or education, or interfere with his physical, mental or moral development. (UNDRC)

In Principles 7 and 9, the UNDRC departs from the normative view of childhood presented in the 1924 GDRC, which envisages a world in which many children gain their education through working and in which childhood is not strictly quarantined from the economic sphere. There is the recognition that working children, beginning now to be framed as a special case, need special protections from exploitation and harm, as covered in Principle 7:

The child shall have full opportunity for play and recreation, which should be directed to the same purposes as education; society and the public authorities shall endeavor to promote the enjoyment of this right. (UNDRC)

The relegation of children to certain places deemed acceptable for them (home, school and the playground), and making an exception or special case, even to the point of demonization or criminalization (Bar-On, 1996), of children who occupy other spaces is a topic we take up in more detail in Chapter 6.

1989 UN CONVENTION ON THE RIGHTS OF THE CHILD (UNCRC)

The 1989 UNCRC (UN, 1989) builds on these two earlier attempts to codify the rights of children but departs from them in several key respects. The UNCRC attempts to account for the various dimensions which impact on the lives of children – the economic, social, cultural, and civil and political dimensions – and to frame rights for children in respect of all of these. This undertaking has been described as both 'innovative and integrationist' (Ramesh, 2001) relative to the earlier documents of the League of Nations and the UN. For example, the 1924 GDRC does not allude to the civil or political dimensions of children's lives at all. The 1959 UNDRC only alludes to these once, in Principle 3, which refers to the child's right to an identity and a nationality, both pre-conditions for citizenship.

By contrast, the UNCRC addresses the civil and political rights of children in a number of articles, to produce a politically contextualized vision of children and their rights. Articles 7 and 8 of the UNCRC address the child's rights to identity and nationality. At birth every child is to be 'registered immediately' (Article 7) ensuring legal personhood and citizenship. Notably, these articles follow directly from the statement at Article 6 of the child's 'inherent right to life', signalling the importance of the political and civil dimensions of the child's life. In Articles 13, 14 and 15, the rights of children to freedom of expression, thought, conscience, religion and association are outlined. Further embedding a vision of the child as a subject, capable of functioning in many respects like an adult (albeit within a presumptive liberal-democratic context and without adult-like responsibilities), the rights of the child to privacy are outlined in in Article 16.

CHILDREN'S RIGHTS IN THE POLITICAL RIGHTS LANDSCAPE

The rights-based framework of the UNCRC centres on children's rights and reframes needs as rights, with the need for provision and protection becoming rights. It emphasizes rights for children to *do* things in addition to having things *done to* and *for them* by adults. Thus, the child is conceptualized as an active, independent person with rights, interests and agency (Lansdown, 1994). The emergence of the concept of children's rights derives from a long history of the conceptualization of rights as a means of assuring recognition and participation in the political process which dates from the eighteenth-century European Enlightenment (Archard, 2011). In the twentieth century, following the conclusion of the Second World War, the conception of human beings as holding inalienable rights underwent a resurgence, largely as a reaction to the atrocities of the war, particularly the Holocaust and the systematic persecution of ethnic and other minorities (political dissidents, homosexuals, people with disabilities) under the Third Reich. In 1948, the General Assembly of the UN adopted the Universal Declaration of Human Rights (UNUDHR) (UN, 1948) in an effort to ensure that the events of 1939–1945 would not be repeated. In so doing, it assisted the turn to rights-based political action by a range of groups who considered themselves implicitly or explicitly excluded from the right to political participation and representation, which emerged in the following decades. These groups included, in the US context, the civil rights movement that laid claim to the rights of African Americans and members of other minorities. Internationally, such claims were made for women, gay and lesbian people, the disabled, and, through the activism and advocacy of others, children and even animals.

Garnering popular appeal, the quest for rights-based solutions to long-standing inequalities marked the period from the late 1950s and readily became linked to what has been called identity-based politics. Certain rights accorded to 'humanity', progressively since the period of the Enlightenment, and enshrined in the UNUDHR were in fact rights accorded to, or only able to be exercised by, the normative human being – the white, originally property-owning male, who was assumed to be heterosexual and able-bodied. In settler-colonial societies such as Australia, Canada, New Zealand and the USA, the wave of rights-based political action included the mobilization of Indigenous peoples for political rights, which, in this period, focused on rights to land of which they were dispossessed with the arrival of the Europeans (Scholtz, 2006).

In the most radical articulations of children's rights – as outlined by Cohen (1980) – children are held to be rights-bearing individuals, oppressed by adults and adult society, in need of liberation, and fully capable of a range of activities from which they are excluded, including sexual relations and marriage. The UNCRC's approach to children's rights is tempered by the articulation of the concept of the child's evolving capacities to understand and exercise the rights he or she bears. The concept of the evolving capacities of the child is central to the UNCRC's attempt to balance earlier protectionist and welfare approaches to children – which, by definition, highlight the vulnerability of children – with its rights-based agenda, which seeks to emphasize children's capacities to act and think for themselves and participate in key decisions affecting their lives. There is a large margin for discretion in the determination of when an individual child may have acquired the requisite capacities to assume the full range of participatory functions envisaged in the UNCRC. Some children – irrespective of their ages and capacities – will never readily be able to do so without seriously fracturing the family and community structures in which they live, whereby the notion of individual rights is subordinate to more communitarian principles of the needs and interests of the group to which the child belongs. The determination of whether a child has this capacity has emerged as an area of debate on which the advice of 'child experts' such as psychologists is increasingly called upon – particularly in legal proceedings concerning children.

OVERVIEW OF THE PROVISIONS OF THE UNCRC

The UNCRC is divided into three parts containing 54 articles. Of these, 40 of the 41 contained in Part 1 of the Convention are substantive in nature, providing definitions (including the definition of a child at Article 1) and outlining the rights of children and corresponding obligations of states and other parties in a variety of domains. The remainder of the Convention – Article 41 at the end of Part 1, Articles 43 to 45 in Part 2 and Articles 46 to 54 in Part 3 – deal with the processes within the UN and in signatory states in adopting the Convention.

A useful taxonomy of the 40 articles of the UNCRC – the 3Ps – has been developed by commentators to deal substantively with the rights of children. The 3Ps classifies the substantive articles of the convention in respect of three kinds of activity – provision for children, protection of children and participation by children (Hammarberg, 1990; Roose and Bouverne-De Bie, 2007). Some commentators have extended this to 4Ps to include prevention, arguing that the prevention provisions of the UNCRC are significant enough to warrant their own classification (Ramesh, 2001). However, for the purposes of this discussion the prevention provisions are dealt along with those dealing with protection.

All provisions are underpinned by the principle of the best interests of the child, which is explicitly mentioned on six occasions in the UNCRC, in Articles 3, 9 (twice), 18, 20 and 21. The rights to adequate provision for normal development and protection from harm are features of the earlier GDRC and UNDRC but substantially elaborated and extended in the UNCRC. The element of prevention is new to the UNCRC (as is the concept of children having rights of participation), extends the earlier idea of protection and places an increased onus on governments and others to anticipate harms to children and work to prevent them.

PROVISION

With respect to provision, the UNCRC qualitatively expands the conceptualization of provision from the basic provision outlined in the first article of the GDRC. The GDRC holds that a child 'must be given the means requisite for its normal development, both materially and spiritually'; the 1959 UNDRC expands that provision to 7 articles covering material and spiritual provision, provision of education, provision for children with disabilities, and the provision of love, understanding and an atmosphere of affection, whether within the child's own family or in other forms of care. Building on the 1959 Declaration's more qualitative conception of the range and kind of provision and nurturance needed by children, to which they are entitled as a right, the UNCRC's articles on provision include 10 articles (Articles 6(2), 9, 19, 23, 24, 26, 28, 29, 31 and 37) which map an extended range of requirements that extend well beyond food and shelter and love as necessary to the normal development of the child.

PROTECTION AND PREVENTION

In addition to articulating the rights of children to be protected from various sorts of harm, the UNCRC goes further than the 1924 and 1959 Declarations by stipulating that children are also entitled to measures that prevent harms occurring to them. The kinds of harms encompassed are preventable disease, in the calling for preventive health care regimes (Articles 23, 24); prevention of accidents (Article 24); prevention of children becoming exposed to, or involved in, the use and trade of illicit drugs (Article 33); prevention of different forms of sexual exploitation of children (Article 34); and the prevention of the abduction, sale and traffic of children. The nature of these harms, a number of which involve criminal activities, and the measures required to prevent them occurring or at least, preventing them involving children, clearly call for more systematic, legal and governmental approaches than those required by protective measures envisaged in the 1924 and 1959 Declarations. They also imply the possible need for intergovernmental approaches, as in the case of prevention of inter-country abduction and trafficking of children. The practical implications of Article 38, which regulates the participation of children in war, are discussed in more detail in Chapter 6.

PARTICIPATION

Perhaps the most significant innovation in the conceptualization of children in the UNCRC occurs in the articles which take up the issue of the child's right to participate in a range of activities, including those which may be described as political or civil in nature. It is these articles which signal the most important conceptual departure from the paternalism of the 1924 and 1959 Declarations. These two earlier documents claim to enshrine the rights of children, but neither document really envisages children as rights-bearing individuals with the capacity to exercise agency and to express their views.

Children's age-related capacities to exercise – or even to understand – rights remains a challenge in the conceptualization and actualization of children's rights, and is the subject of great debate within several disciplines including philosophy, human rights studies and childhood studies (Freeman, 1992; Federle, 1994; Pupavac, 1998, 2001; Harris-Short, 2003). While in no way resolving these challenges, the UNCRC attempts to articulate a vision of the child as a rights-bearing individual with an increasing, age-related capacity to know, understand and exercise these rights, and imposes corresponding obligations on individual adults (particularly parents), society at large and governments to inform children of their rights. This includes obligations to assist and support children in exercising their rights appropriately – that is, with the paramount principle of the best interests of the individual child in mind. Shaped by the rights-based movements which emerged from the 1960s, the UNCRC articulates rights for children in terms which shift the conception of children and their rights from 'protection to autonomy, from nurturance to self-determination, from welfare to justice' (Freeman, 1992: 3).

The rights of children to (age-related degrees of) participation, autonomy and self-determination are articulated in Article 12 which outlines the children's age- or maturity-related capacities actively to participate in decisions concerning them and in a range of political, social, civil, intellectual and cultural activities which are underpinned by principles of liberty and freedom. Article 12 states:

1. States Parties shall assure to the child who is capable of forming his or her own views the right to express those views freely in all matters affecting the child, the views of the child being given due weight in accordance with the age and maturity of the child.

2. For this purpose, the child shall in particular be provided the opportunity to be heard in any judicial and administrative proceedings affecting the child, either directly, or through a representative or an appropriate body, in a manner consistent with the procedural rules of national law. (UNCRC)

When Article 12 is read alongside the articles briefly described above – which outline the rights of children to participate in political and civil activities, to think, speak and express themselves in a variety of media, hold beliefs and associate freely, and to exercise all of these rights along with a right to privacy – it can be seen that the UNCRC goes much further than anything in the 1924 or 1959 Declarations in outlining the rights of children and in providing them with opportunities for the exercise of these rights. The rights articulated in Article 12 apply to situations outlined in other articles in the convention, all of which must be assured by the state and other parties. Thus in Article 9, which deals with circumstances in which children are separated from one or other of their parents and for whom legal or other proceedings may be needed in order to determine residence, parental care or out-of-home care arrangements, it is stated at 9.2 that:

In any proceedings pursuant to paragraph 1 of the present article, all interested parties shall be given an opportunity to participate in the proceedings and make their views known. (UNCRC)

Article 12 makes it clear that the child concerned must be considered to be one of the 'interested parties' in such legal proceedings, and that where the child 'is capable of forming his or her own views' the state must 'assure' that the child has 'the right to express those views freely in all matters affecting the child, the views of the child being given due weight in accordance with the age and maturity of the child'. While subject to a determination made by others that the child has the maturity to take this position, and bearing in mind the principle of the best interests of the child, this provides the child with both the opportunity to participate in proceedings and express views, and some assurance that those views will be given 'due weight' in the final decision concerning the child.

The concept of the agentic child – that is, the child with agency – within a rights-based framework is a significant contribution made by the UNCRC, which partially displaces earlier paternalistic, protectionist and welfare frameworks and their conception of the child as primarily an object of the actions of others. The agentic child envisaged by the UNCRC also reflects the influence – or dominance – of liberal-democratic formulations of personhood, which privilege the individual and individual rights (such as the right to privacy) over community. As discussed further below, for all its claims to universalism, the UNCRC assumes Global Northern normative political and economic conditions that are unevenly experienced in other parts of the world. Child agency exercised in domains not envisaged by the UNCRC as appropriate to children – children working on the streets of cities of the Global South, for example – is problematically situated in the UNCRC (Bar-On, 1996; Ennew, 2000). The formulation of the agentic, rights-bearing child who has some scope for self-determination theoretically opens up the possibility of a direct relationship between the child and the state which potentially compromises the authority of the family over the child.

BALANCING THE RIGHTS OF PARENTS AND CHILDREN

There is, then, a set of tensions within the UNCRC which surrounds the respective rights of children (including the right to know and be raised within their families) and the rights of families, specifically parents, given that the UNCRC imposes certain limits on the exercise of parental authority where the exercise of this authority might limit or deny a child's right as articulated in the UNCRC. Nonetheless, in its Preamble the UNCRC is emphatic on the principle of the 'fundamental' importance of families, specifically with respect to raising children, stating that member states are:

> Convinced that the family, as the fundamental group of society and the natural environment for the growth and well-being of all its members and particularly children, should be afforded the necessary protection and assistance so that it can fully assume its responsibilities within the community,
>
> Recognizing that the child, for the full and harmonious development of his or her personality, should grow up in a family environment, in an atmosphere of happiness, love and understanding [...]. (UNCRC)

While recognizing the need to afford the 'necessary protection and assistance' to families in raising children, Article 5 is directed specifically to 'responsibilities, rights and duties' of parents and extended family to support the child in exercising rights under the convention:

> States Parties shall respect the responsibilities, rights and duties of parents or, where applicable, the members of the extended family or community as provided for by local custom, legal guardians or other persons legally responsible for the child, to provide, in a manner consistent with the evolving capacities of the child, appropriate direction and guidance in the exercise by the child of the rights recognized in the present Convention. (UNCRC)

This article outlines the state's obligations to respect families and also imposes an obligation on families: 'to provide [...] appropriate direction and guidance in the exercise by the child' of rights recognized in the UNCRC. As noted by some commentators, the UNCRC establishes the possibility of a triangulated relationship between the state, the family and the child and adds a new dimension to the politicization of children and what has been described as a politics of contempt for models of family and child-rearing outside the norms envisaged by the UNCRC (Nieuwenhuys, 1998). While in many circumstances, the family will act on the child's behalf in dealing with the state, the UNCRC opens the possibility for the child to deal directly with the state and to do so against the wishes of the family – indeed, to report breaches of the UNCRC and other inappropriate or illegal conduct by parents to the state. As discussed in Chapter 6, on the question of access to education, where this might be opposed by parents on gender or economic grounds, children are theoretically empowered to go directly to authorities and complain of the contravention of their rights by their parents. Indeed, a UNCRC 'success' story posted on the UNICEF website celebrates the achievement of an Indian girl in defying her parents by working with UNICEF local representatives and against her parent's authority on the matter of her being forced into an early marriage at the cost of her education (UNICEF, 2013).

Many children require protection by the state from their own parents and this need underpins state child protection regimes, which have the authority to remove children from parents and, under certain circumstances, to terminate parental rights to authority over children. However, by enshrining the child's capacity to deal directly with the state independently of parents and family (and even against their wishes), and increasing the range of issues on which the parents might be called to account for actions relating to the child, one almost inevitable implication of the UNCRC is the flattening of differences between the status and authority of parents and children before the state and the consequent emergence of 'paranoid' parents apparently uncertain of their authority and expertise to deal with their children in the face of professional child experts and legal frameworks which mandate particular approaches to children (Furedi, 2001).

While paranoia might be a feature of parenting in the Global North, as argued by Pupavac (1998, 2001) an implicit infantilization and pathologization of adults inheres in many articles of the UNCRC; this differentially implicates adults and parents in the Global South. For many adults in the Global South, accepted practices in raising children, views on the status of children, and capacities to provide their children with the quarantined childhood of schooling and leisure are outside the vision being articulated in the UNCRC. This places these adults in a position of moral deficit as falling short of the universally accepted standard of adulthood and parenthood demanded by the UNCRC. Likewise, the nations to which such parents belong fall short of the model of modern nationhood imagined in the UNCRC and risk becoming what Pupavac calls 'pariah nations' (Pupavac, 2001). Pupavac argues that the UNCRC, with its legally binding authority on signatory states, takes the surveillance of parents and others dealing with children to new heights: it authorizes a particular model of parenting (which is underpinned by the parents' responsibility to support the child's capacity to exercise the rights it enshrines) and encourages chains of monitoring, surveillance and reporting which might commence with the child reporting parents to the state.

AN AFRICAN ALTERNATIVE TO THE UNCRC

For many nations in the Global South, the UNCRC's emphasis on the rights of the child and its silence on the corresponding responsibilities of the child to its parents and wider community are unworkable and potentially damaging to the family and community structures that support children and to which children actively contribute. The African Charter on the Rights and Welfare of the Child (ACRWC) (1990) is a document prepared by the African Committee of Experts on the Rights and Welfare of the Child (ACERWC) and is an African regional-specific alternative to the UNCRC. The ACRWC re-directs the UNCRC's focus on rights to a wider range of considerations. At Article 31, the ACRWC articulates a set of responsibilities for African children.

> Every child shall have responsibilities towards his family and society, the State and other legally recognized communities and the international community. The child, subject to his age and ability, and such limitations as may be contained in the present Charter, shall have the duty;
>
> (a) to work for the cohesion of the family, to respect his parents, superiors and elders at all times and to assist them in case of need;
>
> (b) to serve his national community by placing his physical and intellectual abilities at its service;
>
> (c) to preserve and strengthen social and national solidarity;
>
> (d) to preserve and strengthen African cultural values in his relations with other members of the society, in the spirit of tolerance, dialogue and consultation and to contribute to the moral well-being of society;
>
> (e) to preserve and strengthen the independence and the integrity of his country;
>
> (f) to contribute to the best of his abilities, at all times and at all levels, to the promotion and achievement of African Unity. (ACRWC, 1990)

While possibly prescriptive and directive in ways which might be held to compromise the child's right to freedom of thought and other freedoms expressed elsewhere in the ACRWC, the articulation of the duties and responsibilities of children is an attempt to moderate the emphasis on individual rights of the UNCRC. It attempts to rebalance the vision of childhood from one of rights, as articulated in the UNCRC, to one where access to rights is balanced by obligations to respect 'parents, elders and superiors' in addition to a range of responsibilities to the family, community and nation. For many, the installation of the global child of the twentieth century in a position to which rights but no concomitant responsibilities inhere is a philosophical and moral flaw in the UNCRC.

The ACRWC also attempts to counter what the representatives of the African states perceived to be the Eurocentrism of the UNCRC, through positing a cultural and moral framework that exists outside the Global North. Throughout the document, reference is made to 'African cultural values' in which children will be raised and regarding which they will show observance and respect. While many Africans and Africanists might dispute the degree to which a pan-African construct such as

'African cultural values' can be identified or realized, the universalizing tendencies of the ACRWC are specified as applying only to Africa and African children – they are not imposed on the children of the world. Nor do they establish a standard by which the treatment of children in other parts of the world is to be judged.

UNIVERSALISM AND CULTURAL RELATIVISM

As indicated by the moves taken by African nations to develop the ACRWC, major concerns exist in the Global South with respect to the universalism of the UNCRC. This concern runs along two main trajectories. The first is general and philosophical and relates to the degree to which the UNCRC, in its conception and reliance on the concept of individual rights, emerges from distinctively Global Northern political and philosophical foundations which are inherently at odds with the dominant communitarian and non-individualistic principles of many communities in the Global South (Harris-Short, 2001; Pupavac, 2001). As argued by Lewis, the global institutionalization of a rights-based framework for children effectively erases other, more appropriate models for thinking about children, which exist outside the Global North. To predicate the advancement of children on a rights-based agenda is to tie children's interests to a philosophical and political position which is not shared outside the Global North and to impose a standard for the care and advancement of children which is largely alien to many cultures and which, in any case, many nation-states are ill-resourced to facilitate (Lewis, 1998). By implication, any demurring from the rights-based approach is then erroneously read as a failure to support children's interests and advancement rather than as a reservation about the rights-based approach as the best or only way to achieve these goals.

The second concern is more specific and relates to the operation of the provisions of the UNCRC with respect to particular traditional cultural practices. The UNCRC states that agreement on the following 54 articles has been achieved '[t]aking due account of the importance of the traditions and cultural values of each people for the protection and harmonious development of the child'. However, many practices – including female genital mutilation (FGM) and child marriage – remain at once traditional cultural practices and in contravention of children's rights as articulated by the UNCRC. FGM is nowhere specified in the UNCRC, but remains a vexed and controversial issue in the reconciliation of the universalist reach of the UNCRC with cultural practice in many parts of the world, especially African nations.

Muteshi and Sass (2005) provide a detailed study of the prevalence of, and moves to abandon, the practice of FGM across Africa. They demonstrate that many African cultures provide contexts where girls and women strongly believe that genital 'cutting' is necessary for hygiene, femininity, identity, coming of age, religious observance, and acceptance within their communities and by prospective sexual partners. The harmfulness (and, to many, distastefulness) of FGM must be balanced against a range of other potential harms in abandoning the practice in advance of broad-based cultural change which may take years to achieve. Further, moves to criminalize or sanction the practice may simply cause it to go underground and deprive girls of medical treatment in the event of infection or other complications from the procedure (ibid.). While FGM is an abhorrent practice to many in the Global North, it remains deeply and complexly embedded in many societies. To one view, the practice is a violation of the rights of the girl child. From another perspective, to cease the practice while views about its cultural centrality persist is to risk exposing girls who have not had the procedure to a range of other potential harms. A girl whose genitals remain intact but who, by reason of this, is ostracized by her family and community and considers herself deformed, unclean and unworthy (ibid.) may have one right upheld, while other rights have been violated.

BEYOND THE UNCRC: THE RENEWED EMPHASIS ON DEVELOPMENT AND CHILD WELL-BEING

In 2000, 11 years after the adoption of the UNCRC, the UN adopted the Millennial Development Goals (MDGs) which set targets for development across eight fields, to:

1. Eradicate extreme poverty and hunger

2. Achieve universal primary education

3. Promote gender equality and empower women

4. Reduce child mortality

5. Improve maternal health

6. Combat HIV/AIDS, malaria and other diseases

7. Ensure environmental sustainability

8. Develop a global partnership for development. (UN, 2000a)

While not formally announcing a retreat from the rights-based approach to children articulated in the UNCRC, in the view of some commentators, the adoption of the MDGs is a tacit recognition by the UN and the global community that pursuing children's rights without redoubled attention to the conditions of poverty and under-development in which many children live is misdirected. The work of Gareth Jones (2005) and Yehualashet Mekonen (2010) highlights the (re-)focus in global thinking and practices on the advancement of children in the light of the commitment to the MDGs and identifies the emergence of the relatively new concept of child well-being in the arena of global childhood policy. The concept of well-being is not necessarily tied to rights, and stands to be enhanced by higher levels of material provision, but may exist in a range of conditions. Nevertheless, well-being signals a more holistic approach to the children and the conditions in which they live as distinct from attempting to impose on all children, irrespective of their material and cultural circumstances, a universalized concept of rights. Research also indicates that well-being is a concept to which children can relate, thus opening the possibility of children participating more actively in policy determinations (Ben-Arieh, 2005; Thoilliez, 2011).

REFLECTIONS ON THE UNCRC

The UNCRC dominated global children's policy for more than a decade with its rights-based approach to advancing the condition of children across the world and represents a high point in the construction of the global child, possessed of rights, agency and capacities for self-determination. This does not necessarily mean that this has coincided with a high point for children of the globe who, as Freeman (1992) observes, were not even consulted in its formulation. Assessments of the achievements of the UNCRC and the pursuit of children's advancement through the articulation (if not the realization) of their rights may take time and further research.

The rights-based approach to children of the late twentieth century arose out of the earlier welfare or protection regimes. Each of these conceptual frameworks for the advancement of children reflect prevailing intellectual and political currents of their times. There are signs that the dominance of rights-based thinking on children is now giving way to a more holistic consideration of child well-being as the basis of global policy and action. In the journey from the protection of children to the rights of children and now it seems the well-being of children, children nonetheless remain largely subject to policy and approaches to which they have little input. While they remain objects of global concern and action, considerations of what a child is and how children's interests are best advanced rarely actively include the voices and views of children themselves.

Further reading

Harris-Short, S. (2003) 'International human rights law: Imperialist, inept and ineffective? Cultural relativism and the UN Convention on the Rights of the Child', *Human Rights Quarterly*, 25 (1): 130–81.

Quartly. M. (2010) 'The rights of the child in global perspective', *Children Australia*, 35 (2): 38–42.

UNICEF (2007c) *Protecting the World's Children: Impact of the Convention on the Rights of the Child in Diverse Legal Systems*. Cambridge and New York: Cambridge University Press and UNICEF.

Part Two

CASE STUDIES IN THE MEANING OF CHILDREN AND CHILDHOOD

5

THE HABITUS OF CHILDHOOD: HOME, SCHOOL, WORK

- A child's habitus is embodied within and framed by 'family', in all its possible forms, through the child's earliest interactions with place and space.

- The places and spaces of childhood that attract the most attention from researchers and policy-makers are the home, school and work.

- Case studies quickly demonstrate that the dominant notions of the appropriate spaces and places of childhood are not homogeneous, whether within or between nations.

- As there are multiple expressions of habitus, children interact with place and space in multiple ways.

In Part One of *Global Childhoods*, we have looked at the effects of Global Northern notions of childhood as they have been shaped within the cultures of developed countries, and as they have been disseminated around the globe through international policies embedded in political interventions and the delivery of aid. In Part 2 we turn to look at a series of case studies to begin analysing the diversity of childhood within and between cultures: in developed, developing and underdeveloped countries. These case studies offer examples that bring into question the universalizability of the dominant concepts and ideas mapped out in Part 1. In this first chapter of Part 2, we start this contextualization of children and childhood by examining the spaces and places associated with childhood: home, school and work.

In the affluent Global North, child labour laws have existed since the nineteenth century and the lives of many children are now relegated solely to the (private) ordered and professionally managed places of home and school, in which (public) places of structured or unstructured 'play' are also comprehended. These are physical environments in which – we imagine – children are cherished and cared for, nurtured and educated to reach their full potential. Yet, data from countries around the world show that 'home' and the privatized places of childhood such as 'school' are not and have not been unconditionally safe or equitable for children. Rather, they may be places of physical, sexual and psychological harm and abuse, and their benefits made unevenly available on the basis of class, ethnicity and gender. Further, as we have already seen from historical evidence, children have had socially and culturally approved roles in all three of these places over time, and the boundaries between home, school and work are not and never have been clearly or completely demarcated.

In the Global South, home may be configured very differently from the stereotypical nuclear family of the Global North. Where many children lack access to education, the places of childhood may be quite public (on the streets, in factories and in sweatshops), and children's activities may co-exist across our three spatial categories. In short, while it may be tempting to assume that the spaces of home, school and work are separate and discrete, this is not the case anywhere in the world. Nevertheless, these specific places all represent aspects of children's lives with which researchers into childhood are concerned.

THE HABITUS OF CHILDHOOD

Starting with the earliest efforts to re-conceptualize childhood as a period of being (Alanen, 1988; James and Prout, 1990; James, Jenks and Prout, 1998; Jenks, 1982; Qvortrup, 1991), research that explicitly addresses children's use of or positioning within space has repeatedly made use of Bourdieu's notion of habitus (1977, 1984). Habitus is the interpenetration of our social, cultural and physical environment – the faces, places and spaces – that we as social beings inhabit, through which we know ourselves and by which others identify us. Habitus is generally conceived of in terms of adult embodiment. However, given that it is a phenomenon acquired, embedded and embodied over a lifetime, Bourdieu's notion of habitus, implicitly, is a matter of great concern in the study of children and the conceptualization of childhood. Habitus is laid down in the body from infancy and therefore is an experience of childhood. Or more properly, childhood is crucial to the foundation and shaping of habitus.

Bourdieu's habitus provides a particularly effective analytical framework for interpreting the nature of place in relation to childhood, as it allows the places of childhood to be nuanced both as separate and interconnected spaces rather than viewed simply as discrete geographic locations. Home, school and work are what Bourdieu has termed 'fields of play', in which children are gaining knowledge and levels of expertise that (in)form their habitus. As Bourdieu has noted, habitus is first formed within the family, or the spatial realm of home, but it is affected by the institutional structuring of the various fields of play that make up the habitus (1984), the most dominant of which are school and work. What that 'family' might be need not be restricted to the nuclear family; we take family, and therefore the home, as encompassing a broad sense of kin or kin-like relationships.[1]

We physically and psychologically *embody* the social and political spaces – *the fields of practice* – we inhabit and/or identify with, a process which Bourdieu argues begins with our earliest childhood experiences. The possession of expertise in the 'rules of the game' in any such field of practice, our *cultural capital*, is the knowledge we possess, whether straightforwardly (through structured education) or less obviously (through informal learning, like manners), acquired in keeping with and related to our social class. We might also have *symbolic capital*: or prestige, relating to how well we are able to 'play the game'. *Cultural capital* involves a degree of choice or 'good taste' that extends to and is inseparable from the material sense of taste that motivates our preferences in what we eat and that is embedded in the experiences of childhood:

> it is probably in tastes in *food* that one would find the strongest and most indelible mark of infant learning, the lessons which longest withstand the distancing or collapse of the native world and most durably maintain nostalgia for it. (1984: 79)

Taste and our choices or dispositions towards something like food, in turn, affects the physical shape of the body in its 'dimensions (volume, height, weight) and shapes (round or square, stiff or supple, straight or curved) of its visible forms, which express in countless ways a whole relation to the body' (1984: 190). While the forms habitus takes are not homogeneous, it is possible to argue that the praxis (that is, lived actions in the moment) that leads to the formation of habitus is observable across cultures, in children's earliest negotiations over power, over the consumption of food (Gillen and Hancock, 2006).

That might mean that someone who is from a particular background and as a result is highly skilled in the rules in a given 'field of play' will have both the symbolic and cultural capital that will allow him or her to ask questions or reactively offer relevant information. In a situation that values that knowledge, being skilled in the 'game' will ensure the most appropriate response and outcomes. For example, in a medical consultation, the capacity of the patient not only to answer the questions posed in taking a medical history but to volunteer further information without being prompted is likely to increase the likelihood of an accurate diagnosis and treatment. Someone faced with the same set of circumstances but with less (or simply different) cultural and/or symbolic capital, whose capacity to 'play the game' is more limited, may fare less well, even when the situation might appear favourable to him or her. So, if local understandings of embodiment and disease (cultural and symbolic capital) are not taken into account in the delivery of foreign medical aid into a community, the likelihood of inaccurate diagnoses and ineffective treatment arises (see Pienaar, 2013).

The novels of Charles Dickens provide pertinent examples from fiction that help expand upon the idea of the habitus of childhood. Dickens repeatedly introduces child characters who are skilled in 'fields of play', and who possess appropriate levels of symbolic and cultural capital for their habitus to succeed in the 'game': although, they may be ill-prepared and ill-equipped to cope with a shift into the habitus of another class. The Artful Dodger in *Oliver Twist* (1838) is a prime example of a child who is an expert 'player' on the streets and in the slums of nineteenth-century London. He has all the capacities to thrive within the habitus that has been formed within his 'family', namely, Fagin and the other child pickpockets with whom the Dodger was apprenticed in the art of theft to the point of becoming adept in his trade.

Conversely, Pip in *Great Expectations* (1860), whose elder sister and blacksmith brother-in-law constitute his family, is proficient enough in the habitus formed in his apprenticeship at the forge to be resourceful in his encounter with the escaped convict and murderer, Magwitch. However, his habitus does not prepare him for exposure to the middle-class cultural and social expectations of Miss Havisham and her protégée, Estella. Even when Pip acquires economic capital and is given training in the cultural and symbolic capital of a middle-class habitus, his lack of expertise leaves him open to ridicule and abuse. The title characters of *Oliver Twist* and *David Copperfield* (1850) offer similar examples of children who are 'out of place' and have to negotiate the boundaries around symbolic and cultural capital in the fields of play in which they find themselves. While these are fictional models, Dickens's novels were both influenced by and highly influential on the child reform movements in England which, as outlined in Chapter 3, spread across the Atlantic to the USA. Thus, Dickens's child figures assumed an important place in the internationalization of sentimentalized norms of childhood and remain directly connected to the dominant and internationalizing models of children and childhood that have stemmed from them.

It is implicit in Bourdieu's ideas of fields of play that adults (parents, teachers, lawyers, doctors, policy-makers) have the upper hand when it comes to symbolic and cultural capital in the formation of habitus, and therefore a dominant position in relation to the child's habitus. These 'structuring' and institutional adults have the recognized capacity to define and delimit the child through monitoring and directing his or her body, and how and where it is situated as he or she 'becomes' an adult. In this dynamic, as in developmental interpretations, childhood has generally been conceived of as a stage in a process, whereby one becomes imbued with habitus. The sociological project begun by Alanen (1988), James and Prout (1990), and James, Jenks and Prout (1998), explicitly recognized the importance of family habitus while also rejecting the notion of the child as *only* a 'becoming' adult. Their aim was to validate childhood as a period of 'being' in its own right (Qvortrup, 1991), and to recognize children as agents in their own right. In this binary opposition of being/becoming, until relatively recently, adulthood has been characterized as a state of being in which one is fully imbued with one's habitus, no matter what one's level of expertise in any given field of play.

More recently, following on the breaking down of dichotomies in the reconceptualization of adulthood as a state of *both* 'being and becoming', Uprichard (2008) has argued for this approach to be extended to children and childhood. While sociologists like Alanen, James, Jenks and Prout and others shifted the discourse on children and childhood to emphasize their 'being', which enabled a view that 'presents children as agents of their own social worlds' (ibid.: 305), Uprichard finds concentrating solely on the 'being' child unsatisfactory for two reasons. As we saw in Chapter 1, socialization has often been presented as the binary opposite to developmental theories, and Uprichard argues that to favour 'being' in opposition to 'becoming' merely leads to socialization being mirrored by developmentalism in an unhelpful dichotomization. Her second objection is that it does not take into account the 'future' experiences of the projected adult – which children are aware of and incorporate into their daily lives. However, she admits that the 'becoming' child appears implicitly and explicitly in research: 'In other words, the two constructs of the child are already being used together. [Uprichard] simply argues that they are done so more often and more explicitly' (2008: 306).

Much like phenomenological arguments that have sought for reconciliation between rather than a privileging of either the mind or the body in talking about embodiment (Merleau–Ponty, 1962), Uprichard believes the sociological and psychological, present and future, nature and nurture, being and becoming, are inextricable.

> There is a need, therefore, for a multi-disciplinary construction of the 'child', which fits with children's own constructions of their experiences of child-hood. [… which] is *not* to say that the biological base of childhood is a forceful determinant. Rather, it is acknowledging that children do become adults and the kinds of adults they are likely to become are shaped by the kinds of child-hoods they are experiencing today. (Uprichard, 2008: 311)

Like Uprichard, we interpret childhood as a period of both 'being and becoming' and children as both social agents and persons in a flux of formation.

This interplay of being and becoming can be seen implicitly at work in research into habitus at the site of the child's body, in which habitus is implicitly and explicitly theorized as formed within the frame of 'family' and what constitutes family may be as varied as what constitutes a child or childhood. The three fields of play – home, school and work – are used to interrogate and critically engage with not only the effects but also the boundaries of habitus, and the appropriate spaces and places of childhood.

HOME: FAMILY HABITUS, CHILD-HEADED HOUSEHOLDS, AND CHILDREN ALONE

Habitus is formed in the 'home' which is both a physically located place or space, and more importantly, the people who live within and around it. These notions have significant potential for application to the social theorization of the lived experience of childhood. In whatever form it takes, the family is the key determinant in the production of habitus. Childhood is structured within the family's sense of what is appropriate to their habitus (Bourdieu, 1984; Tomanovic, 2004). Bourdieu's study of 1960s Parisian society in *Distinction* (1984) amply demonstrates that habitus differs, at a very basic level, on the basis of class or socio-economic status. His theoriza-tion of capital (social, cultural, physical, symbolic and economic), fields, taste and disposition is an extension of his concern to understand the determinants around how the human body both reflects and instantiates all levels of our background and environment. Differential access to capital leads to disparate experiences of habitus in childhood. To expand our point we will begin by looking at one example from the wide range of studies of children's habitus.

In a longitudinal study of two groups of Serbian children, one working class and one middle class, we find a detailed comparative example of how 'the habitus is inculcated as much, if not more, by experience as by explicit *teaching*' (Jenkins, 1992: 76, cited in Tomanivic, 2004: 343, her emphasis). The families' differential access to and 'allocation, distribution and use' of social, cultural and economic capital has persistent effects on children's habitus (ibid.: 343). In particular, children's use of urban space, their taking part in cultural activities (being) and their ideas of possible futures (becoming), can be demonstrated to result from their family habitus.

Interviews with each of these groups of children, conducted in 1993–4 and again in 2000, studied how (or whether) they used and moved through urban spaces, and revealed that their use of space was tied 'to temporal routines and everyday activity schedules' (Tomanovic, 2004: 344). The working-class children tended to stay home with the family and the middle-class children tended to go out into urban spaces, because they are socialized to do so by their parents. Middle-class children were familiar and comfortable with going to theatre, children's movies, having dinner out, etc. The working-class children were not and therefore did not, partly because they lacked the means to do so but also because it was not within their habitus, as shaped by their parents' example. This limited 'their spatial mobility to their suburban housing estates and the immediate surroundings' (ibid.: 345).[2] Those from a middle-class background had their time highly organized for them, whereas amongst the working class children, there was 'little structured and very little controlled time, but at the same time few activities' (ibid.: 346).

In this, a direct relationship is drawn between economic capital and cultural or symbolic capital (Tomanovic, 2004: 347). Middle-class children attend institutions (music lessons, foreign language classes, sports, theatre) and undertake activities designed for them; working-class children access culture in private realms (radio broadcasts of neo-folk music, television, walking) that are at the same time less structured. What is immediately obvious from this one study is that the higher the class, the closer children come to the UNCRC model of agentic and actively participatory childhood. The working-class children's 'significant actors' (ibid.: 351) – those who shape the habitus – were their immediate and extended family, and neighbours. The middle-class children's experiences were shaped by their families but they were also introduced to wider networks of friends and friends' parents via their more dispersed social activities. Across classes, their everyday lives are 'shaped directly by family habitus and lifestyle as it is externalized in the use of space, the organization of time and cultural tastes' (ibid.: 354):

> At the same time, family habitus activates different kinds of capital for (and by) children and thereby constructs different childhood practices. (ibid.: 356)

The habitus of childhood has elements that are socially and even culturally cross-cutting, but not universalizing. The general notion of habitus is a generalizable variable across class and culture as a process of both being and becoming, formed in the 'home'. What that home consists of and the constituents of that family determine, particularly during childhood, the places and spaces of childhood and how the child relates to their surroundings. In this example from the Global North, the notion of childhood and children as defined by the UNCRC is clearly recognizable – innocent, at play, learning, protected, nurtured by adults – but there are also points of departure from any straightforward norm of childhood habitus, along class lines.

Family of whatever kin or kin-like formation is generally assumed (across cultures) to have one or more adults in the role of care-giver and/or economic provider. As we have seen in relation to the UNCRC and as discussed in a later chapter with respect to orphans and adoption, one of the prime drivers in national and international policy around children is that they are to be cared for; and that a child alone or unsupervised is considered to be inherently at risk. Children who form and maintain a family unit or household without the day-to-day guidance of an adult problematize this imperative; as well as the allied notion of children subordinate to adults, and as incapable of forming a family unit *on their own* (Payne, 2012).

The actions of children who form Child Headed Households (CHH) are often characterized as the product of 'agency in the face of adversity': that is, their capacity to act is only noticed and comes up for discussion 'precisely, and it often seems only, because they live in situations of permanent crisis' (Payne, 2012: 399). Ruth Payne's interviews with young Zambians who have become heads of households after the death and/or serious illness of adult members of their families, render a rather different picture. Despite their own sense of their lives as essentially 'ordinary', they are consistently the objects of and patronized by social workers, government bodies and aid agencies. In CHH children exert 'everyday agency' that deserves recognition of their actions and capacities as being as 'important and legitimate' as their 'need of protection' (ibid.: 400). Payne openly calls into question the universalizability of interventions that are embedded in UNCRC assumptions, arguing that those adults who are intent on intervention, 'should pay greater attention to children and young people's own perspectives of their lives, rather than using definitions and categories (e.g. CHH, orphan, etc.) founded on externally derived notions of them as vulnerable and "in crisis"' (ibid.: 400).

These young people, while classified as children under the UNCRC and seen by adults proposing interventions as abnormal, un-childlike and out of place, are coping in an everyday and normal way. Individual CHH members can therefore resent adults and/or guardians being inserted into their lives, or losing their position of responsibility when a debilitated adult recovers. The frictions caused by this 're-childing' of the agential child are similar to those experienced in the reintegration of demobilized child soldiers, as we shall see in Chapter 6. This is not to deny that these young people are living in 'precarious situations', rather that, while they know and admit that they face difficulties, 'this was not the only framework, or even the predominant one, through which they understood their realities' (Payne, 2012: 405). Their roles as functional household heads and the legitimate structures in which they operate are at odds with assumptions about children's agency that are implicit in the policies being applied to them. These are, in turn, founded in 'discourses of crisis and survival for "children at risk"' (ibid.: 406), as founded in the UNCRC.

Such complex and challenging situations require more appropriate social interventions which are not only more culturally sensitive but which are also 'rooted in
local knowledge *from* CHHs, not *local level* knowledge *about* CHHs (e.g. from local
NGOs, other community members, etc.)' (Payne 2012: 406). These young people
are providing the frame within which younger members of the household/family
are inculcated into their wider habitus, in a non-standard yet legitimate family form,
while at the same time both being and becoming heads of households in their own
right. In doing so, as in other family formations, they are setting the conditions of
possibility for the embodiment of cultural, social and symbolic capital. While they
are put at a disadvantage by having to compete for resources on the same basis as
adult-headed households, at the same time these young people in CHH are implicitly treated as agents within their wider culture.

Conversely, young people of similar ages and relative competencies, who are without a physical 'home' due to war or other crises, have been actively removed from
their families when they have sought asylum in the UK (Crawley, 2010). Heaven
Crawley's (2010) interviews with young teenagers separated from their parents and/
or families, because their age was disputed, tells a story of disempowerment and abuse
as they were questioned over their application for asylum in the UK. The interview
techniques used by immigration officers that Crawley describes appear to be based
on psychological or developmental principles which, on the one hand, are intended
to treat an interviewee as rational – in separating him or her for individual assessment. However, in practice, the interviewers treat these asylum-seekers as if they are
'guilty', and are patronizing, disbelieving and 'rude'. In short, they treat them *like
children*, even though they simultaneously consider them to be 'unchildlike': '[based
on 2007 figures] over a third (35%) of all asylum seekers who arrive claiming to be
children are age-disputed and treated as adults' (Crawley, 2010: 167). The confronting life experiences that these young people have undergone (generally in war) are
downplayed, dismissed or ignored.

In each of these examples, the notions of the family and the context of home –
national, local and familial – as the seat of habitus are problematized. Class differences show that habitus clearly affects one's perception of what is an appropriate
place or space in which to circulate: the CHHs undermine the assumption that
the 'home' is only functional when headed by an adult 'carer', and the treatment of child asylum seekers demonstrates that the inability to think outside of
rigid norms of 'family' and 'home' can lead to the institutional abuse (rather than
protection) of children who have already been exposed to atrocities. In each of
these examples of non-standard homes, the children within them have significant
agency, are confident in their habitus to a large degree, and in their being and
becoming.

SCHOOL: INSTITUTIONS, REGIMES AND CONTROLLING CHILDHOOD

As we have demonstrated, 'home' and the family is the primary site of the formation of habitus: this can in turn affect the approach to, experience of and

outcomes from education. Bourdieu was clear that institutions, and in particular educational structures (Bourdieu and Wacquant, 1992), affect the ongoing shaping of the habitus. So, family habitus sets the tone for a child's interaction with formal education, but that may undergo revision during the schooling experience. The importance of education – in its broadest sense – has already been touched on in the discussion of home. We saw that what the middle-class parents chose to instil in the habitus in terms of after-school education, on the basis of greater economic capital, affected their children's social, cultural and symbolic capital. The working-class children were not as closely monitored in their activities, but by the second series of interviews their approach to education was much more pragmatic and strategic than their 'cultured' middle-class counterparts, in that they were actively planning the employment and later life outcomes of their 'becoming'. Nevertheless, there is a clear separation between the places of 'home' and the places of 'school' (Tomanovic, 2004).

In theoretical approaches, national plans and international policy, 'school' may be understood as spatially constituted in a wide range of forms; however, the general expectation of schooling practice is that it should begin with early childhood care and education (ECCE). In a global context, that frequently involves the programmatic influencing of the national education policies of developing and under-developed countries, so that they meet the agendas of donor nations and/ or international organizations such as the UN and/or the World Bank (Molla, 2013). To elaborate we will look at a comparison of the incursion of early childhood care and education (ECCE) policies in two cultures, Norway and Ethiopia, where 'it is possible to identify some similarities between how global discourses on education and rights affect children in different local contexts' (Kjørholt, 2013: 245).

Applying Global Northern notions of children and childhood through education programmes in developing countries is shown to be not entirely beneficial, particularly when it is contesting and transforming 'local knowledge and notions of childhood' (Kjørholt, 2013: 246). In Norway, the global discourse on ECCE has turned to seeing children as objects of 'human capital' and there has been a 'growing emphasis on children as *users* and *consumers* in Nordic countries' (ibid.: 248). In this, education is being characterized as a 'bazaar' (ibid.) in which children may select the education-du-jour. These moves are underpinned by Global Northern notions of what it is to be human that are based on values of individual liberties and rights implicit in the UNCRC, which are being exported with aid programmes and children's parliaments, under the auspices of bodies like UNICEF, where it is unclear 'what implications this has for children and the variety of different local lives in countries in the global South' (ibid.: 249).

In her interviewing of children who have attended such children's parliaments in Ethiopia, Anne Trine Kjørholt provides two illuminating quotations. One is from a young girl, who makes clear she knows she is able, and is prepared, to threaten her parents with reporting them to the children's parliament if they do not send her to school. The other is from a young boy who recognizes that if he does go to school, his family will suffer economically: 'who is going to do my part of the work?' (Kjørholt, 2013: 250). Ethiopia has a fragile economy in which children's contribution to the family economy can be crucial to everyone's survival (ibid.: 250). The direct application of external values, rather than being helpful, can in fact be destructive and ignores the place of local knowledge and expertise.

The Global North values child-centred education but this is itself shifting to a neo-liberal approach of students as human capital, which privileges the child as the means (becoming) to his or her own end (a citizen). As we have argued, the imposition of a global norm and ideal of children and childhood may be an agent of compromising existing cultural, social and political structures. In Ethiopia, children are being organized, by external adults, to aim for individual rights-based existence at the cost of local knowledge that is more likely to lead to sustainable livelihoods. In short, they are losing local knowledge about survival such as local plants that can be eaten.

> This deterioration of local environmental knowledge is connected to wider processes of social and economic change such as increased urbanisation and deforestation (Ali and others, 2013), albeit unintentionally contributing to a further risk of poverty for children and their families. (ibid.: 252)

Kjørholt (p. 252) is in favour of improving education, but argues that it must be sustainable and more than 'detaching children from their rural ways of life, without giving them the opportunity to benefit from the rewards of modern education'. Overall, the applicability of rights discourse is debatable unless it is opened out to include further concepts (Kjørholt, 2013: 253). That is, enhancing education through aid must take into account both the local and national habitus, the existing strengths of local interconnections between 'home' and 'school', or risk entrenching poverty. So, the habitus of the child is being redirected by external (adult) influences away from the public spaces of traditional knowledge and learning and into the privatized space of (inadequate) formal education.

To return to our discussion of the experiences of asylum-seeker children, many asylum seekers are housed in situations where 'home' is barely distinguishable from 'school': that is, where both places are within the boundaries of a detention or asylum centre. Children living and learning in Danish asylum centres exhibit the ill-effects of these spaces on their identity, at least partly as the result of an institutional effect (Vitus, 2010). They are restricted to a place of school/home where there is little sense of time passing and, therefore, of a 'future'.

In the case of the individuals Vitus discusses, these children are not necessarily separated from their families (or only partially, in choosing to stay with siblings rather than a parent in some instances) but their family habitus is forcibly changed in its temporal structure. Vitus describes the destructive effects of leaving children of a wide range of ages '"hanging" in time and space' as they await asylum application outcomes, often for years. That 'hanging' takes place in the classrooms where they are given limited access to education and no sense of what may wait for them 'outside'. 'Social positions and dispositions (which [Bourdieu] calls "habitus") determine agents' anticipation of the future and the strategies agents apply as reactions to the possibilities offered and the temporal structures in which they are positioned' (Vitus, 2010: 28). In a situation where these children cannot imagine a future, where any future 'ceases to be a point of reference for the fact of their existence at all' (ibid.: 40), they have no power in their 'being' and no sense of the possibilities of 'becoming', which leads to despair. School, far from offering them pathways or imagined possibilities, becomes a time-wasting or time-filling exercise.

Where the child is able to imagine a future, and home and school are more discrete spaces, habitus nonetheless affects a child's capacity to 'play the game' in the 'field' that is education. Dominant cultural views are imbued through habitus within the family home and, in one study of US high schoolers, it is argued that the girls studied may be better able and 'may be more encouraged to make use of their cultural capital to succeed in school' (Dumais, 2002: 44) than their male counterparts. Amongst this cohort cultural capital, while influential, did not raise students' examination scores in and of itself, rather, three interlinking factors led to success: ability (to play the game), (family) habitus and economic capital (ibid.: 59). Family habitus may affect not only 'high' academic achievement but also the desire to take part in school activities in the first place. Fitzgerald and Kirk (2009) found that for disabled youth their family's approach to introducing them to engaging in sport varied between being supportive and enabling of them taking part, or denying the ability to do so. This had flow-on effects on the identity of these disabled youth, within the family and in relation to their bodies/embodied identities (ibid.: 471). Those who were supported were more confident and had a more complete sense of social identity, in contrast to those who were not and who, as a result, were less confident and more dependent on their families.

Relatedly, class habitus is not a straightforward indicator of 'success' in schooling and future employment prospects. As we saw amongst Tomanovic's study of Serbian working- and middle-class children, by the time the working-class children had reached their teens they were more pragmatically prepared for their future lives in having clear goals and plans for employment, whereas the middle-class children were generally unfocused. Similar results are seen in students at two US high schools with broadly different social demographics (Threadgold and Nilan, 2009). This study showed middle-class students appear to be overly optimistic about their prospects: 'those higher in cultural capital showed a more casual, relaxed and individualized approach towards the future' (ibid.: 64). Conversely, working-class students (at Montesano high school) are more realistic and more reflexive. They are therefore better adapted to expect more of themselves if they want to achieve their educational and employment goals. Montesano youth thought they would be judged as inherently deficient in the middle-class job and labour market, 'at the level of the "self"', and that only dedicated hard work on their part could overcome this' (ibid.: 64). In the USA, where the national habitus supports achievement through self-realization, their preparedness to 'work hard' constitutes significant expertise in rules of the game.

In this small sample of studies we can see that education, or the spaces and places of 'school', are a site of global contestation. The imperatives of the UNCRC and the later Millennial Development Goals to promote education can be delivered in ways that are demonstrably harmful to individuals, families and societies if not conducted with sensitivity to local conditions (Kjørholt, 2013). 'Home' and 'school' also clearly interact in ways that enable shifts in habitus, and are both affected by and have effects on the wider social conditions (Kjørholt, 2013; Threadgold and Nilan,

2009; Dumais, 2002), particularly in relation to temporal issues and their capacity to imagine the future selves they may become (Fitzgerald and Kirk, 2009; Vitus, 2010; Dumais, 2002; Tomanovic, 2004). That 'adult' self is expected to be a working self, but as Kjørholt suggested, the being and becoming child may already have a recognized position in the spaces and places of 'work'.

WORK: RIGHTS, AGENCY AND FUTURES

There is a strand of childhood studies that considers children's appropriate work as being 'school', whereas our concern here is with a child's capacity to take part in economic activity, whether formal or informal. However, one discussion from the 'school as work' stream of thought is of relevance here. Larson (2004) cites Le Compte's idea of the 'hidden curriculum' of the classroom – as constituted in 'work values, responses to authority, orderliness, and behaviour patterns that socialized children for future work' (Le Compte (1978) cited in Larson, 2004: 375) – as a means of providing structure and motivation for disabled children. Children have their own definitions of what is 'work' and 'play' in the classroom: or, it could be said, they recognize the political structure of educational imperatives and the spaces in which they have agency. Larson argues that education *is* work for disabled children, in expecting them to engage in what is thought of as children's 'work' as occupational therapy and thereby acquire agency.

It is taken for granted that the capacity to work and the activity of gainful employment is an indicator of agency, at least for adults. Children's 'work' is generally conceived of as 'to play and to learn' – or perhaps to perform 'chores' in the home – even though as we saw in Chapter 2 this has not always been the case. The notion of children's habitus including them acting as economic agents is now problematic. We have already begun to see that in some instances the blending or balancing of education and work in developing or under-developed countries is both inevitable and even desirable (Kjørholt). We have also seen, in Chapter 3, that between the activities of the ILO and the policies flowing from the UNCRC, nations with developing or under-developed economies who have ratified the ILO Convention (1973) have set a minimum age for employment lower than the recommended 15 years of age. Nevertheless, the proposition that children should be able to balance work and education remains contested.

There is an ongoing interplay of arguments against children working, that flows on from the rights discourse of the UNCRC and which takes place in a complex landscape of dependent relationships where children's voices need to be more fully included (Jones, 2005). In surveying the arguments from children's rights Jones calls for research that will

> demonstrate more clearly that improving rights can deliver changes to livelihood opportunities. In particular, we must explain why many children who are aware of their rights, do not work, do attend school and live within strong families will be poor in later life, while some who work, miss school and do

not live within nurturing relationships manage to break out from poverty. (Jones, 2005: 340)

We can see that studies like Kjørholt's go some way to doing so. Relatedly, habitus is a determinant of both school participation and the decision to work, each of which may be further influenced by complex local, cultural, social, economic, individual or familial factors. Rather than taking an 'either-or' approach, Jones cites Grootaert and Patrinos who argue for more attention 'to be given to the condition of work in order to enable children to strengthen capabilities and empower them to negotiate better conditions [...] , or insurance programmes to reduce income variability and basic health programmes targeted to the very poorest households'. (Grootaert and Patrinos 1999, cited in Jones, 2005: 340).

In the developed world, those who do not succeed or fit into standard educational institutions may find themselves (permanently) marginalized from work (Chadderton and Colley, 2012). The social service structures in the UK that, on the face of it, are intended to transition youth into work may actually end up locking them out of it. The employment agencies and social service organizations, under pressure to minimize the number of people 'on the books', can make youth feel hounded into applying for positions for which they are unsuited and/or untrained, just to meet bureaucratic targets. The unemployed youths interviewed by Chadderton and Colley related narratives of serial rejection of their applications, for positions they knew they did not have the skills to perform. The outcome of this failure of schools to find a way to accommodate the habitus of the individual 'difficult' students is creating what the authors call a disposable generation. School then can be seen to be a means of restricting rather than enhancing work prospects of some children.

Also in the UK, and in common with earlier examples of views of future employment based on interviews with working- and middle-class children, Pimlott-Wilson (2011: 112) argues that family habitus remains the prime shaper of children's aspirations for employment, even if they are also capable of aspiring to something beyond the expectations of their family habitus. Leaving aside the effects of education, there is a direct connection between how children understand their habitus and their likely future working lives. Children have the capacity to actively redirect 'their own life paths and the simultaneous influence of social conditions' (Pimlott-Wilson, 2011: 113) and '[h]abitus is therefore not totally restrictive, allowing individuals to encounter new experiences and alter their path, as well as trammelling them into familiar ones' (ibid.: 116). In each of these examples, the discourse on work remains intertwined with education, no doubt influenced by the wider discourses flowing from the UNCRC and the ILO, whereby the only conditions under which children should be working are in careful balance with education.

Our final example of working children, in public space, uses an historical example to argue for an utterly contemporary theoretical approach to children's use of space and place in general. Judy Gillespie argues, like Uprichard, for a view of children as, and the habitus of childhood as a site of, both being and becoming that takes place in the context of spatial and temporal negotiation. Taking an example outside the bounds of the shaping forms of institutions, she looks to urban history to show how children have been – and she argues remain – capable of great agency in public space. Her approach is both theoretical and pragmatic, as an urban planning theorist. She uses the case of 'Newsies' – that is, children who sold newspapers on street corners in the late nineteenth and early twentieth centuries in major US cities. 'Newsies' showed a capacity to use space and to organize themselves as effective social, economic and political agents. They were experts in the fields of play of their habitus. Gillespie shows how the roots of urban planning were conjoined with those of slum reform, and the removal of children from the streets is a direct result of such reforms (an argument that can be extended to the general clearing of the urban commons of 'common' people).

In nineteenth-century policy and urban planning discourse, children were viewed as 'becomings', adults in formation, which 'meant that the problems of urban space, children, and childhood were inextricably intertwined; if children were the raw material out of which the future would be fashioned, looking at the tenements and slums of New York, Chicago, and other large cities, the reformers were fearful of the future' (Gillespie, 2013: 72). Newsies were not necessarily homeless, even if they were on the street from early in the morning until late at night: many of them brought in money indispensable to the family economy. At different times, they organized against the newspaper publishers for whom they worked in disputes over pay; collected donations in cases of individual 'Newsies' in need; and formed alliances akin to union-organization. Like the usurped leaders of CHH discussed above, they were also resistant to local policy or statutes that aimed to exert adult control over them in the form of 'adult superintendents': 'The results were predictable: the newsies pulled together to undermine efforts by adults to regulate their activities and city after city abandoned enforcement activities' (Clopper cited in Gillespie, 2013: 74).

This ultimately led to urban planning reforms that saw, what Gillespie characterizes as an enclosure of the urban commons, whereby the appropriate public spaces of childhood were redefined as purpose-built playgrounds and parks, children were debarred from their places of employment and lost their capacity to create their own spaces. A child on the street was a child out of place, an approach that we can immediately see has parallels in the policy initiatives in present-day developing and under-developed countries. Gillespie asserts that parents have come to view high-rise living as child-unfriendly and suburban sprawl as 'safer' in a world where children are expected to spend their time in or around the private and monitored spaces of 'home' or 'school' (such as Tomanovic's study). Gillespie (2013: 77) argues that, whether or not they feel equipped to effect change in what is an 'adult-centric' field, nonetheless, 'the planning profession is intimately implicated in both the being and becoming of the youngest inhabitants of its cities' and that they should be child-sensitive rather than adult-centric in their future planning.

PLACING CHILDREN

This chapter draws on work by historians, sociologists, human geographers, anthropologists and scholars in the fields of development studies to provide a critical overview of key issues and debates in the spatialization of childhood, using global examples. Further, we ask readers to consider questions about the spatialization of childhood in a range of contexts. For example, it is far from clear that all instances of children at work are to be condemned as deplorable (Kjørholt, 2013). Some would argue that, in the absence of universal basic education, work can be viewed as a form of tutelage and instruction, which equips children without access to formal schooling with skills they can use to their advantage (Kjørholt, 2013; Jones, 2005). There are demonstrable instances where children have resisted and continue to resist and subvert their relegation to designated spaces and roles (Gillespie, 2013; Payne, 2012). The difficulty lies – for theorists, agencies and governments alike – in thinking beyond current frameworks to re-imagine the *places* of childhood and the roles of children in society and the economy.

Although education is treated by some authors as a habitus in and of itself, in Bourdieu's terms it is not: it is a field of play. As we saw above, education is one of many interpenetrating social and cultural fields that go together to create the embodied habitus of the individual. Education, while important in the formation of habitus, is one of the constituents of the broader habitus, a field of play to which class will determine one's access to, expertise in and capacity to succeed 'in the game'. It is a source of cultural, social, symbolic and even physical capital (through sports and sponsored meals). Like Pip in *Great Expectations*, education (or fate) may take us out of the habitus into which we are born but it is difficult to succeed fully in the acquisition of the full knowledge of the rules of the fields of play of another class.

Practical examples from children's lived realities dealt with in this chapter make clear that, while the concept of habitus is applicable in different cultures, the forms habitus takes are not straightforwardly analogous, interchangeable or universal. Nevertheless, in formulating the habitus as embedded and embodied, Bourdieu has opened the way for a much more textured and deeply layered understanding of social knowledge(s) and, for our purposes, a way of framing three physical spaces assumed to be appropriate to childhood as fields of play: home, school and work.

While we have seen that the majority of theorization around childhood in the Global North has involved (formal) education, questions remain around just what are the 'places' of education and the realities of when and where children might find their 'schooling'. The history of childhood from Erasmus onwards takes schooling as a fundamental focus of the appropriate 'place' for children between the ages of infancy, when 'home' is the space of childhood, and the working life of the late-teenager and adult. Erasmus was tutor to upper-class young males so his 'classroom' was, to a great extent, the adult world of palace politics and courtly dining halls. He was not working in the regimented and physically violent schoolrooms of Foucault's nineteenth-century France or the open-plan mixed classes of contemporary student-centred learning. While the UNCRC enshrines the universal right to education, we still need to be more open in defining what constitutes 'schooling' and the places in which this might take place. Is the space of schooling a workshop, is it a classroom, is it a patch of ground under a tree, is it a courtyard within a compound, is it a secular space, is it a religious space? Or is it, as is increasingly the case in parts of Africa, available via a mobile phone for children on the move or whose work commitments prevent them from attending school?

Like education, home is a field of play, but also an expression of class and a physical representation of our social and cultural capital. The decorations and the furniture we have represent an externalization of our expectations of what is correct for our wider habitus. Our place in society and our economic capital determine to a great extent where, how and in what manner we live. Home in the Global North may be a house, an apartment, a farm or a car; in the Global South, it might be one of these options but it also might be a compound, a village, a slum, or an island. How can we conceive of home as a place in a way that comprehends the complexity and variety of domestic spaces? This may involve a quarter-acre block, a single room, the street, a whole village and its surroundings. And it is a space from which school and work may be inextricable. To sum up, even the UNCRC recognizes that work is a necessity for some children and modifying earlier pronouncements on the need for children to be in formal education, has recognized that in some instances economic necessity requires that there is, rather, a balance between work and education.

NOTES

1   For example, Bourdieu's earliest theorizations of habitus are based on the *Kabyle* in the 1950s, a grouping of Bedouin people of Northern Africa who lived within a tribal social formation, as described in *Outline of a Theory of Practice* (1977).

2   Tomanovic (2004: 345) admits this data is culturally relative – children in a study from London were more likely to stay at home, children in Finland were more likely to be more independent and exploratory. However, the wider point holds, that class habitus affects children's relationship with space and social activities.

Further reading

Bourdieu, P. (1977 [1972]) *Outline of a Theory of Practice*. Tr. Richard Nice. Cambridge: Cambridge University Press.

Bourdieu, P. (1984 [1979]) *Distinction: A Social Critique of the Judgment of Taste*. Tr. Richard Nice. Cambridge, MA: Harvard University Press.

Bourdieu, P. and Wacquant, L.J.D. (1992) *An Invitation to Reflexive Sociology*. Chicago: University of Chicago Press.

Gillespie, J. (2013) 'Being and becoming: Writing children into planning theory', *Planning Theory*, 12 (1): 64–80.

Tomanovic, S. (2004) 'Family habitus as the cultural context for childhood', *Childhood*, 11 (3): 339–60.

6

CHILDREN AND DISASTER: 'CHILD SOLDIERS' AND ORPHANS

- Child soldiers and orphans are two categories of 'unchildlike' children that have prompted global concern and intervention since the *Geneva Declaration of the Rights of the Child* (1924).

- The lived experiences of 'child soldiers' are more complex than the polarized representations in the media, or as affirmed in the *Optional Protocol on the Involvement of Children in Armed Conflict* (UN, 2000c), and there is no simple distinction to be made between 'victims' and 'perpetrators', or 'coerced abductees' and 'decision-making agents'.

- Understandings of what constitutes an orphan differ between official definitions provided by bodies such as UNICEF and the ICRC and popular representations, creating the inaccurate belief in the Global North that there are millions of 'orphaned' Global Southern children in need of rescue through adoption and other interventions. At the same time many children with parents are vulnerable, prompting UNICEF to shift its emphasis from orphanhood to vulnerability and favouring the term 'unaccompanied children' over orphans.

- Significant tensions exist in approaches to the support of children separated from their families through war and disaster: between child-focused or rights-based approaches that emphasize care options which include extended family and community and welfare-based approaches that often amount to child rescue.

INTRODUCTION

By reason of their relative powerlessness, children frequently experience extreme hardships during, and in the aftermath of, war and disaster (Alam, 2010; Enarson and Phillips, 2008). Images of the suffering of children in both socio-political and natural catastrophes form a staple of modern news media coverage, whether during the fall of Saigon in 1975, the 2004 Boxing Day tsunami, the 2010 earthquake in Haiti, or in the demobilization of militarized children from any number of armed conflicts around the globe (Holland, 1985). Children affected by socio-political and natural disasters are frequently more susceptible than adults to the immediate dangers and diseases that flourish in conditions of devastated infrastructure. Further, children endure the long-term impact of war and disaster, through dislocations of family, interruptions to schooling and other perils, including death and injury from unexploded ordnance such as landmines (UNICEF, 2006).

In line with the twentieth-century globalized focus on the welfare, protection and rights of children, several child agencies have focused on both orphans and child soldiers. This emphasis has led to international policy and treaties around the treatment of such children. Children in each category are seen as imperilled and placed in situations which are *unchildlike* – that is, situations that are not compatible with a normative vision of children and their needs.

While recognizing the dangers and privations to which many child soldiers and orphans are exposed globally, our aim in this chapter is to complicate understandings of these two categories of children with reference to tensions between child welfare and child rights approaches to children and their capacities. These approaches in turn reflect epistemological differences in the conceptualization of the child as *being* and the child as *becoming*, as discussed in earlier chapters. Drawing attention to a range of research on both child soldiers and orphans (unaccompanied children) and approaches to children in war and disaster, the chapter aims to introduce readers to the complex debates that surround these two categories of children.

CHILD SOLDIERS, ORPHANS AND SURVIVORS: A BRIEF OVERVIEW

Children have never been excluded from war, whether as active participants or as members of civilian populations overrun during armed conflict. The vicious treatment of infants and small children, emblematic of innocence and helplessness, features strongly in the demonization of various foes and characterizes nearly every phase of colonization as reported in the earliest records, most often in describing the malign tendencies of 'uncivilized' first peoples or 'the enemy'. Over the past 20 years or more, the representation of armed conflicts, particularly in developing countries on the African continent but also throughout Asia and South America, has continued this tendency (Lee-Koo, 2011).

From our brief history of childhood, we know that boys as young as seven were apprenticed as active participants into both the land and sea forces of European nations and the US from at least the seventeenth century until the early twentieth century (Marten, 2002; Paris, 2000). Underage youths who 'ran away' to both World Wars continue to be celebrated as brave individuals (Bishop, 1982; Van Emden, 2005), and armed forces in the Global North target youths in recruitment campaigns, on the basis that life in the military develops valuable citizens and enhances individual capacities (Lee-Koo, 2011). Yet, our current responses to militarized children can range from pride in heroic young citizens in the making;

to pity and calls for leniency for exploited innocents; to outrage at the atrocities committed by 'barbaric' youth brigades; to wonder at the survival and redemption stories of former child fighters.

Similarly, bound by prejudices and assumptions concerning the capacities and resilience of children which derive from the affluent Global North, contemporary responses to the plight of orphaned children, particularly those orphaned by disasters, frequently activate deep-seated 'rescue' responses (Briggs, 2003; Doyle, 2010). In some circumstances, these responses have been acted out in rescue missions aimed at the evacuation of children from disaster zones. Such actions are endorsed by the Geneva Conventions under the Additional Protocol I (ICRC, 1977) with strict processes in place which insist on evacuation as a temporary response to be accompanied by measures to ensure the child's identity is not lost and that re-unification with family is facilitated post-emergency.

Since the end of the Second World War and during both the Korean and Vietnam Wars, one form that this kind of rescue operation has taken has been for children to be removed from their countries of origin and adopted into foreign families (Zigler, 1975; Choy, 2007; Bergquist, 2009; Fronek, 2009, 2012). The prevalence of adoption as a response to the predicament of children in emergencies led to a specific article (Article 21) on inter-country adoption (ICA) being included in the UNCRC, in which it is stated that the removal of any child for inter-country adoption must only be undertaken as a last resort, where all other care options for that child have been exhausted, and that in overseeing the transnational adoption of its children, state parties 'shall ensure that the best interests of the child shall be the paramount consideration' (UNCRC, 1989). Notwithstanding this article, inter-country adoption as a result of interventions in disaster zones remains an area of concern, involving dubious legality and in some cases the criminal trafficking of children (International Social Services, 2010).

Child rescue narratives overlook both the long histories of self-reliant children and child-headed households (CHH) around the world, and other interests of the children (in addition to the need to be safe from immediate danger) which are potentially compromised by rescue. These include the need to be within their own communities, their need for continuity, and the fact that even when parents have died, children may have affective ties with many others including other children in similar situations, members of extended families and communities. As we have already explored in the previous chapter's discussion of CHH in relation to home as a place of childhood, CHH are prominent in research on the natural and socio-political disaster of HIV/AIDS-affected communities in Africa and elsewhere. However, what researchers term 'orphan competent' communities challenge prevalent assumptions of children's inherent vulnerability and (in)competence in circumstances of both socio-political and natural disasters.

Notwithstanding a growing body of research on the capacities of children to cope and provide for themselves under certain conditions and their resilience, the rescue narrative continues to have appeal in responses to the plight of children in disaster (Briggs, 2003; Doyle, 2010; Murphy et al., 2010; Fronek and Cuthbert, 2012b). In general terms, part of the longevity of this narrative – which authorizes adults to step in and intervene even to the extent of removing children from the circumstances in which they find themselves – is that it endorses received understandings of the respective roles and responsibilities of adults and children. The role of adults is to take control and, by reason of their superior capacities, to offer assistance and care to children who, by their natures, are vulnerable and less competent.

Some emergency situations are so dire that interventions such as evacuation are needed. As noted above, the evacuation of children in war-time emergencies is explicitly allowed for in the Geneva Conventions Additional Protocol I (ICRC, 1977) – but, such evacuation is framed as being temporary only, with family reunification as soon as circumstances allow being a prime objective (ICRC, 1977; Dixit, 2001). Even temporary separation from family may do more harm than good, as is highlighted in reviews of research literature on the evacuation of children in war and disaster (Dixit, 2001; Fronek and Cuthbert, 2012b). The impact of war and other emergencies is compounded for children when combined with family separation and dislocation from community and environment. Overwhelmingly, the evidence points to better outcomes for children facing disasters, including war, when their affective and social networks remain intact.

The Machel Report (Machel, 1996) outlines the potential harms faced by children separated from caregivers and evacuated during crises, including their potential exploitation on the inter-country adoption market. In the event of imminent danger, the report recommends families be evacuated rather than separating children from caregivers. The same point is made in the International Committee of the Red Cross (2004) inter-agency guiding principles for unaccompanied and separated children (ICRC, 2004), which state that inter-country adoption in the country of asylum is normally not considered in the interests of the child. Thus, we need to be critically attuned to whose interests are being served when child rescue and adoption narratives are mobilized.

Many proponents of child rescue approaches to children in emergency situations advocate for child rescue from an interested perspective. They seek children for the purposes of adoption and promote adoption-driven evacuations and removals in contrast to more child-focused approaches, which might place adoption on a care continuum for children in emergencies that also includes efforts at family preservation, family re-union, and community support (Mezmur, 2009). The latter approach is that supported by the UNCRC (1989), the ICRC through both its Protocol additional to the Geneva Conventions (ICRC, 1977) and its inter-agency guiding principles on unaccompanied children (ICRC, 2004), International Social Services, UNICEF and international protocols and agencies.

A WORLD OF ORPHANS?

While not all children in disasters are orphaned and not all orphaned children exist in circumstances of disaster, there is, as we discuss below, considerable blurring between these categories of children who are linked as objects of concern and in need of intervention. This, we suggest, arises from assumptions in the Global North which favour the nuclear family as the optimal unit for the raising of children and tend to co-opt all children whose support is not immediately recognizable as being orphaned. In the wake of the HIV/AIDS epidemic, which has devastated populations in many parts of the developing world and especially many poor African nations, and in other large-scale disasters, the figures of the unsupported child and the child in disaster have assumed considerable prominence as objects of global concern, policy focus and intervention. Interventions to assist such children are not without controversy, as with the illegal removal of children from Haiti in 2010 for adoption by families in the US (Dambach and Baglietto, 2010; Hague Justice Portal, 2010).

While our discussion proceeds on the assumption that children left orphaned or otherwise unsupported and children in emergency situations need appropriate care and support in order to grow and develop normally, we foreground differences in views as to what form this support should take. These differences highlight tensions in prevailing views on children and childhood with respect to the degree to which some children, or children of a certain age, may be competent to put in place their own care arrangements with community support, and the contrasting views which assume that children can never be competent to provide this support and their proper care requires a wholesale intervention (often akin to the rescuing of the child from these circumstances).

Any consideration of the category of the orphan child must begin with understanding what the term means and how it is used. Popular and sentimentalized understandings of the word orphan in the Global North take the term to mean a child who has lost both its parents and is thus at risk of being wholly unsupported and in need of family-based care and shelter. It may be noted that with the progressive nuclearization of families in the Global North from the time of the advent of industrialization and accelerating in the first half of the twentieth century, the relative isolation of many nuclear family units significantly amplifies the emotional and material consequences of the death of one or both parents and results in the concept of orphanhood taking on tragic dimensions.

The current definition of orphan used by UNICEF differs from this popular understanding, as it is used to refer to a child who has lost at least one parent (single orphan) in addition to children who have lost both parents (double orphans). Thus, when UNICEF or other bodies cite statistics for orphaned children – for example, the figure of 132 million orphans worldwide given by UNICEF in 2012 – the very large numbers cited include children who may have at least one parent living. Thus UNICEF advises that of this 132 million children classified as orphans only 13 million have lost both parents, the majority have the support of at least one parent and extended family members. Salient misunderstandings arise from this terminology:

> However, this difference in terminology can have concrete implications for policies and programming for children. For example, UNICEF's 'orphan' statistic might be interpreted to mean that globally there are 132 million children in need of a new family, shelter, or care. This misunderstanding may then lead to responses that focus on providing care for individual children rather

than supporting the families and communities that care for orphans and are in need of support. (UNICEF, 2012b)

As this UNICEF explanatory note indicates, even children who have lost both parents may not live entirely unsupported, as they may have the support and care of extended family or community.

UNICEF and other agencies that focus on children in emergency situations have been at pains to address 'misdirected' (Doyle, 2010) assumptions about children in emergencies and orphanhood and to tackle Eurocentric assumptions about the appropriate care of children in such circumstances. In the last 20 years, there has been a determined shift away from using the word 'orphan' in favour of the term 'unaccompanied' child, as in this statement by the UNHCR in 1994:

> Unaccompanied children are those who are separated from both parents and are not being cared for by an adult who, by law or custom, is responsible for doing so. The children should not be described as "orphans", but as "unaccompanied children". It cannot be assumed that unaccompanied children in Rwanda and in the refugee camps are orphans. The status of being an orphan always requires careful verification since the term "orphan" is sometimes used in the region for children who have lost one parent. Even though some children have come from orphanages in Rwanda [...] many, if not most, alleged orphans have living parents [who] may have entrusted their children to an orphanage as a security measure or to ensure adequate provision of food and shelter. (UNHCR, 1994)

This statement further highlights differences in global understandings about how and where children are best, or most appropriately, supported and raised. Assumptions in the Global North are that children should be cared for within the family structure known as the nuclear family, and that anything less than or different from this mode of care represents a deficit. Of course, with high rates of marital dissolution and single-parent households in most Western societies, and the widespread phenomenon of the 'deadbeat dads' (that is fathers who fail to maintain contact with and financial support of their children), many children around the world live effectively as 'single' orphans.

In recognition of the fact that orphanhood itself may not necessarily equate with vulnerability and lack of support *and* that many children remain vulnerable even when they have two parents, UNICEF is in favour of de-emphasizing orphanhood as necessarily equating with vulnerability and replacing this with a focus on a wider range of factors which may lead to children being vulnerable (UNICEF, 2012b). In line with this approach, UNICEF and other child-focused aid agencies such as the ICRC (2004), de-emphasize individualized approaches to children akin to child rescue actions in favour of more holistic support for the communities that provide care for children left temporarily or permanently unsupported through war and other disasters (UNICEF, 2012b). This contextualized approach to the care of children is aligned with the emergence in recent years, as discussed in Chapters 3 and 4, of the more holistic child well-being approach in international and national children's policy, and brings a slow recognition that the facts of being poor, or 'orphaned', or resident in the Global South do not in and of themselves create conditions justifying intervention, rescue or adoption by foreign nationals (Smolin, 2007).

DO ORPHANS NEED ADOPTION (OR DOES ADOPTION NEED ORPHANS)?

A realm of global activity in which the category of orphan is most hotly contested is that of inter-country adoption (ICA), in which proponents of the adoption of children routinely point to the large numbers of orphans globally – mobilizing images of children who are totally unsupported and in need of family-based care – for whom inter-country adoption is posited as the only solution to their plight. This argument is in contradiction to the advice of UNICEF, the UNHCR and other international agencies, arises from different understandings of the term orphan, as outlined above, and is then enmeshed in different and competing views of the place of inter-country adoption as a response to children in need, relative to a range of other care options. These differences are outlined effectively by the African scholar Benjamin Mezmur who equates adoption-driven approaches to child rescue with serving adults' *rights to a child* for the purposes of family formation, and aligns more holistic approaches to child placement and care, which might include ICA in particular circumstances, with addressing the *rights of the child* (Mezmur, 2009).

In addition to confusion around the term 'orphan', there is, we suggest, a global politics at work by which some in the Global North seek to perpetuate the use of the term and the particular meanings it generates – of vulnerability, of the need for rescue, and the need for adoption into a loving northern home – for particular reasons. Legally an orphan is the only category of child who may be made available for adoption. In order to be made available for adoption by foreign nationals, therefore, a child must be certified as an orphan. While adoption proponents argue that orphans need adoption, and that only adoption into a loving home can provide the child with what it needs to grow and develop normally and fulfil its potential, this position ignores a growing range of child-care regimes which are available to children in their own countries and is in clear contravention of the UNCRC (UN, 1989), the Hague Convention on ICA (1993), and statements by UNHCR (1994) and the ICRC (2004). It is perhaps more correct to say that the inter-country adoption market needs a steady supply of orphans to meet demand for children for family formation. Efforts within the global children's movement to keep more children in their home communities and the retreat from the notion of orphanhood as necessarily equating with vulnerability and need have not been good for ICA, whose numbers are now in global decline (Selman, 2012).

While ICA developed in response to the plight of children in war-time emergencies – primarily the Korean War (1950–53) – it has since been regularized as a route to family formation for a range of adults who for biological and social reasons cannot have children of their own (Cuthbert, Spark and Murphy, 2009). Thus, over the second half of the twentieth century, ICA grew as a demand-driven phenomenon.

This is distinct from a needs-driven phenomenon in which ICA is viewed and prac-tised primarily to meet the needs of genuinely orphaned or unsupported children for family-based care when all other possibilities have been exhausted. As we outline in the next section, natural disasters have also created circumstances in which chil-dren temporarily separated from parents or members of extended families have been constructed as 'orphans' and subject to removal (in some cases mass removal) from their countries of origin for the purposes of adoption.

CHILDREN IN DISASTERS

Children are particularly vulnerable in times of emergency, crisis and disaster whether this is caused by war or natural events such as earthquakes, floods or fire. However, the children of some countries are more vulnerable than others – in under-developed countries where, for example, social supports and emergency response infrastructure are less developed, emergencies can have devastating and long-term impact on com-munities, including children. One of the additional risks the children of the Global South face in disasters is the application of what has been called 'misdirected kind-ness' (Doyle, 2010) in the form of removal or 'rescue' by adoption agents. The main difference between such rescue attempts since the Second World War is that children have been removed permanently for the purposes of adoption, rather than tem-porarily evacuated. In war-torn Vietnam, post-Ceauşescu Romania, and in response to natural disasters in South-East Asia and the Caribbean, significant numbers of children were subject to mass removal by foreigners for adoption (Bergquist, 2009; Brookfield, 2009; Rotabi and Bergquist, 2010; Selman, 2011; Fronek and Cuthbert, 2012a, 2012b).

In assessing the appropriateness or otherwise of this response to the plight of chil-dren in emergencies, it is worth asking whether such an intervention could occur in more developed countries.[1] Can we readily imagine that mass evacuation and adop-tion by foreign nationals would have been considered appropriate responses to assist some of the thousands of US children affected by Hurricane Katrina in 2005, or Australian children displaced by the catastrophic bushfires in the Australian state of Victoria in 2009, or by the floods in the states of Queensland, New South Wales and Victoria in 2010–11, or the serial earthquakes which devastated the New Zealand city of Christchurch and its surroundings in 2010 and 2011? Can we imagine US, Australian or New Zealand children, many of whom might have one or both par-ents who survived the disaster, being airlifted from their communities for adoption by foreigners, with their names and identities permanently changed? Why, therefore, does the permanent removal for adoption of children from disasters in poor nations *appear* acceptable?

Different criteria pertain in Global Northern nations, due to differences in the levels of infrastructure and, both flowing from this reality and extending beyond it, assumptions about the competence of these nations to manage their own emergen-cies, with targeted and limited support from other nations. When disaster strikes in the Global South, a range of other considerations and what we might call global

North—South imaginaries come into play as an effect of both long-standing assumptions based in colonial histories and the ongoing effect of aid and development cultures. The relative lack of infrastructure to cope with emergency situations places aid-receiving nations in the Global South in an inferior position. The Global North, with its advanced economies and technologies, stands in relationship to the Global South as an adult to a child. The Global South is frequently imagined as quite child-like in its need for funding and assistance. As noted by several commentators, the quintessential image of the plight of the Global South, the child in famine/disaster/war/poverty, serves as an emblem for these parts of the globe, and through its ubiquity has come to represent the Global South in the popular imaginary of the North (Holland, 1985; Thorne, 2003; Jones, 2005).

When disaster strikes in the Global North, as with Hurricane Katrina in the USA in 2005, the communities are credited with capacities to get themselves back on their feet and to recover, even when it is acknowledged that post-disaster responses could have been better managed. Further, in such contexts, reunification is a priority for children separated from their parents – as was the case post-Katrina (Fronek and Cuthbert, 2012b). In the 2011 Australian floods, where the scale of post-disaster recovery was likened to the aftermath of war, the immediate post-disaster focus was on building community resilience (ABC, 2011; Brandenburg et al., 2007). Both implicitly and explicitly, re-uniting dislocated children with their families, keeping children in these communities and, to the extent that they are capable, involving children in community recovery processes are considered central to the task of post-disaster recovery. These objectives are in line with all international protocols on the care of children and communities in disaster.

Another set of dynamics is at work when disaster strikes the Global South (Nicolas et al., 2009). Heightened calamity and rescue discourses produce an homogenously apocalyptic view of disaster zones in the Global South. The disaster zone is constructed as a place where no care for children appears possible (Fronek and Cuthbert, 2012b). Following the argument of Pupavac (1998, 2001) on the infantilization and pathologization of the Global South in aid and other discourses, portrayals of disaster zones in the developing world see all victims reduced to 'children' in their need for aid. Frequently, aid and disaster recovery projects funded by foreign donors bypass local community structures and support networks, further rendering adults in the affected communities powerless and childlike (Fronek and Cuthbert, 2012b), and as passive recipients of recovery assistance rather than as active participants in their own recovery in partnership with foreign aid donors. The people, culture and nation caught up in disaster are represented as near to wholly dysfunctional. Adults are systematically disempowered, local care structures for children and vulnerable people are overlooked, and many children who are not in fact orphaned, are treated as orphans without adequate care or support, in need of rescue (and available for adoption) by adults from the Global North.

Such a view, which runs counter to international aid protocols as we have seen, aligns with the needs and interests of the international adoption market for which emergencies in the form of disaster and war represent significant opportunities for the sourcing of children for adoption. This is especially the case since the introduction of the *Hague Convention on Protection of Children and Co-operation in Respect of*

Intercountry Adoption (Hague Conference on Private International Law, 1993) which has dramatically reduced the numbers of adoptable children being made available through regulated channels on the global adoption market.

It has been argued by several scholars that proponents of ICA who posit adoption as the most suitable way of dealing with children in distress have a significant interest in perpetuating the use of the term orphan and the misunderstandings that arise from the differences between official definitions and popular understandings of its meaning (Smolin, 2012; Fronek and Cuthbert, 2012b). Thus, an organization called The Orphan Foundation which has as its aim 'removing barriers to adoption' states that there are 163 million orphans in the world for whom adoption into a loving American home is an objective worth striving for (The Orphan Foundation, 2008). Australian celebrity adoption proponent, Deborra-Lee Furness (the wife of actor Hugh Jackman) paints a similar picture; she advocates an end to the needless delays imposed by Australian 'anti-adoption' bureaucracies that are preventing these 'millions of orphans and unwanted children' finding loving Australian homes (Furness, 2008, 2013).

For Furness and many other proponents of ICA, any attempt to regulate the practice of ICA, to de-emphasize the term orphan or to preference holistic in-country community support in poor communities, communities affected by HIV/AIDS or in the aftermath of war and other disasters, is seen as anti-adoption (Fronek, 2009; Poe, 2010). The conceptualization of the needs of the child in disaster and distress which emphasizes holistic support to children in their communities, works against the sentimentalized 'rescue' narratives which have underpinned the history and practice of ICA for over 60 years.

The intertwined histories of war and disaster and inter-country adoption from the second half of the twentieth century to the present highlight the contestations around the category of the orphan child and the child in disaster and the difficulty, in this conflicted space, of identifying what might be in the best interests of children, both with respect to their immediate safety and longer-term considerations. An equally contested space is that occupied by child soldiers and children caught up in armed conflict to which we turn in the second half of this chapter.

CHILD SOLDIERS AND CAAFAG

As detailed in Chapter 3, the history of the UNCRC is rooted in nineteenth-century child labour reform and child protection movements at the national level. It is also based in the internationalization of policies aimed at global reform in the treatment of children that came in the wake of the two World Wars of the twentieth century. There we saw that the first stage of attempts to recognize 'the rights of the child', by the League of Nations, was a direct response to witnessing of the effects of the First World War on children. More particularly, the violence perpetrated against children in the Second World War – in concentration camps, and in the orphaning and both social and family dislocation experienced by children in the aftermath of the war – was germinal in the reformulation of those earlier efforts into the UNCRC. Yet in the Second World War, children were not uniformly victims of the war; many were enthusiastically militarized, whether through enlistment or paramilitary youth organizations, while others aided or took part in resistance movements. As a child living under Nazi occupation in the Netherlands, the actress Audrey Hepburn, one of the earliest UNICEF ambassadors, famously acted as a courier and messenger for the Dutch resistance. She was just one of thousands of otherwise ordinary children to do so across occupied Europe. Further, those children who were displaced and disposed were not necessarily passive in their repatriation. For example, Ian Serrallier's children's classic *The Silver Sword* (1956) fictionalizes the true story of children independently and competently travelling from Poland to Switzerland in the wake of the war.

The agentic rights-bearing child that emerges from the UNCRC, who has access to schooling and opportunities for sports and play, is a child of optimism and peacetime. With respect to the prospect of war and the prospect of children's active involvement in war, the UNCRC shifts the discourse from that of rights and agency back to that of welfare, protection and vulnerability. Article 38 of the UNCRC specifically calls on governments to avoid the direct involvement in hostilities of people aged under 15. The *Optional Protocol on the Involvement of Children in Armed Conflict* (adopted by the UN General Council in 2000, coming into force in 2002, hereafter the *Optional Protocol*) extends that effort, but first we will outline just who this document is intended to cover.[2]

Prior to the *Optional Protocol* (UN, 2000c) the 'subjects' at issue — we cannot call them 'agents' as they are not constructed as full agents — were referred to as 'child soldiers'. In response to concerns that this term leaves out many of the ways in which children are affected by armed conflict, this has been replaced by the broader term, 'children associated with armed forces or armed groups' or CAAFAG. For ease of reading, we will continue to use the term 'child soldiers' throughout this chapter, but in doing we are including the fuller definition of CAAFAG. Just who is comprehended within the acronym CAAFAG is set out in the *Paris Principles and Guidelines on Children Associated with Armed Forces or Armed Groups 2007* (hereafter, the *Paris Principles*):

> 2.1: "A child associated with an armed force or armed group" [CAAFAG] refers to any person below 18 years of age who is or who has been recruited or used by an armed force or armed group in any capacity, including but not limited to children, boys, and girls used as fighters, cooks, porters, messengers, spies or for sexual purposes. It does not only refer to a child who is taking or has taken a direct part in hostilities. (UNICEF, 2007b: 7)

The definition, then, is based on a clear differentiation from the child who circulates in the stereotypically 'proper' spaces of childhood, of 'home' or 'school'. The document as a whole assumes that that the activity of such a child is involuntary, or at least coerced (for persons below 18 are not supposed to be able to give fully informed consent). We can also see from the tasks listed that the child's possible activities might also be seen as 'work' (an 'unchildlike' activity).

Article 1 of the *Optional Protocol*, on which the *Paris Principles* are based (UNICEF, *Guide to the Optional Protocol*, 13) puts the onus on states to ensure that those under 18 are not sent into active service, and that they are not recruited for or used in armed conflict by non-government militia. This proscription is very much based on a notion of children as vulnerable and subject to coercion. Article 2 goes on to affirm that there shall be no compulsory recruitment (conscription) of those under 18. However, by setting the minimum age for recruitment at 15, Article 3 allows countries such as the USA, the UK and Australia (and others) to retain the ability to enlist young volunteer recruits with parental/guardian consent, as long as they are not deployed in active warfare. Article 4 sets out the inequality between State and non-State militia, as the latter are not to recruit (compulsorily or voluntarily) anyone under 18. The intent and import of the document, then, is very much an extension of the protective elements of the UNCRC.

The implementation of the *Optional Protocol* therefore has a number of possible effects for children. The use of children over 16 in regular forces is largely uncontentious and those states that want to retain the right to enlist these 'children' are prepared to keep them out of active service. But what of child soldiers, who are allied with armed forces within conflict zones, as defined in the *Paris Principles* and in contravention of the *Optional Protocol*? Children in war are part of a much more intensive interest, particularly from those in agencies either required or committed to uphold the *Optional Protocol* in their delivery of aid. In turning to discuss the ways in which child soldiers are dealt with on the ground, most often by aid agencies or researchers working with them, we will see that the assumptions of the UNCRC and the *Optional Protocol* are not so easily mapped onto children's lived experiences.

'AIDING' CHILD SOLDIERS

The vast majority of the literature that deals with child soldiers is retrospective. Research is based on the provision of aid to, or the re-conceptualizing of, children, male and female, who have returned from experiencing life in an armed militia in one or more possible roles, and is reliant on memory and the post-war narration of experiences. Such children might have been active fighters, or might have taken on support roles (cooking, acting as bearers). They might also have been used as sex-slaves. Just what roles they played – active or supportive – features large in the demographic data collected by most researchers, particularly those interested in the children's ongoing mental health.

Second, the focus is almost exclusively on children in developing or underdeveloped countries (Betancourt et al., 2011; Mæland, 2010; Brett and Specht, 2004). Where child soldiers form a part of a regular military force, particularly in developed countries, under-18s do not attract the same kind of concerned research. This is perhaps because, in line with compliance with the *Optional Protocol*, youth recruits in developed countries are not deployed on active service; but, as Lee-Koo (2001) argues, it is also because their military service is much more likely to be constructed as a path to productive citizenship. It is the child soldiers in developing and under-developed countries who attract the most concern and condemnation, and who are constructed as either abused or demonically 'unchildlike'.

Third, as noted, much of the research on child soldiers is aimed at, or is a part of, efforts to deliver aid to war-affected areas. Much research is therefore explicitly allied with the preconceptions and the aims of the bodies delivering the aid. There are many aid initiatives aimed at preventing children from becoming 'victims' of war; but aid generally comes with conditions attached concerning who may receive it and how it may be deployed. Accordingly, what is researched is, to some extent, dependent on how aid is delivered. The major donors and/or aid providers to war-affected countries are from international agencies, many either under the auspices of the UN or who are committed to the UN's policies. The assumptions of what it is to be a child soldier and how best to 'aid' children post-conflict are therefore likely to be based in the UNCRC's conceptualization of the child.

There are three stages that are of interest to such agencies: the children before they became soldiers, their experiences during armed conflict (as monitored after the fact) and their lives after demobilization. Each of these stages can be dealt with from the theoretical perspective of the 'becoming' or the 'being' child. In the first stage, the child may be seen as the standard developmental child, bucolically innocent; or, as a proto-agent living in (overwhelmingly) impoverished circumstances that regularly lead to civil unrest in under-developed countries. In the bulk of the literature on child soldiers these are the assumed states prior to entry into armed conflict. In the second stage, while at war, the 'becoming' child is generally characterized as abused and forced into committing atrocities, vulnerable and malleable in the hands of malevolent adults/leaders. More rarely, there is an acknowledgement that children at war are also 'being', that is, agents able to take up arms for a cause that they see as offering the possibility of change.

In the third stage, after returning from the battlefields, the 'becoming' child is seen as needing to be reintegrated into a community and society that will 'cherish' and care for them as they continue their interrupted progression from child to adult. This approach almost always implies that the child is re-childed. Attempts at re-childing a 'being' child can lead to frustrated and disempowered individuals (see Chapter 5). Such efforts at re-childing may also lead to re-radicalization if the basic socio-economic and political circumstances have not changed (McMullin, 2011). McMullin argues that the shaping of the 'child soldier' according to the terms of the UNCRC and the *Paris Principles*, with its concentration on reintegration, ironically often makes nothing better and sometimes even worsens conditions for the child.

VICTIMS IN NEED OF TREATMENT

The main way of responding to the perceived post-conflict needs of child soldiers directly reflects the treatment of adult returnees from most modern wars, particularly those that have attracted UN intervention: that is, disarmament, demobilization and reintegration (DDR). In the DDR of children returning from armed conflict, youth are demobilized to temporary holding camps once disarmed, and then attempts are made to reintegrate them into communities. Much of the psychologically premised research has been carried out at the point of reintegration. This is the site of the child soldier as a 'victim in need of treatment'.

There is a strong sense of child soldiers requiring medical 'treatment' – whether from psychologists, psychiatrists or physicians. For example, there is a lot of concern to monitor the mental health of returned child soldiers, on the assumption that they are likely to be suffering from PTSD. This is most obvious in the cluster of psychological studies on child soldiers in a number of countries of Africa. One of the best-known researchers and commentators in this field is Therese Betancourt, who along with her co-authors has conducted widely cited, longitudinal studies of former child soldiers in Sierra Leone and Northern Uganda. Conducted in collaboration with community groups and aid agencies, Betancourt et al. (2010a, 2010b, 2011, 2012) are concerned to trace the levels of PTSD and other mental health problems amongst returned child soldiers, the levels of reintegration into their communities and to follow returned child soldiers' development into adulthood. Betancourt et al. argue that the effects of experiences of witnessing or perpetrating 'intense physical violence' (2010a: 1078) become more obvious over time along with the long-term effects of reintegration (or lack thereof), and that what appears to be unproblematic or at least not obviously problematic in (late) childhood leads to mental health issues in adulthood. Betancourt and her colleagues are openly concerned to treat the 'becoming' child, who has been 'deprived of their rights to the care and protection of their families, and denied education and other developmental opportunities' (Betancourt et al., 2010a: 1078).

For each of their studies Betancourt et al. (2010a, 2011) drew on large pools of male and female subjects from communities in refugee camps, comparing the mental health indicators of returned child soldiers with their peers who remained in communities during the wars, cross-correlating the data for gender differences. Collecting and reporting their data at intervals, they variously observed that how well returned child soldiers are accepted by their communities is a determinant for their mental health outcomes (2010a, 2011, 2012); the effects of gender on community acceptance and reintegration, and on resilience (2011); and the efficacy of different treatment protocols for boys and girls (2011, 2012).

Their findings are that the female child soldiers in their cohort had less access to schooling, citing education as a high indicator for reintegration and confidence (see also Angucia et al., 2010), and are stigmatized as having been sex-slaves. Boys were more likely to have been active combatants (42 per cent vs. 28 per cent) but each gender was just as likely to have been exposed to or to have perpetrated violence; girls were likely to be more anxious and aggressive than their non-child soldier peers. The boys who were raped (5 per cent) were shown to suffer more psychological effects in the long term than the girls (44 per cent), who suffered but were not completely debilitated (2011). The longitudinal nature of Betancourt et al.'s studies provides support for later findings about resilience and adaptation amongst returnees, with girls being more stigmatized and more likely to suffer depression immediately after repatriation (2010b), but more resilient and better at coping in the long term, returning to culturally accepted gender behaviours such as 'being kind' to regain a degree of acceptance (see also Jordans et al., 2012).

Relatedly, Annan et al. (2009), in their qualitative study of male returned child soldiers in Northern Uganda, find a polarization on the basis of resilience, between child soldiers who continue to be 'lost' to their communities and those who reintegrated. They argue that the deciding factor appears to have been the level of acceptance they achieved, that is, not facing discrimination from their (displaced and encamped) family and friends. Klasen et al.'s (2010) early intervention study of 'positive adaptation' amongst Ugandan former child soldiers found that of the 30 per cent in their sample who were found to be resilient, gender was not a factor but socio-economic status was (with higher status producing greater resilience). In their comparative study of nearly 600 male and female returned child soldiers and their non-militarized peers in Burundi, Jordans et al. (2012) report that 69.4 per cent of the child soldiers joined voluntarily.

All the above studies are intertwined with the deployment of aid at the final point of DDR (reintegration) and are concerned with psychological treatment and/or psychologically informed education. Other approaches to the child soldier as 'victim in need of treatment' are more concerned with the physical after-effects of having been a child soldier. A member of the Save the Children Fund (Uppard, 2003) characterizes returned female child soldiers in Sri Lanka very much as vulnerable innocents, but is concerned to address their physical health. Female child soldiers, many of whom have been sex-slaves, are likely to have acquired STIs; to have long-lasting physical effects (sterility) if not treated; to be branded as 'whores', socially excluded and ignored in statistics.

How well do these approaches, all clearly premised on developmentalist assumptions, stand up to scrutiny? The lack of efficacy of the education programmes for girls reported in several studies is unsurprising, particularly if schooling is experienced as a form of 're-childing' by someone who has achieved agency. The reported raised levels of aggression and anxiety in these studies (Betancourt et al., 2011) not only show that child soldiers do not have an easy time adapting to expectations of their communities but imply that returning to limited agency after chaotic and abusive, but nevertheless agentic, experiences is in some ways a poorly thought-through approach. Further, Angucia et al.'s reporting of the input of adults in directing the returnees to return to education suggests a similar dynamic to the CHH in Chapter 5. We saw there that when youth have had experience with responsibility it is harder for them to return to former familial dynamics of subordination.

It may be that the girls' greater resilience to sexual abuse (Betancourt et al., 2011) has something to do with the gender expectations of their habitus; that it is, sadly, with a recognized possibility that they are open to sexual abuse within their gender habitus (whereas boys are not). Further, the reporting of higher rates of 'depression' amongst girls who have been used as sex-slaves (Jordans et al., 2012) may have as much to do with the temporal proximity of the study to demobilization and factors such as re-childing, given the reported resilience in long-term studies (Betancourt et al., 2011). Indeed, resilience in general may also be related to the individual's capacity to recover rather than a given developmental stage being crucial to future health, much as there have been adult returnees from many wars who have been resilient and coped perfectly well in later life and others who have been comprehensively destroyed (BWHO, 2012).

There are also instances where outcomes are reported that are clearly undermined by the data. For example, Jordans et al. (2012) claim that their interviewees are not 'really' volunteer recruits, at the same time as they document explanations given by child soldiers for joining militia (vengeance, ideology, prestige, fear, material benefit, peer pressure, social exclusion) that speak of rational decision-making, not all of which can be interpreted as coercive. Annan et al.'s study (2009), incidentally, supports McMullin's (2011) contention that children have reasons for deciding to join militia that lie in pre-existing socio-political circumstances, including unsupportive family relationships, lack of employment and lack of education, to which many of their interviewee child soldiers were returning. Hamnett (2008) also discusses the wider circumstances behind children becoming soldiers: poverty, lack of opportunities of all kinds, war and disease. The delivery of aid that is based on education and skills-training intended to prepare returnees for work often fails to recognize that there is no work to which those skills can be applied and there is little recognition of these young people as 'agents in their own right'.

AGENTS IN THEIR OWN RIGHT

The discussion of children's reasons for taking part in armed conflict, as reformulated to recast them as victims, disempowers them in a way that is patronizing (Jordans et al., 2012). Yet there is implicit recognition within the *Optional Protocol* that young people below the age of 18 may consciously choose to join a state's armed force, often as a means to waged and subsidized education and training (Lee-Koo, 2011); it seems illogical that all child soldiers in non-state militia are then necessarily victims, as is often portrayed in the literature on child soldiers. The construction of children as 'a distinctive type of human being' in the UNCRC is challenged by the lived experiences of such child soldiers, for just as a proportion are brutally forced to become soldiers, others are conscious volunteers (Bhabha, 2006: 1532).

At the same time, as children's reasons for becoming soldiers might have been strategic and based in socio-economic conditions affecting both them and their non-militia peers, they may be demobilized into 'a range of structural and often pre-existing challenges that may even be among the roots of war, such as social inequality and chronic poverty, [that] can account for ongoing psychological distress in its aftermath' (Vindevogel et al., 2013: 757). International DDR aid that does not extend beyond an immediate period of resettlement is unlikely 'to mend the war-affected surroundings at all socio-ecological levels' (ibid.: 763). It is therefore also reasonable on the part of communities to be cautious in reintegrating former child soldiers, for once it is accepted that they are not just 'misguided children' but politically conscious agents, it is clear that their path to returning to a non-militarized life is more than a matter of 're-childing' the child.

There is also a problem in making clear distinctions between the *Paris Principles'* definition of the child soldier and children living (and acting) in sites of conflict. As Pedersen and Sommerfelt (2007) argue, there are many conflicts in which children may be involved where it is difficult to delineate easily between those affected and those participating. Children in armed gangs in Brazil, for example (though one could as easily give examples from Guatemala or the USA), are exposed to war-like violence. Pedersen and Sommerfelt argue that 'one should focus on armed conflicts that are organized in a war-like fashion, regardless of whether or not the conflict is formally regarded as war' in order to frame the 'social indicators' of child soldiers (2007: 255). Indeed, there is evidence from anthropological research that in such circumstances it is possible that child soldiers are 'socialized' into violence. For example, in Bosnia during the break-up of the former-Yugoslavia, children were observed 'playing war' and were not discouraged by adults from doing so; such war-like play became a normalized part of their lives (Korbin, 2003). Further, it is clear that some child soldiers join armed militia as committed agents and retain that agency and commitment into adulthood (Kanagaratnam et al., 2005).

More critical of under-examined assumptions in the developmentalist (psycho-logical) literature, Shepler's (2005) ethnographic study of former child soldiers in Sierra Leone and their parents, teachers and community leaders, reveals how strategically each group manipulates the UNCRC view of child soldiers as 'innocent' and 'apolitical'. Returnees, many of whom were already active social and economic agents before they became fighters, recognize what is expected from the variety of audiences they encounter and put on the appropriate social mask of 'non-agency' to get what they desire (aid funds, education, reintegration, forgiveness, acceptance), while still speaking about their experiences in terms of their agency amongst their fellow former soldiers (Shepler, 2005: 199–200). In a complementary manner, the local adults sensitized to the discourse of the UNCRC appear to consciously, and paradoxically, use the UNCRC to re-infantilize these former soldiers into the space of respect for adults. Shepler describes how techniques 'primarily from the fields of education, psychology and social welfare' (Shepler, 2005: 207) are used along with the discourse of 'human rights' (ibid.: 208) to 'discipline' the agentic and 'being' child soldier back into the community. Thus, 'if we see a former child soldier as only traumatized (though he or she may well *be* traumatized), we miss all the other aspects of his or her reintegration, most importantly the social aspects' (ibid.: 208).

At a broader level, the UNCRC model of the child may contain the seeds of inefficacy for the deployment of aid. In his study of DDR programmes in Angola, Jaremey McMullin (2011) argues that post-conflict attempts at DDR were based on an unhelpful universalizing model of the child that excluded child soldiers and 'rendered them invisible' (2011: 750–2). That is, those who did not fit the model of the vulnerable victim were left at the margins. Further, in implementing DDR and UNCRC-based aid, children of the Global South are contrasted with children of the Global North, and thereby used to police the boundaries of the normative 'sacred child' which 'performs a containment function [...] that erases discussion of victims and perpetrators across a vertical, international axis and that absolves international states, donors and institutions of obligations to cast child rights in terms of access to better political and economic conditions locally, nationally and globally' (ibid.: 760). In so doing, whole societies, specifically those with high populations of young people which are almost exclusively nations of the Global South, are by extension infantilized and their young constructed 'as dangerous, destabilizing and crippling to development' (ibid.: 760).

Similarly, Lee-Koo (2011) provides an excellent example of the binary juxtaposition of the acceptable Global Northern youth soldier and the unacceptable Global Southern 'barbaric' child monster. Based on close readings of representations of children in the two domains, from the Coalition to Stop the Use of Child Soldiers and the Australian Defence Force (ADF) 'Gap Year' recruitment campaign (for 16–18 year olds), she demonstrates how the Global South's child soldier is constructed as alone, vulnerable and 'out of control' in contrast to the ADF's productive citizen-in-the-making, 'and reinforces pre-existing notions of the global South as a morally defunct zone of tragedy' (Lee-Koo, 2011: 731). Lee-Koo argues that aid agencies aiming to increase humanitarian intervention and to garner support from the Global North rely on a form of imagery that is colonial in flavour, stemming from 'distant powers (including states and transnational organizations) which seek to maintain asymmetrical power relations [...] in order to conduct humanitarian operations' (ibid.: 735). The representation of child soldiers of the Global South silences their on-the-ground needs, their range of capacities and the possibility that they are agents motivated by complex socio-political circumstances (ibid.: 740).

In the research we have canvassed in this chapter, it is logical that the 'becoming' child dominates much of the discussion of children in disasters, as these children are the immediate object of international aid that is subject to the provisions of the UNCRC, its related Optional Protocols and other aid-governing documents. Complementing and problematizing the UNCRC view of children who are caught in the wake of war and/or disaster are arguments that deepen our understanding of children as subject to the wider social and political forces (the habitus) into which they have been socialized. This characterization of child soldiers and orphans of disasters more often comes out of discussions in the social and political sciences, which are critical of approaches to assisting children that do not take into account the child's capacity for agency, that do not acknowledge that children are not uniformly 'victims', and in which we encounter again the 'being' child.

NOTES

1   The argument in this paragraph is adapted from a discussion published in Fronek and Cuthbert (2012a).
2   There are 129 signatories to this Protocol, and 152 parties. (http://treaties. un.org/, accessed 22 September 2013).

Further reading

Hague Justice Portal (2010) Haiti earthquake and intercountry adoption of children (http://www.haguejusticeportal.net/index.php?id=11382).

Furness D.-L. (2013) National Press Club: Adoption Crisis Forum (Speakers Deborra-Lee Furness, Dr Jane Aronson, Dr Karyn Purvis and Louise Voigt), 13 November 2013 (http://www.abc.net.au/news/2013-11-13/national-press-club-adoption-crisis-forum/5089322).

International Social Service and the International Reference Centre for the Rights of Children Deprived of their Family (2009) Earthquake in Haiti: Intercountry Adoption Cases (http://www.iss-ssi.org/2009/assets/files/news/haiti_position%20CIR_ENG.pdf).

Lee-Koo, K. (2011) 'Horror and hope: (Re)presenting militarised children in global North-South relations', *Third World Quarterly*, 32 (4): 725–42.

McMullin, J. (2011) 'Reintegrating young combatants: Do child-centred approaches leave children – and adults – behind?' *Third World Quarterly*, 32 (4): 743–64.

Machel, G. (1996) *Promotion and Protection of the Rights of Children: Impact of Armed Conflict on Children* (Machel Report). United Nations Department for Policy Coordination and Sustainable Development (DPCSD) (http://srsg.violenceagainstchildren.org/sites/default/files/documents/UN%20Resolutions/A-51-306_Machelstudy.pdf).

Mæland, B. (2010) *Culture, Religion, and the Reintegration of Female Child Soldiers in Northern Uganda*. New York: Peter Lang.

7

THE CHILD AND THE NATION: CASE STUDIES IN THE PERSECUTION AND FORCED REMOVAL OF CHILDREN BY THE STATE

- Nationalist rhetoric frequently positions children as central to the future of the nation, but not all children are equally valued by the state.

- Some children, by reason of their class, ethnicity or the political ideology of their parents may be deemed by the state to be a threat to the future of the nation or 'surplus' to requirements.

- Children may endure mistreatment through neglect or abuse, but on occasions this may amount to systematic, state-sanctioned persecution and forced expatriation of children by the state.

- Children, by reason of their future potential, may be the target of politically motivated social engineering: genocide, ethnocide and ideocide have particular impact on children and may even focus specifically on children.

- Historical examples of the systematic persecution of children by the state gave rise in the course of the twentieth century to international treaties for the protection of children.

INTRODUCTION

Through the course of the nineteenth and twentieth centuries to the present, children have come to assume increased political significance for nations and the international community (see Chapters 3 and 4). The welfare, development, and rights of children have become subject to national legislative regimes and increased scrutiny by the international community to the extent that the status of a nation's children stands as an index for the development and advancement of the nation. In national statements, both formal and informal, national leaders espouse the cause of children, linking the welfare and status of children to its future prospects. In this sense, the 'becoming child', the child valued for his or her future potential as a citizen/worker/soldier/parent of future citizens, is emblematic of the nation and its own becoming.

Anxieties about the state of the health of children prompt apprehensions about the future of the nation as we saw in Chapter 3 with reference to the rise of child obesity as a national and international issue. In the early twentieth century, concerns about the health of children (and the quality of mothering they received) prompted maternal and child health movements in the UK, Canada and Australia, as an early intervention of government and science into child rearing (Lewis, 1980; Comacchio, 1983; Arnup, 1994). Similarly the National Policy for Children developed by India's Ministry for Women and Child Development reiterates a florid statement on the value of children to the nation articulated in the 1974 policy it replaces, identifying the children of India as the nation's 'supremely important asset' (Government of India, 2013). Similar statements are made by governments, political leaders and child-focused organizations around the world. For example, commenting on the child provision in the 2011 US Federal budget, the Children's Defense Fund, a national advocacy organization for children, noted that even in tough economic times, the budget reflects the 'understanding that investing in children now will ensure a more stable economy and a healthier, more competitive workforce in the future.' (Children's Defense Fund, 2012). Early Childhood Australia, the Australian advocacy organization, promotes the same view, balanced by a statement of children's intrinsic value: 'Young children are precious in their own right and they are the future of the nation' (Early Childhood Australia, n.d.). While children are in large part dependent on the nation to initiate and maintain policies and programmes for their development, the nation sees its own future as dependent on the future human capital represented in its children.

However, there are frequently gaps between national rhetoric on the value of children and the programmes put in place to support them. Not all children within a given nation may be valued equally by that nation. While it is commonly assumed that children may fall victim to violence perpetrated by enemy or aggressor nations, it is also the case that children have fallen victim to state-sanctioned violence and persecution within their own countries.

In this chapter we present two case studies which enable us explore some darker aspects of the relationship between the child and the nation. Our focus is on the ways in which, under certain nationalist regimes or the imperatives of empire, nations have engaged in the systematic persecution or forced expatriation of children. Our discussion is embedded in some general considerations of the relationship between the nation and children and a more specific discussion of children and political violence, with reference to the impact of genocidal regimes on children. From these discussions, we turn to our two case studies: the 'disappeared' children of Argentina under the military rule of the generals in the 1980s, and the forced migration of children from Britain to colonies and former colonies which commenced in the 1620s and persisted until 1967. We contextualize these dark episodes in the state's treatment of children against a backdrop of similar experiences of other groups of children: children in several genocidal regimes, the forced removal of Indigenous children in North America and Australia, and the mass expatriation of South Korean babies born to single mothers in state-sanctioned inter-country adoption programmes. Before we turn to these case studies it is necessary to provide some background to the subject of children and the nation.

NATIONALIST VIOLENCE, STATE TERROR AND THE CHILD

While nations make claims about the nurturing of children, in reality modern history is crowded with examples of children whose experiences at the hands of state authorities have been otherwise. Speaking broadly, we can divide the failures of the state with respect to the proper care of children into two categories: failures of omission and of commission. However, it may be argued that there is a large grey area between these categories, where failures of omission in the duty of care owed to children by the state are so long-standing and pervasive that they begin to take on another complexion.

Child abuse in institutions in which children were resident or which they attended for schooling largely falls into this category of failure to protect children from harm, but with elements which spill into the grey zone mentioned above. The contemporary reckonings resulting from inquiries in Ireland into prolonged systemic abuse, including sexual abuse, of children in Catholic institutions, highlight the gross failure of governments in Ireland over many years to subject these church-run facilities to proper monitoring and, in some cases, to respond appropriately to reports of abuse (Commission to Inquire into Child Abuse [Ryan Commission], 2009). Australia is another nation which has engaged in a grim reckoning of failures of the state to provide the appropriate care for children.

In Australia, this reckoning has led to many state- and federal-level inquiries into children's welfare since the subject was first opened up in the ground-breaking Stolen Generations inquiry into the forced removal of Indigenous children from their families, published in 1997 (HREOC, 1997).[1] Three national apologies have been delivered: by Prime Minister Kevin Rudd to the Indigenous Stolen Generations (Rudd, 2008) and institutionalized children and former forced imperial child migrants (Rudd, 2009); and by Prime Minister Julia Gillard to the mothers and their now adult children who were separated by past forced adoption practices (Gillard, 2013). These apologies acknowledge the damage inflicted by past policies which saw children, both Indigenous and non-Indigenous, removed from parents, institutionalized, abused, in some cases stripped of their identities with little chance of re-connecting with their families (Cuthbert and Quartly, 2012, 2013).

In his apology to adults who had endured institutionalization and forced imperial migration as children, Kevin Rudd elected to represent the failure of the Australian nation as one of omission: 'You were in no way to blame for what happened to you because it was the nation who failed you. The institutions the nation created for your care, failed you' (Rudd, 2009). In the light of the fact that the Australian Federal government and several states actively solicited the migration of English children to provide ready sources of labour, the framing provided by Rudd is open to dispute.

Nonetheless, it is possible to distinguish between children suffering through neglect or failures of the state to protect them from abuse and mistreatment, and the suffering of children who are targets of political exclusion and violence implemented in the name of national regimes from which they should have expected protection. Some key ideas from scholarship in this field set the scene for our case studies.

In *Imagined Communities*, his influential book on the hegemony of nationalism, Benedict Anderson theorizes the nation as an 'imaginary' construct, subject to limits and yet sovereign (Anderson, 1983: 49). The nation is imagined because citizens of even the smallest nation cannot know each other personally and hence must be able to imagine their connectedness and commonality as citizens in order for the nation to cohere. This national imaginary or nationalist spirit – the 'imagined community' of the book's title – is the powerful glue of nations. The national imaginary fosters fellow feeling and a sense of common purpose amongst citizens and, equally, may foster fear, suspicion and even hatred of outsiders, non-citizens and minority groups within the nation whose 'difference' challenges assumptions of national cultural coherence. The nation is limited in the sense that it is defined by its borders, which de-mark the extent of its sovereignty and the point at which the sovereignty of one nation rubs against that of another.

The nation is also limited in the sense that it is exclusive. In the decade leading to the joining of the colonies into a federated whole in 1901, the founding fathers of the Australian nation imagined a community that was white and of European extraction, and the nationalist rhetoric on which the nation was built emphasized this exclusivity (Threadgold, 2002). It is no coincidence that the first piece of legislation enacted by the new Australian parliament was the Immigration Restriction Act (1901), which enabled the so-called White Australia Policy, and ensured the dominance of Australia's European (British) population. The imagined community of the founders of the Australian state emphasized this cultural/racial cohesion to the exclusion of Indigenous people and members of other ethnic groups (Chinese, Japanese, Afghans) who had contributed to the establishment of colonies and their industries and enterprises including horticulture, pearling and transportation. In this way, Threadgold argues, national imaginaries posit equations between national identity and ethnic or cultural identity that rarely exist in fact. In consequence, some groups are excluded from the nation while others are marginalized within it. Although not themselves citizens, children are central to these nationalist imaginings.

In European settler-nations such as Australia, Canada, the USA and New Zealand the imposition of the nation-state constructs on territories formerly inhabited by Indigenous peoples was achieved first through the dispossession and then exclusion of Indigenous populations from control of land. Exclusion from, or marginal participation in, the polity followed. Indigenous peoples, once defeated by the colonizers, ceased to be 'enemies' and became instead 'problems' to be managed by the new nation. An important component of the management of the 'native' problem in settler-societies in Australia and North America was focused on children, as national governments directed attention to Indigenous children in efforts to assimilate them to the dominant culture. The complementary work of missionaries in this endeavour is discussed in Chapter 3.

Widespread child removals from Indigenous communities took place in Canada, the USA and Australia from the late nineteenth century. Indigenous children, including many so-called 'half-caste' children, were programmatically removed and sent to native schools and children's homes in an effort to make them 'white', to fracture their links with their communities and culture and to educate them to be serviceable to the nation. These interventions – the subject of the aforementioned national apology in Australia delivered by the Prime Minister Kevin Rudd in February 2008 – have been labelled by Indigenous people and some scholars as genocidal in their intent and in their impact on Indigenous cultures, languages and communities (Barta, 1985; Markus, 2001; Innes, 2001). Until well into the twentieth century in Australia, governments and other agents involved in this activity, including churches, believed it to be in the best interests of both Indigenous children and the nation.

National cohesion, national integrity and national reorganization have also been banners under which other genocidal, ethnocidal and ideocidal actions have been undertaken. As argued by several scholars, most notably, Arjun Appadurai (2006), the mix of nationalism, ethnic and cultural identifications and affiliations (which frequently cross national boundaries as in the cases of transnational diasporic communities) and various fundamentalisms has resulted in forms of political unrest and violence characteristic of the late twentieth and early twenty-first centuries.

The presence of ethnic and cultural minority groups within the nation, and their claims for basic or fuller inclusion in the polity, is an irritant that challenges nationalist mythologies of cultural unity and cohesion, predicated on equations between nation and culture. Especially when overlaid on old enmities, Appadurai argues that the assumption that national identity is coterminous with the cultural identity of a dominant group within the nation and excludes minority groups has given rise to serial attempts at genocide, ethnic or cultural cleansing or ethnocide, as evidenced by atrocities in Rwanda, Cambodia, Burma, Bosnia and Darfur. In these dark events, a dominant ethnic/cultural group which equates its identity with that of the nation (or the nation in its purest and most authentic form) seeks to cleanse the nation of cultural or ethnic minority groups through actions that lead to genocide or attempted genocide.

Genocidal political and military violence has direct and indirect impact on children in targeted communities. One particularly invidious form of political violence which specifically implicates children is the mass rape of women in subjugated populations. Rape has occurred throughout recorded history. The raping of women in war and conflict may take the form of isolated or opportunistic acts of lawlessness committed by individual soldiers, or form part of more or less co-ordinated campaigns of terror intended to further disempower, degrade and humiliate subject populations. The UN estimates that between 20,000 and 50,000 women and girls were raped during the Bosnian conflict in the early 1990s. During armed conflict in the Democratic Republic of Congo, approximately 1,100 rapes were reported each month, with an average of 36 women and girls raped every day. Estimates are that over 200,000 women and girls have suffered from sexual violence in that country since armed conflict began (UN, n.d.).

More recently in the field of genocide studies, scholars have identified particular features of rape during armed conflict or political unrest and insurgency which align this activity with genocide (MacKinnon, 2006), specifically, in situations where the raping of women from particular groups is accompanied by assertions of ethnic- or race-based power. In such situations the 'blood' and genetic material of the subjugating or dominant group is forcibly introduced into the subjugated community with the intention of eradicating this group.

Female survivors of such politically motivated rape report statements made by the men who raped them which bear out this intention of genetic conquest, as in this report by a victim of rape in the Bosnian genocide of the 1990s:

> [S]ix soldiers came in and all of them raped me. They cursed me, insulted me, said there were too many Muslim people and said a lot of Muslims [Bosniaks] were going to give birth to Serbian children. (Cited by Berman, 2012)

Armed subjugation of the Muslim Bosniaks is thereby extended through sexual subjugation of Bosniak women. By diluting Bosniak 'blood' with that of the non-Muslim Serbians, the Serbians seek to compromise and weaken the identity and integrity of the Bosniak population.

Similarly, in one account from the bitter inter-ethnic conflict in Darfur in 2005, the reporter notes the frequency of rape as a political tool of subjugation and intimidation. As in the Bosnian example above, the assertion of one ethnic 'blood line' over another informs this violence:

> Kalma isn't the only place where multiple accounts of rape have surfaced. Some 120 miles away, in the town of Mukjar, two men separately described women being brought into a prison where they were being held and raped for hours by Janjaweed [Arab militia].

> They said the assailants shouted that they were 'planting tomatoes' – a reference to skin color: Darfur Arabs describe themselves as 'red' because they are slightly lighter-skinned than ethnic Africans. (de Montesquiou, 2007)

This rape is genocidal in intent as it seeks to compromise the continuation of these subjugated communities by tainting and complicating the ethnic and genetic identities of the children born to these rape victims. To the extent that the capacity to reproduce the next generation within a particular community signals a future for that community, forcing the women of the community to bear the children of the enemy is a violent delimiting of that future both symbolically and materially. This practice highlights the sinister yet huge symbolic importance of children as human capital for the nation and for particular cultural or ethnic groups within the nation. With no children, there is no future.

The children born as a result of such rape are socially and symbolically stigmatized by the circumstances of their conception. Such children are often marked by their visible difference from their mothers and their communities – as in the 'planting tomatoes' reference in Darfur, where the children of Arab Janjaweed fathers may have a lighter skin colour than their non-Arab Sudanese mothers. These children frequently become a painful symbol and reminder of the conflict into which they were born. They can face rejection and ostracism, along with their mothers (and sometimes by their mothers, who are unable to accept them), or by their mothers' family and community because they carry the 'blood' of the enemy or persecutor.

THE 'DISAPPEARED CHILDREN' OF ARGENTINA – THE IDEOLOGICAL CLEANSING OF ARGENTINA

While differences in ethnicity and culture form the basis of genocidal violence in these examples from Bosnia and Darfur, politics and ideology form the basis of state terror against children in the following case study from Argentina.

The story of the 'disappeared' children of Argentina shares many of the elements which characterize the practice of genocide and genocidal rape, as illustrated above in the Bosnian and Darfur examples Other elements illustrate further the complex relationships between children and the state, the symbolic value of children in political and ideological conflicts, and the material effects these relationships and symbolisms can have on the lives of children.

In the period between 1976 and 1983, the government of Argentina was taken over by an extreme right-wing junta of five generals who engaged in a period of state-sanctioned terrorism aimed at purging Argentina of left-wing political influences and opposition. The resulting reign of terror of the generals was referred to officially as the National Reorganization Process (*Proceso de Reorganización Nacional*), the aim of which was to re-instate pure or authentic Argentinian national values and remake the nation along these lines. This reign of terror also became known as the 'dirty war': a war pursued by the state against its own citizens through the systematic kidnapping of dissenters, intellectuals, academics and university students, journalists, trade unionists and others associated with voicing opposition to the junta, or even suspected of holding different views.

The victims of this terror became known as *los desaparecidos* or 'the disappeared'. It is estimated that between the years 1976 and 1983, over 30,000 Argentinians 'disappeared'. On one occasion, 60 high school students from Manuel Belgrano High School in Buenos Aires were 'disappeared', apparently for having joined a student council at the school – an activity deemed by the junta to be subversive, degenerate and un-Argentinian (Goldman, 2012). Victims were abducted as they walked to and from work or school; as they stepped off public transport; and in terror raids on private houses and apartments in which whole families were taken and never seen again (ibid.).

The systematic attempt by the generals to cleanse the nation of political dissenters is akin to genocide, but undertaken on ideological rather than ethnic or racial grounds (Schabas, 2000). The generals sought to rebuild the nation and its population along what they considered to be 'authentic' Argentinian principles and values, a process of re-organization and purification that required the cleansing of the population politically and ideologically. Appadurai (2006), in his study of several episodes of violent national cleansing in the twentieth century, uses the term ideocide to describe the motivation and effects of this kind of persecution. In Argentina, the project of National Reorganization provided an ideological rationale allowing the generals to persecute and murder their own political enemies and opponents by framing these individuals and organizations as enemies of the nation. That is, the nation, or the particular version of the nation imagined by the generals, served as the rationale for a regime of state terror against fellow Argentinians, including large numbers of children.

In addition to the abduction, torture and death of dissidents, distinctive elements emerged in the 'dirty war' with respect to the treatment of infants and very young children who were either 'disappeared' with their parents, or born to women who were pregnant when seized (Abuelas de Plaza de Mayo, n.d.). In many cases, very young disappeared children and infants born to pregnant women in detention camps were spared death – sometimes their pregnant mothers were kept alive until they delivered, only to be executed shortly after the birth. These children then became the subject of a particular ideocidal intervention. They were removed from detention and adopted into military or other families sympathetic to the junta (Abuelas de Plaza de Mayo, n.d.; Arditti, 2007). The children were given new birth certificates and new identities with their adoptive families; their connections with their families of origin were severed completely as, importantly, were their links to the social and political lives of their parents within banned trade unions, political opposition or guerrilla groups and dissident organizations. In this way, what may be described as the ideological or political inheritance of these children – along with connections with family and culture – were disengaged and the children were re-made as 'purified' children of the National Reorganization. Possibly up to 500 children of dissidents were adopted into families sympathetic to the regime (Abuelas de Plaza de Mayo, n.d.).

It was largely through the work of a small group of grandmothers of young children who were 'disappeared' with their parents, or born to women known to be pregnant when abducted, that the scale of this part of the dirty war has come to light (Arditti, 2007; Goldman, 2012). These individual women joined forces while searching for their children and grandchildren and began to organize and mount a regular vigil in the Plaza de Mayo, a large square in Buenos Aires, calling themselves the Abuelas de Plaza de Mayo (the grandmothers of the Plaza de Mayo), as they explain on their website:

These children are the children of our children, who have also disappeared. Many babies were kidnapped with their parents, some after their parents were killed, and others were born in clandestine detention centers where their mothers were taken after having been sequestered at different states of their pregnancies.

We, the babies' grandmothers, tried desperately to locate them and, during these searches, decided to unite. Thus, in 1977, the non-governmental organization called Abuelas (Grandmothers) de Plaza de Mayo was established, dedicated specifically to fighting for the return of our grandchildren. We also relentlessly investigated our children's and grandchildren's disappearances, in hopes of finding them. (Abuelas de Plaza de Mayo, n.d.)

The dogged persistence of the Abuelas in searching for their grandchildren – which resonates through the searches of other children and parents separated by the state, such as Australia's Stolen Generation of Indigenous peoples – testifies to the gross violation of family and identity entailed in these actions. The Abuelas' highly publicized campaign 'Do you know who you are?' (Arditti, 2007) highlighted that haunting questions remained for young adult Argentinians born in the years of the dirty war, as to whether they were in fact 'disappeared' children placed in other families. The assault on rights to connection with family and identity led the Argentinian delegation to the UN to advocate for the inclusion of the so-called Argentinian clauses, dealing with identity, in the UNCRC (UN, 1989; Sikkink, 2008).[2] The Argentinian experience also led to the recognition of a specific human right – the right not to endure forced disappearance – in a convention adopted by the UN in 2006 (McCory, 2006).

What can be seen at work here – both in the terrorism of the generals and the resistance of the Abuelas – is the profound connection between children and the future. Not only did the generals deal with the present political threat posed by their adult enemies and opponents, but they also sought to extend the authority and reach of their programme of National Reorganization into the future through their dealings with the children of their enemies. Through being placed in families sympathetic to the regime, the disappeared children of the reign of the generals were educated and raised in political and ideological (and social and cultural) environments which were different from – indeed antagonistic to – the values and beliefs of their own birth families. In some cases, the adoptive parents of these children were implicated in the torture and death of their parents. In this way, these children – some of whom came to know the story of their origins and identities much later in life – were deployed by the military dictatorship in a process of politically motivated social engineering, which aimed to ensure that the state of Argentina could be finally 'cleansed' of left-wing, subversive and 'terrorist' elements. This was done by eliminating one generation of enemies of the state and attempting to convert the children of these enemies to the extreme right-wing principles of the military dictatorship and its supporters.

This element of the project of National Reorganization had a devastating impact on many of the disappeared children who later came, in horror, to know the truth of their origins and the fates of their birth parents. It had equally devastating consequences for others who, being challenged with suggestions that they were part of the disappeared generation of Argentinian children, refused to believe these claims and clung to their adoptive families and the values they represented.

As we see in the next case study, the large-scale intervention in the lives of children involving their forced removal from families (and their expatriation) in the interests of the nation is not restricted to militaristic reigns of terror: it was a feature of England's management of the poor and other 'undesirable' elements of the population for centuries.

SURPLUS TO NATIONAL REQUIREMENTS – THE EXPATRIATION OF 'UNWANTED' BRITISH CHILDREN AND THE POPULATION OF EMPIRE

As depicted in the films *The Leaving of Liverpool* (ABC and BBC, 1992–93) and more recently *Oranges and Sunshine* (Loach, 2010), poor children from the British Isles were transported to former British colonies, Australia, South Africa, Rhodesia (now Zimbabwe), Canada and New Zealand. Child deportation has a history as long as that of British imperialism and colonization. The mass transportation of children to the Americas goes back as far as 1618, when 100 children were shipped from the City of London to Richmond, Virginia. More children were transported at the request of the Council of New England in 1622. The precedent for the flow of poor, abandoned, marginalized or criminal children from Britain to the colonies was established and was maintained intermittently for the next three centuries, resurging in the early twentieth century, well beyond the time when such a practice should have been countenanced (Kershaw and Sacks, 2008: 9). Reflecting on this grim history, the Child Migrant Trust, established in 1987 to advocate for the rights of former child migrants, suggests that the British state used child migration as a social welfare option for the management of poor children for centuries (Child Migrant Trust, 2012). While total numbers are hard to estimate, when children purposefully transported are combined with those who elected transportation in preference to long jail sentences for crimes committed, the potential numbers swell to many tens of thousands (Kershaw and Sacks, 2008: 13).

The mass, involuntary transportation of children from Britain to her colonies of North America shares features with the cross-Atlantic trade in slaves, which saw hundreds of thousands of Africans transported to the Americas to endure lives of harsh and unpaid labour and take on the status of chattels of their owners. The British children transported first to North America, later to other or former colonies in Africa and Australasia, were destined to serve as farm labourers, apprentices, domestic maids and servants. They were not paid wages but received board and lodging in return for their labour. Some enjoyed conditions comparable to adopted children (bearing in mind that the labouring child was a norm at this time), but many were treated as chattels and as a source of unpaid labour.

The American War of Independence ended cordial relationships between Britain and its former colonies for the time, but the hunger for cheap child labour persisted in the growing American settlements that were now expanding rapidly beyond the New England area. This demand resulted in the transportation of children within America in an attempt to address both labour shortages on the frontiers and the problem of poor and idle children in the rapidly growing cities of the eastern states. As we have noted at several points in this book, gangs of poor and idle children on the streets prompt an ambivalent response to the child in danger and the child as danger.

In the early period, child labourers were transported by wagon train to settlements outside the cities. With the advent of the railways, large numbers of poor children, many of them Irish, were scooped off the streets of cities such as New York and Boston and transported to the frontiers on what became known as 'orphan trains'. The phrase to be 'put up' for adoption derives from the practice of putting the children up on railway platforms for the inspection of local families seeking an extra pair of hands for chores (again, much like slave market practices). Many were not orphans at all. The scale of this internal migration was immense: it is estimated that 200,000 poor children from cities in the east were boarded onto orphan trains for the west between 1854 and 1930 (Warren, 1998).

With respect to transportation from Britain, many forced migrant children in the later period were institutionalized in work farms run by philanthropic organizations such as Fairbridge and Barnados, or by the Catholic and other churches (Bean and Melville, 1989; Gill, 1998; Hill, 2001; Kershaw and Sacks, 2008). Dr Thomas Barnado was a prominent figure in child migration schemes to Canada, South Africa and Australia and spoke of the children he deported as 'Bricks for Empire Building' (Kershaw and Sacks, 2008: 9). The last mass transportation of English children for Australia left Liverpool in 1967. Many of the children on board this vessel – like thousands before them – were destined for lives of unpaid labour and abuse in the new country, their status not materially different from that of slaves.

Graphically highlighting the long historical delay in seriously addressing children's rights, it is worth considering that British children (and many Irish children in Britain and later children from the British territory of Malta) were subject to involuntary transportation and the gross curtailment of their liberty more than a hundred years after the passing of the Abolition of Slavery Act of 1833, which abolished slavery in the British Empire, and the Thirteenth Amendment to the Constitution of the United States in 1865, which outlawed slavery in that jurisdiction. Recalling our observation in Chapter 3, that the movement to prevent cruelty to animals preceded organized attempts to prevent cruelty to children, this long gap highlights the degree to which the rights of children remained obscured – even with the rise of rights-based political movements – until well into the twentieth century. Of course, the children who were vulnerable to transportation were the children of the poor and of marginalized groups, such as the Irish, in overcrowded British cities.

The proponents of imperial child migration schemes as practised from the late nineteenth and into the twentieth centuries, made claims about the benefits this transportation would bring for the children themselves. Philanthropists such as

William Fairbridge, who established the Fairbridge Farms which received large numbers of deported children in South African Rhodesia and Australia, romanticized the prospects that awaited poor British children in the colonies:

> Train these children to be farmers! Not in England [...] Shift the orphanages of England to where farmers and farmers' wives are needed, and where no man with strong arms and a willing heart would ever want for his daily bread. (Fairbridge, *Veld Verse*, quoted in Kershaw and Sacks, 2008: 142)

In reality the reasons for their transportation had much more to do with the interests of other parties: the British nation that sent them away and the developing colonies and later newly independent nations that received them. Quite clearly, children who could not advocate for themselves were used instrumentally by their nation in the service of empire: they served as highly expendable and transportable units of labour. Authorities in England were spared the expense of supporting impoverished children in alms houses, orphanages and other institutions; streets and lanes were cleared of 'problem' children who would inevitably grow to become 'problem' adults and represent a further drain on the public purse. Addressing the issue in the British Parliament in 1922, an advocate for child migration responded to a call from the Premier of the Australian state of South Australia for up to 6,000 child migrants and stated that:

> If this were done it would relieve the State of a certain amount of money for the public purse, and also provide Canada and Australia with a very large number of juvenile immigrants. (Cited by Bean and Melville, 1989: 90)

The further benefit of these schemes was the provision of white population stock for English colonies and former colonies. In Australia, as in other settler-colonial societies, a key historical anxiety has been the generation of a sufficiently robust Anglo-Celtic population to secure first the colonies and, from 1901, the fledgling nation from the real or perceived threat of the surrounding non-white population, both that of Indigenous Australia and the surrounding and highly mobile populations of the Asia-Pacific region.

In some cases, parents were told that their children were destined for better lives in warmer climates, where education and training would equip them for more productive and serviceable lives in their new countries. The title of the film *Oranges and Sunshine* (Loach, 2010) alludes to this utopian vision of poor children from a cold climate growing strong in climates of abundant sunshine and fresh fruit. The reality endured by many of these children was quite different. In many cases, parents were not informed that their children were being transported and children were told that their parents were dead or did not want them.

A major inquiry into forced imperial child migration from the United Kingdom to Australia was undertaken by a committee of the Australian Senate. The inquiry commenced in 1999 and reported to the Australian parliament in 2001 (Parliament of Australia, 2001). The report provides ghastly insights into the lives of these children and the long-term damage many experienced as a result of their treatment.

As has been revealed in the submissions received by the Senate inquiry and by the investigative work of Nottingham social worker Margaret Humphreys, who established the Child Migrant Trust in 1987, many children who were transported in this way experienced harsh lives of penury, hard labour and abuse (including sexual abuse), and received little or no formal education. However, transcending accounts of the physical hardships and privations of their lives, and central to the testimonies of suffering of many of these transported children, is their loss of identity and connection with family and community, a loss they have shared with the disappeared children of Argentina and the Indigenous Stolen Generations.

The treatment of these children highlights the ways in which children may become arbitrarily subject to both national and imperial imperatives. In the case of the forced imperial child migrants, the dual needs of the sending nation and receiving colonies/nations were met through their deportation, which was then represented as being in their best interests.

Tragic irony runs very deep in the Australian example. For as British children were being forcibly expatriated and transported to Australia, Indigenous children were simultaneously being forcibly removed from their parents in the interests of white nation building. The English and Australian states would seek to distance themselves from charges of having conducted a 'dirty war' on their own children and claim that the transportation of poor English children to new lives in Australia and the removal of Indigenous children from their families was driven by good – if in retrospect terribly misguided – intentions. It is sobering to consider that actions such as these can be committed under the rule of law (on which both the British and Australian states with their Westminster modes of government pride themselves), and not under the rule of the gun, as in Argentina.

CHILDREN AND THE NATION: FINAL OBSERVATIONS

Nationalist rhetoric frequently aligns the interests of the nation with those of its children and links the future of the nation to their capacities. In reality this is not always the case. Some children are excluded from the national imaginary with material and sometimes deadly consequences for them. National imperatives may require certain children to be eliminated, expatriated or re-made as the children of others – as occurred to several hundred 'disappeared' children in Argentina under the National Reorganization Process.

As we have seen, there are children who have been subject to persecution by the state by reason of their ethnicity, their class or the political commitments of their parents. Regrettably, examples of this far outnumber the limited case studies we have been able to include in this chapter, and the list is long: Jewish, Slavic and Gypsy (Roma) children exterminated under the racial purification schemes of the Third Reich; children persecuted and killed along with their parents under Pol Pot's regime in Cambodia; children persecuted and killed in Rwanda, Bosnia, Burma and the Congo. These examples all relate to the perilous condition of childhood in regimes of terror and totalitarianism.

As we have also seen, unspeakable things are done to children under conditions of settled, even democratic, government. The governments of Britain and Australia – held up as model liberal democracies and champions of political freedom on the global stage – colluded over an extended period of time in the forced expatriation of poor British (and Irish and Maltese) children to Australia (and elsewhere) in order to satisfy imperatives in each nation: the need to spare the English state of the burden of their care and the need for sturdy (white) cheap labour for nation building in Australia. While not commonly raised in this context, the record of South Korea with respect to the expatriation of nearly one million children in state-sanctioned inter-country adoption programmes in preference to the development of social welfare programmes for their support, or the revision of repressive codes of sexual morality that ostracize unwed mothers, does not sit well with South Korea's status as a developed nation. As characterized by Tobias Hübinette, South Korea stands as an 'orphaned nation' in respect of this shameful national failure to its own children (Hübinette, 2005, 2006).

There are, as we argued in Chapter 4, grounds for reserve and scepticism regarding the appropriateness and efficacy of a rights-based framework as mandated by the UNCRC (1989) for addressing the needs of children. However, the magnitude and persistence of gross exploitation of children within their own nations, and the disregard for children as human beings as exhibited in the actions of nations of several complexions up to the present moment, constitute compelling grounds for arguing a need for commitment to the inclusion of children in a human rights framework. We might remind ourselves of how long it has taken for recognition that our treatment of children has not accorded them the rights accorded to adults. One hundred and thirty-four years after the abolition of slavery in the British Commonwealth (and 102 years after slavery was abolished in the USA in the midst of a bloody civil war fought around this issue), poor and marginalized children continued to be transported from England to Australia and elsewhere for lives of unremitting labour, privation and abuse. Finally, as we have also seen, while the persecution of children by the enemy of a nation can readily be cast as barbarism, the persecution and state-sanctioned violation and abuse of children within the nation has frequently been dressed in the clothes of national interest.

NOTES

1 In addition to the Human Rights and Equal Opportunity Commission's inquiry and report into Indigenous child removal, other inquiries include the Australian Senate's Community Affairs References Committee's inquiry into Australians who experienced institutional or out-of-home care as children, the first report of which is entitled *Forgotten Australians* (August 2004) and the second *Protecting Vulnerable Children: A National Challenge* (March 2005). Forced imperial child migration was the subject of an inquiry by the Australian Senate's Community Affairs References Committee, finalized in 2000 in the report *Lost Innocents:*

Righting the Record. Report on Child Migration (Canberra: Parliament House, 2001). At state level, the Queensland government undertook a major inquiry (the Forde Inquiry) into the abuse of children in state institutions which reported in 2001: *The Report of the Commission of Inquiry into Abuse of Children in Queensland Institutions* (Brisbane: Queensland Government Printer, 2001). With respect to past forced adoption practices, there is the inquiry of the Parliament of Tasmania, *Past Adoption Practices* (Hobart, 1999); New South Wales Legislative Council's Standing Committee on Social Issues report into adoption practices of the past, *Releasing the Past: Adoption Practice 1950–1998. Final Report* (December 2000); and The Senate, Community Affairs References Committee, *Commonwealth Contribution to Past Forced Adoption Practices* (Canberra: Parliament of Australia, 2012).

2 These are articles 7, 8 and 11. Article 7 states that 1. The child shall be registered immediately after birth and shall have the right from birth to a name, the right to acquire a nationality and, as far as possible, the right to know and be cared for by his or her parents. 2. States Parties shall ensure the implementation of these rights in accordance with their national law and their obligations under the relevant international instruments in this field, in particular where the child would otherwise be stateless. Article 8 states that 1. States Parties undertake to respect the right of the child to preserve his or her identity, including nationality, name and family relations as recognized by law without unlawful interference. 2. Where a child is illegally deprived of some or all of the elements of his or her identity, States Parties shall provide appropriate assistance and protection, with a view to re-establishing speedily his or her identity. Article 11 states that 1. States Parties shall take measures to combat the illicit transfer and non-return of children abroad. 2. To this end, States Parties shall promote the conclusion of bilateral or multilateral agreements or accession to existing agreements. (UN, 1989).

Further reading

Barta, T. (1985) 'After the Holocaust: Consciousness of genocide in Australia', *Australian Journal of Politics and History*, 31 (1): 154–61.

Human Rights and Equal Opportunity Commission (HREOC) (1997) *Bringing them Home: Report of the National Inquiry into the Separation of Aboriginal and Torres Strait Islander Children from Their Families 1997*. Canberra: HREOC, Commonwealth of Australia (http://www.humanrights.gov.au/publications/bringing-them-home-stolen-children-report-1997).

Jacobs, M.D. (2009) *White Mother to a Dark Race: Settler Colonialism, Maternalism, and the Removal of Indigenous Children in the American West and Australia, 1880–1940*. Lincoln: University of Nebraska Press.

Markus, A. (2001) 'Genocide in Australia', *Aboriginal History*, 25: 57–69.

8

THE VALUE OF CHILDREN

- The values ascribed to children range from the functional and utilitarian, to the emotional, psychological and symbolic. Overwhelmingly the value of children is calculated in terms of the value or benefit they represent to adults.

- The value of children is not universal: it has changed over time and varies in different cultural settings. Within the one social setting, children may be valued differentially depending on a range of variables including gender, class, ethnicity, and citizenship status.

- While evidence of the ways in which children are valued (or not) is everywhere, the value of children has, with very few exceptions (in demography or population studies and the law), not been a concern of academic disciplines until very recently.

- A more holistic approach to the question of the value of children within social and cultural contexts emerged in the mid-1970s with the Value of Children approach, and in 1985 with Viviana's Zelizer's book, *Pricing the Priceless Child: The Changing Social Value of Children*.

- Cases studies highlight some of the variables in how children are valued according to citizenship status and age, or the benefits (economic or affective, social and political) they are imagined as bestowing on adults.

INTRODUCTION

The value of children is frequently framed in terms of what benefits – whether functional and utilitarian or emotional, concrete or abstract – adults perceive that children can bestow on them. In fact, the adult-centredness of considerations of children's value may result in even the most abstract or symbolic of those values – that of innocence, for example – serving important functions for adults and to that degree can also be considered utilitarian. As theorized by Jenks in 1996, the structures of meaning that adults in contemporary Western society build around themselves and their social interactions, and the way they situate themselves in relation to both the future and the past, are highly dependent on concepts of childhood. Childhood has immense symbolic value to adults:

Any assault on what the child is or rather, what the child has evolved into, threatens to rock the social base. The child through the passage of modernity came to symbolize tomorrow and was thus guarded and invested. In the late modern context, where belief in progress and futures has diminished, has the child come now to symbolize the solidity and adhesion of the past? And is it therefore defended as a hedge against an anxiety wrought through the disappearance of the social bond rather than the disappearance of the child? (Jenks, 1996: 130)

The comments of Jenks reflect the values and meanings accorded to childhood in the Global North in the late twentieth century. In other periods in Western history and in other cultures, childhood has been and is valued in other ways.

In one model of value structuring childhood, the child is an active partner in economic production along with adults. In contemporary societies in the Global North, however, many children live quarantined from economic production and childhood is valued in these terms – as a time and a place apart (Stern et al., 1975). Family and the intimacies of the domestic sphere are constitutive of a world in which children occupy a central and valorized position. This is the world to which (we imagine) adults retreat in the evenings, on weekends and on holidays, away from the demands of the workforce and the economy; the capacity of parents to provide sufficiently to produce this cherished haven is to some extent taken as a measure of their economic and moral success. It is an ideal only enabled by the largely invisible and unremitting domestic labour of women, many of whom support it by gruelling double shifts in paid employment and unpaid domestic labour. Nonetheless, the ideal persists, even to the point of cliché, with politicians and other prominent people frequently electing to couple announcements of their resignation or retirement with statements about wanting to 'spend more time with the family'.

In each model, children are valued largely in terms of the benefits they can bestow on adults, relative to differing roles and understandings. As these roles and understandings shift over time or across cultures, so does the value accorded to children themselves or, more accurately, to those children who may be seen as capable of delivering the particular benefits desired by adults. Even within one society, such as contemporary Australia or the UK, different valuations of children compete and not all children are valued equally: evaluation and consequent treatment are squared off against normative ideas of what a child *should* be. At various points in this book, we have noted evidence of ambivalence towards children which informs thinking about children. This may be expressed in terms of contradictory understandings of children in danger, and children as danger. This ambivalence informs considerations of children's value, as against the cost they might represent.

Other variables come into play in the differential evaluation of children. As just one illustration of this, it can be seen that the particular child's relationship to the state – whether as a citizen or the child of a citizen, or the child of an alien – may determine the value of the child in the eyes of the state and the standards of care that individual children receive.

In this chapter, we provide an overview of some key thinking on the value of children. We survey the consideration of children's value as it developed within the specialized disciplines of demography, economics and law. Some attention is directed to the highly influential book by the US economic sociologist Viviana Zelizer, *Pricing the Priceless Child* (1985) and her analytic framework of 'useful' and 'useless' children, which she employs to account for the rise to dominance and normativity of what she calls the 'sacralized child' over the last decades of the nineteenth and early decades of the twentieth centuries. Zelizer's work focuses on the USA, but is applicable with some reservations to shifts in the evaluation of children in other advanced Global Northern economies and increasingly to the value of children in rapidly developing economies outside the Global North.

THE VALUE OF CHILDREN: APPROACHES TO THE QUESTION IN THE SOCIAL SCIENCES

For much of the modern period, considerations of the value of children were of interest in only a handful of disciplines and fields of practice, reflecting the lack of serious attention to children across the main social science disciplines until the relatively recent emergence of childhood studies in history, sociology, human geography and other fields. The contribution of psychology is discussed in some detail in Chapter 1. Demography, or the study of populations, attempts to account for rising and falling birth-rates and led scholars to analyse the motivations driving adults' decisions about whether to have children and how many. The framing of these questions within the dynamic interaction of population, population growth and economic conditions flows from Thomas R. Malthus's influential 1798 *An Essay on the Principle of Population as it Affects the Future Improvement of Society*. Since Malthus, economists, demographers, sociologists of the family and psychologists have attempted to answer one question: Why do some people have many children, others fewer or none at all? (Nauck, 2000: 1).

Law and insurance are other fields in which focused attention has been paid to the value of children. There is a significant body of case law and commentary in the law of torts (being the law of civil wrongs in which the wrong may be addressed through the award of damages or compensation) which interrogates the value of children and calculates this in monetary terms. In the law of torts, attempts to ascertain the value (and the cost) of children arise from consideration of their wrongful deaths, wrongful births and even wrongful lives in order to calculate damages to be made to those – mostly parents – who have been wronged by these adverse events.

WHY DO PEOPLE HAVE CHILDREN? INSIGHTS FROM DEMOGRAPHY AND ECONOMICS ON THE VALUE OF CHILDREN

The dedicated study of population dynamics has been enabled by the rise of systematic population data collection over the course of the nineteenth century; it developed alongside the rise of the discipline of economics and has frequently been treated as a sub-field of (Malthusian) economics. By reason of Malthus's influence, the study of population was preoccupied from its origins with investigations into the optimal level of population growth consistent with economic growth or the wealth of nations, through the provision of a sufficient labour force and a sufficient market for the products of industry.

The logical corollary of this interest is the question of why populations, or sections of the population, continue to reproduce beyond their economic capacities to support this population growth. At a micro-level, this devolved into the question of why the poor generally continue to have large numbers of children despite their limited resources to support them. This counter-indicated population growth was identified as a risk to the wealth of nations by Malthus, as well as placing a burden on the state to care or otherwise deal with those people who could not support themselves. On this point, quantitative assessments of population intersected with qualitative ones: the wealth of nations relied on sufficient numbers of the *right* kinds of people to engage productively with agriculture, commerce and industry. Nations need to develop mechanisms to control or constrain increases in the numbers of people deemed undesirable and hence surplus to requirements.

Over several centuries in Britain, in particular, the national imperative to manage what was considered to be surplus population resulted in the forced deportation of criminals and other undesirables, including the children of the poor, to colonial outposts, as discussed in Chapter 7. In contemporary China, efforts to constrain the growth of the population within the parameters required for economic growth have been expressed in aggressive family planning interventions since the early 1970s and the introduction of the one child policy from 1970 (Anderson and Leo, 2009). Conversely, in Malaysia under the prime ministership of Mohammed Mahathir in the 1980s (Jones, 2013: 30) and in Romania under President Nicolae Ceauşescu at the same time (Kligman, 1998), the imperative of population growth to achieve optimal economic development and other nationalist objectives resulted in misguided pro-natalist policies, with sanctions against families (mainly women) who attempted to exercise birth control. It should not be concluded that pro-natalism is a strategy exercised only in totalitarian regimes or societies in which civil liberties are constrained. As recently as 2004, under the Prime Minister John Howard, the Australian government also embarked on a pro-natalist policy through the payment of baby bonuses designed to promote growth of the native-born population. This policy indicates that for the Australian government of the time, 'Australian' babies were of greater value to the nation than babies acquired through immigration or those arriving on boats as asylum seekers (Dever, 2005). The 'populate or perish' mantra has been a stock of Australian politics and cultural anxiety since white settlement of the continent commenced. This anxiety is grounded in race-based fears that only a robust white population could hold the continent against threats of the 'other', whether the Indigenous population or the peoples of Asia to the North, imagined as teeming and hungry for Australian territory (Murphy et al., 2010). The recent Australian foray into pro-natalism was not accompanied by persecution of women engaged in birth control as in Romania and Malaysia. The Australian campaign was focused on increasing the size of the average Australian family. As articulated by the then Treasurer Peter Costello, Australian parents were exhorted to have three children: one for mum, one for dad, and one for Australia (see Murphy et al., 2010; Dever, 2005).

Beginning in the 1970s, social scientists reframed inquiries into why people have children in an effort more fully to understand the factors influencing population growth and decline. Working to broaden the field of analysis beyond narrowly economic considerations, Hoffman and Hoffman developed what they called the 'value of children' approach to the study of population and fertility. In their 1973 paper, Hoffmann and Hoffman analysed empirical data from a range of sources and established an inventory of dimensions in the lives of adults to which children may add value. Defining the value of children as the 'functions [children] serve or the needs they fulfil for parents' (Hoffman and Hoffman, 1973: 20), their inventory of values (p. 46) is:

1. Adult status and social identity

2. Expansion of the self, tie to a larger entity, 'immortality'

3. Morality: religion, altruism, common good; norms regarding sexuality, acting on impulse, virtue

4. Primary group ties, affection

5. Stimulation, novelty, fun

6. Achievement, competence, creativity

7. Power, influence, ability have an impact on things

8. Social comparison, competition

9. Economic utility

Hoffman and Hoffman contend that these may work in isolation or in combinations as drivers of fertility at the individual and macro levels.

The work of Hoffman and Hoffman incorporates non-economic factors into the analysis of fertility by reference to the social, cultural and psychological value that children may add to the lives of their parents: notably only one of these drivers is related to the economic value or utility of children. Also, importantly, the value or benefit of children is identified by Hoffman and Hoffman as something children may bestow on their parents and is not inherent in the child. Received benefits include helping to mark the attainment of full adult status through the transition to parenthood, or enhancing the adults' sense of self through linking the individual to a sense of immortality, beyond the span of the individual life.

During the middle decades of the twentieth century, parenting in the Global North underwent transformations, under the combined weight of the narrowing strictures of the nuclear family and the burgeoning of expert professions. More tightly planned families resulted in fewer children to whom greater shares of resources including parental time might be devoted. Child, family and parenting professions educated parents to expect not merely to raise children but to devote 'quality time' to them and to seek 'meaningful' relationships with them. In the

Global South, the labour and utility of children – that is their capacity to contribute to the family economy in childhood and to contribute to the support of aged parents in their adulthood – remains an important consideration and motivation for having children. This is not to say that deep, rich and rewarding relationships between parents and children do not exist outside the Global North, but that parent–child and family–child interactions and expectations are framed differently. Such rights as these children are deemed to have are embedded in a cultural context of reciprocal obligation and responsibility. Recalling the African alternative to the UNCRC discussed in Chapter 4 (the ACRWC), one expectation of children in the Global South is that the care they receive from parents and others in their communities will be reciprocated by respect and assistance. For many children, this entails responsibilities to work to contribute to the household economy directly or through their wages.

What may be termed the cultural turn in demography evinced in the work of Hoffman and Hoffman (1973) was also pursued through a major collaborative, cross-national study based at the East-West Centre at the University of Hawaii in the mid-1970s, which further extended and tested the 'value of children' (VOC) approach to understanding the motivations for having children (Arnold and Fawcett, 1975, Arnold et al. 1975; Darroch et al., 1981; Iritani, 1977). As outlined by Bulatao:

> The objective of the VOC project is to develop knowledge about childbearing motivations and the relationship of these motivations to family size preferences and fertility. An assumption of the study is that perceptions of the satisfactions and cost of children have an important influence on decisions about family size. (Bulatao, 1979: x)

An international team of researchers conducted empirical analyses of fertility and generative decision-making in population groups across eight nations – Taiwan, Japan, the Philippines, Thailand, Indonesia, Turkey, the USA and Germany – adapting and varying an inventory of values of children in response to different cultural contexts.

Large cross-cultural and international studies using the VOC approach and based on the East-West Centre's work continued into the 1980s, yielding significant data in many different national and cultural contexts on the motivations of parents for having children and on the values parents perceived to flow from their children. Later work increased the number of value factors parents associate with having and raising children and grouped these into three main categories: economic value of children (e-voc); psychological value of children (p-voc); and the social value of children (s-voc) (Sam, 2001).

Anthropology is another discipline in which study of the value of children is undertaken. Anthropological work has documented the value of children in a range of non-Western cultures. For example, the large comparative study of the economic value of children to parents in Nepal and Indonesia undertaken by Nag et al. in the late 1970s, closely documents the time spent by village children in the following activities:

1. Child care [that is care of younger children]

2. Household food preparation

3. Firewood collection

4. Other household maintenance work

5. Animal care

6. Wage labour (agricultural)

7. Wage labour (non-agricultural)

8. Handicrafts

9. Reciprocal labour exchange, community labour

10. Agricultural work (own land)

11. Production of articles for sale (Nag et al., 1978)

The economic value that children may represent to their parents frequently extends beyond the childhood of the child and into adulthood; the adult child's provision for aging parents represents an important form of social security for the elderly in many cultures. Stern and his colleagues remind us that, until the introduction of social security arrangements for those who were too old or infirm to work, children also played this role in many countries in the Global North (Stern et al., 1975).

Pal (2004) documents the support offered by adult Indians to their elderly parents, which ranges from complete support through co-residence arrangements to partial support. Actions and protests by many of the thousands of Chinese parents who lost their only children in the 2008 earthquake in Sichuan province focused on the economic insecurity they would face as they grew old without a child to provide for them (Radio Free Asia, 2011). This example is cited not to diminish the grief and anguish experienced by these parents at the loss of their children, but to add another important dimension to our understanding of it. In response, the Chinese authorities exempted these parents from the one child policy and allowed them to have children to replace the ones lost in the disaster (Daniell, 2013; Sudworth, 2013).

COMPENSATION FOR THE LOSS OF A CHILD: WHAT 'VALUE' IS LOST WHEN A CHILD DIES?

For centuries English common law has offered parents (or more accurately fathers) the right to sue for damages in the event of the wrongful death of a child in the same way that a master was once able to seek damages for the economic loss sustained through the wrongful death of a servant. In contexts where the value of the child is seen primarily in terms of the economic utility provided to parents through various forms of labour in childhood or the provision of social security to parents in sickness or old age, monetary calculations can be made in terms of what it might cost the parent to replace the child's labour with a paid employee.

However, in the contemporary Global North where children are valued primarily for non-economic reasons, more complicated considerations come into play. The law of torts, which is premised on providing financial compensation for damages understood as present or future financial loss, is necessarily limited in the remedies it can provide when the value of a child is non-economic. The following passage from a law reform commission report in the Australian state of Queensland highlights these difficulties:

> [I]t may be difficult for a parent to claim damages for the wrongful death of a young child. A claim of this kind will fail unless the parent can show either an actual financial loss or loss of services resulting from the child's death, or a reasonable expectation of a prospective benefit of which the parent has been deprived. In the case of a very young child this may be impossible to prove:
>
> [...] the plaintiff has not satisfied me that he had a reasonable expectation of pecuniary benefit. His child was under four years old. The boy was subject to all the risks of illness, disease, accident and death. His education and upkeep would have been a substantial burden to the plaintiff for many years if he had lived. [...] He would have earned nothing till about sixteen years of age. He might never have aided his father at all. He might have proved a mere expense. (Queensland Law Reform Commission, 2003: 33)

In contemporary advanced economies, considerations of the damages to be paid to the bereft parents of a child wrongfully killed do not generally calculate the lost income or financial benefit from the economic contribution that the child would have made to the household had he or she lived. In fact, with respect to many children in advanced economies in the Global North, any monetary calculations that might be made are directed to the expected expenses incurred by parents in raising children.

These costs include housing, clothing, food, and medical expenses, but also an extended period of economic dependence due to an increased period of compulsory education which now extends in many jurisdictions from six years of age to 16, 17 or 18 years. For many families, the period of economic dependence of children may be even longer, as post-compulsory or tertiary education is pursued. In fact, if measured purely in financial terms, the outlay made by contemporary parents in the Global North in raising children is such that it is never likely to be repaid in monetary terms. This highlights the inadequacy of narrow economic thinking in addressing the question of why people have children in the first place and how many they might have.

The news media regularly reports the spiralling costs of raising a child. One 2013 report on the 50 per cent increase in the cost of raising children in Australia between 2007 and 2013 claimed that children 'eat into the family budget like never before' (Morris, 2013). However, the unstated premise of such popular accounts is that no matter what the costs involved, children are worth having as their real value is to be measured in other ways.

WRONGFUL BIRTH, WRONGFUL DEATH, WRONGFUL LIFE

In the Global North the costs associated with raising a child are relatively easier to calculate and tend to exceed the dubious and difficult to determine economic return which parents might expect from their children. A significant body of legal action around children and damages revolves around compensating parents for wrongful births (that is the birth of children which occurred wrongfully due to the negligence of a party, commonly a medical practitioner).

There is also, in many jurisdictions, a related set of actions around wrongful life; these pertain not to the circumstances of the birth itself, but directly to the life of the child. As Mark Strasser explains, 'a wrongful life claim alleges that because of one individual's negligence, another individual is forced to live such an unbearable life that it would have been better for the latter individual never to have lived at all and, but for that negligence, that individual would not in fact have lived' (Strasser, 1999: 33).

Actions for wrongful birth are generally brought by parents who seek compensation for the costs of raising a child that they did not plan or intend to have but whose conception resulted from some wrongful act by a medical practitioner, or compensation for the costs of caring for a child damaged during the birth process through some wrongful act. Actions for wrongful life – a life so impaired by disability or disease that, it is contended, it should not have been allowed to proceed – may be brought by the child against its parents or against medical practitioners or others deemed culpable of the 'wrongful' act which resulted in the child being alive (Strasser, 1999). In cases of wrongful birth and some cases of wrongful life, the costs associated with raising the child, costs to which the parents would otherwise not have been exposed, are calculated in order to inform the sum of damages to be paid by the offending party to the parents, or to the child.

While the costs of raising an unplanned or unwanted child can be readily calculated, courts have traditionally viewed such actions for damages with some distaste when the resulting child is normal and healthy. After all, is not the birth of an unplanned but healthy child a blessing and a joy, irrespective of the costs? How can the life of a child be reduced to monetary considerations? In 1934 an action was brought to a US court by a husband for damages against a doctor who performed an ineffective sterilization procedure intended to avert the life-threatening risk of further pregnancy to the plaintiff's wife. In the event, the wife survived the unplanned pregnancy and gave birth to a healthy child. The judge dismissed the claim for damages, finding that, 'Instead of losing his wife, the plaintiff has been blessed with the fatherhood of another child' (quoted in Kashi, 1976: 7).

Distaste for the notion that damages might be awarded for the unplanned birth of a healthy child highlights the widely prevalent view that children are priceless (Zelizer, 1985), and that to allow damages for the unplanned birth of an otherwise healthy child 'would be against public policy' (Kashi, 1976: 7). More recently, both the High Court of Australia and the Supreme Court (assuming the function formerly performed by the House of Lords) in the UK have confirmed the distaste for awarding damages to parents for the raising of an unplanned but healthy child, even in cases where it is established that the birth was due to some negligence by a medical practitioner:

> A child is not a commodity that can be sold, or otherwise disposed of, in order to mitigate hardship to a parent [...] The recognition of the family as the natural and fundamental group unit of society, which is repeatedly expressed in international instruments, in conjunction with declarations of the need to provide for the care and protection of children, is not easy to reconcile with the idea of the parent-child relationship as something the law will regard as an element of actionable damage. (Gleeson CJ, *Cattanach,* quoted in Fitzpatrick, 2013)

In the contemporary context, actions for the wrongful deaths of children vary significantly, according to culture. As outlined by the Queensland Law Reform Commission (2003), quoted above, there can be no certainty that a child in contemporary Australia – an affluent country with strong social services – will represent anything other than an expense to parents. By contrast, in a well-publicized case in India in 2013, parents sued a railway authority for negligence in the maintenance of its train stock which resulted in their seven-year-old daughter falling from an emergency window on the Kerala Express in December 2012 (*The Hindu*, 2013a). Part of their claim was that they stood to be economically disadvantaged by this loss, as it remains the cultural expectation in India, which has limited social services, that economic support in their old age would be provided by their child (*The Hindu*, 2011, 2013a; Pal, 2004). The court accepted this argument and awarded compensation.

By contrast, in a British case in 2013 (Mail Online, 2013), the court awarded damages for the death of a child, but used different reasoning to reach its conclusions. In this case, the mother sued the hospital which provided care for her and her baby for negligence, which she claimed led to the death of the child. Her claim for damages was made on the grounds that the emotional trauma of the death and loss of her child caused her to be unfit for paid employment for an extended period. The damages awarded compensated her for her lost income by reason of her emotional state following this death. She was not compensated directly for her grief and trauma, nor for the loss of support her child might have provided for her in old age. While damages for the loss of the child were awarded in each case, the reasoning of the courts differed relative to the cultural and economic context.

PRICING THE PRICELESS CHILD: AN ECONOMIC SOCIOLOGICAL APPROACH TO THE VALUE OF CHILDREN

In *Pricing the Priceless Child*, the economic sociologist Viviana Zelizer focuses on the shifting value of children of 14 years and younger in the USA between the

1870s and 1930s and offers a significantly new approach to the way in which the question of how children are valued is both framed and answered. Moving significantly beyond the cultural turn in demography outlined above, Zelizer attempts to understand the value of children in a wider sociological context. She asks a set of broad historical questions about how this value is determined and the factors which caused the way children are valued to change over time. Zelizer acknowledges that the transformation she describes was uneven and complicated by the co-existence of competing views of childhood. Drawing on the work of Ariès and others, she also identifies the long history of the idealized, sentimentalized child which came to dominate US valuations of children and, by extension, childhood. She argues that a confluence of factors led to the establishment of the economically 'worthless' but emotionally priceless child, largely quarantined from the economic sphere, as normative by the 1930s. This profound transformation created 'an essential condition of contemporary childhood' (Zelizer, 1985: 3) in the USA.

Zelizer draws on a rich array of historical data in her study, including data on child labour in the first decades of the century and associated debates, and analysis of legal cases and insurance claims in which parents sought compensation for the wrongful deaths of children. As briefly outlined above, legal considerations of what compensation ought be paid to bereft parents in the event of the loss of a child is historically an important site in which the value of children was calculated.

For Zelizer, notwithstanding the cross-cultural approach of the VOC methodology, the study of the value of children remained overly restricted by economic and rationalist assumptions, such as the assumption that parents make decisions about having children or not on rational grounds with utility-maximizing motivations. Reflecting her sociological approach, Zelizer saw monetary value – the value of money and the monetary value applied to things, including children – as conditioned by a complex of social factors. Hence her description of her work as an inquiry into the 'social value' of children.

Zelizer's analytic framework, based on the dichotomy between the useful and useless (but not worthless or valueless) child, proves to be instructive for understanding the historical transformations which took place in the USA in the late nineteenth century and early decades of the twentieth century. We will return to her ideas in the course of the discussion in the case studies below.

WHAT IS A BABY WORTH?

As a non-biological mode of family formation which has been largely regulated by legislation since the late nineteenth and early twentieth centuries in the Global North, adoption provides a useful window onto prevalent views of family and children at a given point in time (Beretbitsky, 2001). For example, legal criteria regulating the eligibility to adopt a child – the age of adoptive parents, their marital status, whether single people, or openly gay or lesbian people, either individually or as couples, may adopt – offer insights into prevalent views of who or what sort of people may constitute legitimate families (Pringle, 2004; Cuthbert, Murphy and Quartly, 2009). In this case study, we take some 'snapshots' from the history of adoption and the contemporary rise of commercial offshore surrogacy as two modes of family formation that illustrate the value which adults ascribe to children (and the kinds of children most valued) and the values they identify as flowing to them through becoming parents. In the process we also incidentally consider another aspect of the value of a child, namely, the sums of money people are prepared to outlay in order to achieve the aspiration of a 'child of their own', whether through the fees associated with securing adoption or commissioning a baby through a surrogacy arrangements.

Legislated adoption first emerged in the US state of Massachusetts in 1851 (Beretbitsky, 2001). Its history reveals that ideas about who might qualify as suitable adoptive parents have changed, as has the view of what constitutes an adoptable child (see Zelizer (1985) for the USA and Shurlee Swain (2012) for Australia). From the time of pre-legislated and early legislated adoption through to the first decades of the twentieth century, adoption was very much a market for children of serviceable years or middle-childhood – that is children, like the fictional *Anne of Green Gables* (1908) – who could assist with domestic and agricultural chores such as chopping wood, milking cows, sewing, and housework.

The ideal adoptable child in this period reflected then prevailing views of the value of children to families, which included their capacities to perform a range of work. Thus, according to accounts of early German settlers in Pennsylvania, when a boy was born to a farming family, there was rejoicing at the birth of another wagoner, while the birth of a girl was greeted as the addition of a spinster (spinner) or milkmaid to assist with household labour (Stern et al., 1975: 85). Adopted children were not necessarily treated differently from native children – that is, those born to the family. As cited in Chapter 1, Elizabeth Buffum Chace recalled her Massachusetts childhood (between 1806 and 1823) as including household chores and 'manufactures' of candle and cheese making, spinning, weaving and dying. Chace notes that this was labour of which all the children of the house 'whether native or adopted began very early to do their share' (Chace quoted in Stern et al., 1975: 85).

From the mid-twentieth century and continuing into the contemporary period, the child most desired by adoptive parents became the infant or a very young child. How and why this change came about reveals much about the value of children and the benefits or values adults hope to gain from them. For much of human history, infancy and early childhood were perilous periods of life, with babies and very young children facing high risks of early mortality, through disease and domestic accidents such as falling into fires or being trampled by horses. In the absence of safe, reliable infant feeding formulae, sustaining and keeping very young babies alive without their mothers was a major challenge. Accordingly, until well into the twentieth century, infants and very young children were not desired or valued as adoptive children. They represented too great a risk, and too great a cost. Not only were they subject to a range of illnesses, they were economically unproductive and labour intensive; someone, either the adoptive parent or another member of the household, might need to stop productive work to tend to the baby. Hence the preference, from the early period of legislated adoption until the mid-twentieth century, for older, productive children.

The rise of child psychology as one of the expert professions dealing with childhood was largely influenced by the work of English psychiatrist and psychoanalyst John Bowlby (1907–90) whose report, commissioned by WHO, *Maternal Care and Mental Health* (1951) and later adapted for popular audiences as *Child Care and the Growth of Love* (1953), shaped thinking and practice in the field and deepened the post-Second World War 'romance' with psychological approaches to children and family (Vicedo, 2011: 412). Bowlby focused on the early period of infancy and the process of 'bonding', especially mother and child bonding. With this, perceptions of what was at stake and what was possible in the parent–child – or more particularly the mother–child – relationship were significantly expanded. Parenthood became not merely or only a role imbued with authority over (or even possession of) the child, but a role which began to be perceived in larger and more affective terms and with psychological consequences for children's development. Parenthood and the child–parent relationship took on psychological dimensions, psychological responsibilities and psychic pleasures for both parent and child.

With the advent of safe and commercially available infant-feeding formula (Greer and Apple, 1991), the risks of infant adoption declined and, along with the emphasis placed on the importance of bonding from the earliest stages of life, the adoption market in new-born babies came into its own (Zelizer, 1985). By the middle of the twentieth century and particularly in response to the need for women to return to the domestic sphere after their brief exposure to the world of work during the Second World War, a cult of domesticity emerged at the centre of which was an increasingly sacralized, over-determined and scientifically informed bond between mother and child (Lewis, 1980; Comacchio, 1983; Arnup, 1994; Apple, 1995, 2006). This cult ensured that home-bound women had their work cut out for them in raising healthy children (and avoiding psychic harm) and safeguarding domestic peace for the returning wage-earning father. This cult largely reduced women's value and identity to the roles of wife and mother.

By the 1950s, infant adoption appeared as the social policy mechanism that might provide childless couples with a child, allow the mother (often a young single woman) a chance to redeem herself, and relieve the state of the burden of the care of children who might otherwise become state wards and a drain on the public purse (Cuthbert, Murphy and Quartly, 2009). A number of factors converged to make the adoption of infant children relatively risk free and not only acceptable, but desirable. Infant, as distinct from child, adoption also served the interests of secret and sealed adoption in ways that the adoption of older children did not. An infant child adopted into a family would never need to know, and certainly never remember, the other family to which it once belonged.

Sociologist Rosemary Pringle (2004) and feminists including Susan Bordo (Bordo, 2005; Cuthbert, Murphy and Quartly., 2009) reflect on the capacity provided by adoption to make children accessible for the purposes of family formation to a range of adults – older adults, single adults, gay and lesbian adults – who are either biologically or socially prevented from having children of their own. This is what Pringle (2004) calls the expanding demographic of people who seek to access children in order to experience parenthood for the fulfilling emotional and psychological benefits and joys it is held to deliver. Accessing children for family formation and experiencing parenthood has come to assume other values and meanings as well.

In addition to the emotional and psychological value that children may bestow on their parents, adoptive or otherwise, access to children for the purposes of family formation has in recent years come to acquire a sort of political value for marginal groups, such as gay and lesbian people. Within the framework of rights-based political action, as outlined in Chapter 4, the gay and lesbian marriage equality movement is now well established in many countries in the Global North and has succeeded in securing marriage rights equivalent to those of heterosexual couples in some jurisdictions. Parenting equality is another plank in the equal rights political platform. The marriage and parenting equality movement draws from Article 16 in the UNUDHR (UN, 1948) which states that all men and women 'have the right to marry and to found a family'.

While lesbian women have access to a range of reproductive options and the biological capacity to bear a child, gay men's options are more constrained. It is in this context that commercial offshore surrogacy has emerged in the first decade of the twenty-first century as the alternative family formation option of choice for many people otherwise unable to access children for family formation – and, evidence from Australia suggests, the gay community in particular has been active in pursuing this option (Riggs and Due, 2010; Chiang-Cruise, 2011; Whitelaw, 2012; Cuthbert and Fronek, 2014). Thus, for members of groups historically excluded from founding their own families, the capacity to access children for family formation through adoption or surrogacy provides the opportunity for fuller participation in society on terms comparable with heterosexual people, the family being the 'fundamental group unit of society' (UNUDHR, Article 16). Thus for some adults access to children to parent may bestow social and political as well as affective and psychological benefits.

With all their perceived benefits of emotional fulfilment for parents and fuller social and civic participation, the perceived value of children for family formation is such that people are prepared to pay to access this value. Consistent with community distaste for the idea of trading in children, one of the objectives of legislated adoption was to eliminate commercial elements from the transfer of children between families (Swain, 2012; Quartly et al., 2013). The offshore surrogacy arrangements now being undertaken by increasing numbers of couples and individuals from Australia and the UK, openly declare their commercial basis (Cuthbert and Fronek, forthcoming 2014). For Australians seeking to commission the conception and birth of children through surrogacy the costs can range from over AU$100,000 if this is done in the USA, to AU$30-40,000 if surrogacy is pursued in India or Thailand where labour – including reproductive labour – is much cheaper.

Thus, we can see that several answers are possible to the question of what a baby is worth. On the adoption market for around a century a baby was not valued highly at all. Babies were seen as high risk, non-productive and labour intensive, and far less preferable as adoptive children than boys or girls in middle-childhood. From the middle of the twentieth century, the value of babies increased and demand for babies outstripped supply in the USA, as documented by Zelizer (1985) and in Australia, as documented by Marshall and McDonald (2001) and Swain (2012). Older children, with whom bonding might be problematic and who might remember their families of origin (or from whom they may have picked up dubious habits or morals) were no longer valued and bypassed in the rush for babies. When supplies of domestic babies declined with access to reliable contraception among other factors, people seeking babies for adoption went offshore and the inter-country adoption market was born (Cuthbert and Fronek, forthcoming 2014).

The question of what a baby is worth can also be answered another way. The value (or cost) of a baby may depend on whether s/he is acquired through expensive Assisted Reproductive Technologies (ARTs) and whether these are covered under the parents' health insurance. It may also depend on whether the baby is commissioned in the relatively expensive US commercial surrogacy market – where costs can run to hundreds of thousands of dollars – or whether the baby is commissioned in markets in the Global South where reproductive labour is cheaper.

Finally, the value of a baby may be framed affectively through its capacity to provide love and joy to its parents; or politically and socially, through its capacity to allow its parents to participate more fully and on equal terms, along with other parents in society. However, in each of these calculations the value of the baby or child is determined in relation to benefits bestowed on adults.

MANY INDONESIAN CHILDREN IN AUSTRALIAN JAILS VS. ONE AUSTRALIAN CHILD IN AN INDONESIAN JAIL

As indicated in the introduction to this chapter, one salient indicator of the different values ascribed to children dependent on their relationship to the state is the treatment of child refugees, whether with their families or unaccompanied humanitarian minors (UHMs). In Australia, people seeking asylum who arrive illegally by boats, often undertaking perilous voyages from embarkation points in Indonesia and other places in South-East Asia, are routinely detained in detention facilities. Detention in appalling conditions can be prolonged; in many cases it is indefinite. Children have been amongst those detained and Australia's detention of child asylum seekers attracted criticism from the UN in 2012 (UN, 2012), as discussed in Chapter 3. In 2011, two controversies which highlight some contradictions and inconsistencies in the treatment of children, depending on the nationality of the child erupted in the Australian media almost simultaneously.

In 2011 a 14-year-old Australian boy holidaying in Bali with his family was detained by Indonesian police on charges of possessing cannabis. The boy was held in a jail for adult offenders in Bali while his charges were processed through the Indonesian courts, amidst fears that his detention would mean that he would miss Christmas in Australia (Allard, 2011). At about the same time, Mark Plunkett, an Australian lawyer acting for three Indonesian boys whom he alleged were wrongly imprisoned in Australian jails for adult offenders, went public with his claims. In addition, Plunkett claimed that his clients represented a small proportion of the Indonesian minors, some as young as 13, who were languishing in Australian adult prisons in what he characterized as a shameful indictment of the Australian government, tantamount to state-sanctioned child abuse. Plunkett called for an inquiry (Lloyd, 2011). Not only were the three boys incarcerated on dubious grounds, but their detention in adult facilities and the Australian government's failure to notify their parents or the Indonesian government of their whereabouts were in contravention of obligations under the UNCRC (UN, 1989), in particular Article 37. The treatment afforded to these Indonesian boys, Plunkett claimed, would not be tolerated for Australian minors (Lloyd, 2011).

These events and the treatment of the Australian boy on holiday in Bali prompted varying degrees of outrage and concern in Australia. Anger was directed, in particular, to the boy's detention in an adult jail; Indonesia does not yet have a fully differentiated criminal justice system for juvenile offenders (Allard, 2011; *SMH*, 2011). The plight of Indonesian minors in Australian adult prisons was revealed over several months. The Indonesian boys whose prosecution brought attention to this situation were from impoverished seaside villages, and regularly undertook work as deck hands on fishing boats. They had been enticed to serve as crew on boats trafficking asylum seekers to Australia. When intercepted by authorities in Australian territorial waters, the boys were arrested and charged with people-smuggling offences.

Despite the obvious immaturity of the Indonesian boys, they were arrested, manacled and detained along with the adults who employed them. In contrast to Indonesia, Australia does have a fully developed justice system with a capacity for the differential handling of adult and juvenile offenders in the courts and prisons. Australian offenders under the age of 17 or 18 years (depending on the jurisdiction) are processed through a Children's Court in every state and territory, in line with the practice in other liberal-democratic nations in the Global North. This is the Global Northern model which has been enshrined in the UNCRC for emulation in the Global South – so that children in these nations may enjoy the protection and rights enjoyed by children in the North.

In July 2011, the Australian government confirmed that 49 Indonesian minors were being held in Australian jails on people smuggling charges (Barns, 2011; Murdoch, 2011). In his defence of the three boys for whom he acted, Plunkett called into question the scientific wrist x-ray technique used for determining the ages of the children. Devised in the 1930s, the test was based on the normative wrist measurements of predominantly Anglo-American boys of that period. Authorities had ignored the testimony of the boys themselves as to how old they were, preferring the scientific evidence of the test. Plunkett spoke to the boys and, on travelling to their home villages, to their parents and other members of their communities, and established their status as minors. On first meeting with the boys, Plunkett used Australian connections in Indonesia to contact authorities in the boys' village and get news to their families that they were alive and in Australia, something the Australian authorities should have done immediately on their apprehension (Barns, 2011; Murdoch, 2011). Their families had believed the boys were dead, lost at sea.[1]

Over the course of several months in 2011, the Australian press ran stories on these boys, the Australian and the Indonesians, and their fates in the criminal justice systems of these two neighbouring countries (Allard, 2011; Lloyd, 2011). Notably, the boys were apprehended by authorities in each country while engaged in unchildlike behaviour: the Sydney teenager was purchasing cannabis; the Indonesian boys were working as crew at sea. Nonetheless, all the boys were minors. Some media comment pointed to the irony of a situation in which the Australian government expressed outrage at the treatment of an Australian boy in the Indonesian criminal justice system, while it remained obdurate on the incarceration of Indonesian boys in Australian adult jails (*SMH*, 2011). Commentators drew attention to the double standard. Greg Barns noted more than a 'whiff of hypocrisy' in Australia's different response to the plight of these boys:

> Both Indonesia and Australia are signatories to the Convention on the Rights of the Child, although the former has signed with reservations [...]

> Is it too much to hope that Australians, saturated as we have been by media attention on the plight of a 14-year-old boy on holidays with his parents in Bali, will demand that the ... [Commonwealth] government and the opposition pledge to remove young Indonesians, and any other person under the age of 17, from detention immediately? We must be consistent in how we view the rights of children and young people. (Barns, 2011)

Barns also comments on the relative weight given to each case, which reached saturation for that of Australian boy (Barns, 2011). There are some parallels here with studies of the famous 'girl in the well' case in the USA. When toddler Jessica McClure, was trapped in a well in 1987, she became 'everybody's baby' during the course of her ordeal, and the nation held its breath while rescue efforts proceeded (Robinson, 2007). Media analysts have compared the frenzied reporting of her fate to the coverage given to the thousands of child victims of disasters such as the gas leak in Bhopal in India in 1984 or the meltdown in the nuclear reactor in Chernobyl in the then Soviet Union in 1986. Analysis reveals that 69 per cent of all US news audiences followed the story of Jessica McClure (Robinson, 2007), outstripping attention given to the Bhopal and Chernobyl disasters, and even, by a considerable margin, interest in the 2004 tsunami which claimed over a quarter of a million lives in South and South-East Asia, many of them children (Robinson, 2007).

As measured by newsworthiness, one known (American) child appears to be worth more than thousands of unknown and unnamed Indian, Russian or Asian children. Exhibiting some of the same features as the reporting of these incidents, the media coverage of the imprisonment of the Australian and Indonesian boys provides another perspective on the question of the value of a child. For the 49 Indonesian children who languished in Australian jails for adult offenders, the answer appears, in part, to depend on whether the child is the citizen of an advanced nation or a developing one.

VALUES AND CHILDREN

In this chapter, we have argued that the value of children is framed primarily in terms of the benefits – concrete or abstract – which children are perceived as bestowing on adults. A child may represent economic, emotional, psychological or political value to adults, parents in particular. The value of children is neither universal nor constant: it is variable and contingent on a number of factors. Children are valued most according to the degree to which they conform to prevailing ideas of what a child is and should be. Some children are more valuable than others. Unchildlike children, children outside the norms of acceptable childlike behaviour or appearance, may be feared and persecuted. In such cases, the childhood of the child will be overlooked or denied and attention will be focused instead on the criminality, deviance, or otherness of the child.

NOTE

1   The information in this paragraph comes from a conversation between Denise Cuthbert and Mark Plunkett in February 2013. These details are included with Plunkett's permission.

Further reading

Australian Senate. Legal and Constitutional Affairs References Committee (2012) Detention of Indonesian minors in Australia (http://www.aph.gov.au/Parliamentary_Business/Committees/Senate/Legal_and_Constitutional_Affairs/Completed_inquiries/2010-13/indonesianminors/report/~/media/wopapub/senate/committee/legcon_ctte/completed_inquiries/2010-13/indonesian_minors/report/a01.ashx).

Lancy, D.F. (2008) *The Anthropology of Childhood: Cherubs, Chattels, Changelings*. Cambridge: Cambridge University Press.

Zelizer, V. (1985) *Pricing the Priceless Child: The Changing Social Value of Children*. Princeton, NJ: Princeton University Press.

9

FUTURE CHILDREN: IDENTITY AND PERFECTIBILITY

- Just as conceptions of childhood and views of children have changed in the past, so it is almost inevitable that they will in the future.

- We can already discern elements of change underway in the possibilities opened up by biomedical technologies that make possible the physical re-shaping of individuals, both present and future.

- Such technologies, along with practices such as gestational surrogacy, challenge and call into question taken-for-granted notions of family and kinship.

- The modifications to the individual that such technologies make possible enable the remaking of identity and encourage individual perfectibility.

- Such biomedical interventions have implications not only for the individual undergoing them but also for what it means to be a (human) child in general.

INTRODUCTION

We can see as discussed and demonstrated throughout *Global Childhoods* and from the historical contextualization of what it is to be a child that understandings of childhood have changed over time and vary between cultures. Further, in the interpretations of children and childhood as represented through disciplinary frames (sociology, psychology, medicine, law, education), we have seen that what appear to be static taken-for-granted norms about childhood in daily life and culture are in fact perpetually, if imperceptibly, evolving. Given that childhood and children have been understood differently according to time and place, we should be able to agree that those understandings are highly likely to change again in the future. Further, while sometimes patterns of meaning, representation and intellectual conception are repeated in gently modified forms, sometimes revolutionary change occurs.

In the issues and debates covered thus far, it is evident that the seeds of change are already being sown in a range of visions for the future of childhood, as favoured by both national and international agencies. Whether every one of these seeds will germinate and flower remains to be seen. As has been demonstrated in earlier chapters, the UN protocols against child sex trafficking and child soldiers, and the ILO's declarations against the worst form of child labour are clear indicators of international movements dedicated to continuing the minimization of unjust or abusive treatment of people under the age of 18. Relatedly, with the two optional protocols that have been added to the UNCRC since 1989, the signatories to each of these documents have been able to note exceptions for their nation's ratification, in recognition of different contextual realities. So the dominant notion of childhood *is* contested. Further, the implementation of aid around the world, by such bodies as UNICEF, is increasingly reactive to on-the-ground or prominent global debates regarding children. This reactivity can be seen in the directions of current preoccupations in public health, as in the fixation on obesity discussed in Chapter 7, and the trend in addressing such issues at a global level through the increased monitoring and controlling of children's bodies.

Attempts to (re)shape childhood and the lives of children may be seen in arguments from both developmentalism and socialization. This can be seen in interventions that re-child the child, intentionally returning the individual child soldier or child head of household to reinstate and reshape the developmental process, and in early childhood education that seeks to set up the conditions of possibility for the ideal citizen. Where socialization (or re-socialization) is the focus, we have demonstrated that it may do so through affecting the habitus. In either case the object of change is the child's sense of self. Our fictional example of Pip in *Great Expectations* demonstrated that, even if it was not entirely successful, Pip's acquisition of the skills appropriate to the middle classes changed not only his aspirations but also his sense of self: his identity. It is to issues of identity – past, present but especially future – that we turn in this chapter.

In our opening, we alluded to the genealogical documentary series, *Who Do You Think You Are?*, in which identity is constructed as heritage, both social and genetic. All of the participants in the series begin by returning to their own childhoods and familial connections to search out the grounding for their sense of self. By the closing credits, each subject's sense of identity has been challenged, realigned, and in some instances radically reshaped. This notion of a search for identity in combination with the status of children forms a common thread with the case studies explored in our final chapter. In the first case study of future children we begin with an example that relates to children's rights to be hormonally 'reshaped' in the process of 'being and becoming'. In the second case study, we will turn to issues related to the reproduction of future children using examples from past practices of artificial insemination in Australia and move on to explore current practices of gestational surrogacy in India. Finally, we offer some observations on the possibility of 'perfectible' children and childhoods that is implicit in much of the discussion around reproductive technologies.

Each of these case studies involves ethically and socially contentious issues which are publicly (and polarizingly) debated in the Global North. That is, they are matters in which the dominant views of children and childhood are being contested from within the dominant paradigm, in contrast to the case studies up to this point which have been contested largely from 'below'. Nevertheless, each has potential ramifications that extend to the Global South, particularly as they call into question the meaning of children and childhood, whether as developmental or as socialized human beings. Further, while they are geographically specific (in relating to cases in Australia and India) they encompass issues widely debated and intimately connected to the lived realities of children around the world. The first case study relates to children diagnosed with Gender Identity Disorder (GID) (or Gender Dysphoria (GD)) in Australia; the second, to past practices of artificial insemination (AI) and the rights of the adult children of anonymous sperm donors;[1] the third, to the contemporary internationalization of gestational surrogacy, whereby India has become a major destination for 'medical tourists'; and our final remarks, to the capacity to screen and select future children. In each discussion, the capacity of individuals to determine identity and the medical-ethical dilemmas that affect their actual ability to do so are at stake.

FUTURE IDENTITY: A CHILD'S RIGHT TO CHOOSE?

For children diagnosed with GID who are seeking hormone therapy in anticipation of puberty, they and their guardians assert that they have the rational capacities to make life- and body-altering decisions. These children feel trapped in a body the genetic sex of which does not match their gender identity (see Zucker, 2005). In 1989, as part of the near-unanimous signing and ratifying of the UNCRC, mainstream Australia agreed to adhere to a conception of children and a definition of childhood as embodied in that document, and to uphold the rights of children accordingly. In requiring nation-states to act in 'the best interests of the child', the UN explicitly and implicitly promotes an idea of childhood as a time of innocence and vulnerability, and children as not yet rationally competent. Nevertheless, as we have demonstrated, the understanding of childhood promoted by the UN is a historically and culturally contingent construction that is based in normative expectations of children of the developed world (children don't work, they play). We have also canvassed subsequent documents in which the UN and the International Labour Organization (ILO) have shown some understanding of the ability (and need) of some children to combine work and education. Nevertheless, children's rational capacities are treated in general as subordinate to those of adults (Cregan 2013).

In Australia, 18 is the age at which one is generally considered an adult. At 18 one may vote and if found guilty of criminal offences may be sent to an adult prison.[2] In relation to medical treatment, a child is considered incapable of giving fully informed consent and adults – parents, guardians, doctors and judges – remain the primary decision-makers for and about children. However, it has been recognized that a person over the age of 16, while still legally a minor, has the capacity to give informed consent to medical treatment and to have an independent relationship with their medical practitioner (Cregan 2013). Similarly, a 'mature minor' (a child judged intellectually capable of understanding the nature and consequences of the relevant treatment, at perhaps 14 or 15) may be considered able to make decisions about consenting to medical treatment (ALRC 2008 [2013] 68: 44–5).

The treatment of children with GID is a more socially complex and culturally challenging phenomenon than most in the Global North. The condition is defined by a psychiatric diagnosis and is subject to psychotherapeutic intervention, but the medical treatments used to realize the individual child's desired gender identity are hormonal. In Australia surgery may not be performed until adulthood, that is, at the minimum age of 18. The progression to medical treatment, in addition to psychotherapeutic measures in using puberty-suppressing or hormonal drugs, is considered in law to be a 'special medical procedure' (or more properly 'treatment') and as such cannot be consented to by the child, the child's parents or his or her guardians alone. Such treatment requires consent from a judge of the Family Court of Australia, a federal court which has jurisdiction over family law matters in general and this area of law in particular (Cregan 2013).

The Family Court's powers over 'special medical procedures' originated in a court decision in 1992, which aimed to protect the rights and well-being of children from medical interventions that were considered outside the ordinary scope of parents' or guardians' powers. Among the features that define such procedures are the following: there would be grave consequences from an incorrect decision; there is significant risk to the child's best interests as a result of an incorrect decision; or, where the treatment may not in itself 'be grave and irreversible but may be of significant risk, ethically sensitive or disputed' (Family Court, 1998, vii). Further, in approving such a procedure a judge must be satisfied that treatment is a 'step of last resort' (Family Court, 1998, vi). We can hear in these parameters direct reference to the UNCRC requirement that at all times the best interests of the child be upheld (Cregan 2013).

Initially, this overriding of the powers of a parent or guardian was the outcome of 'Marion's Case' in which the parents of 'Marion', a pubescent female child who had a significant intellectual disability in addition to other medical problems, wished to sterilize their daughter to remove the distress she experienced during menstruation (Family Court, 1998, 2). The eventual outcome of the case was that the sterilization was judged to be a 'special case' and that decisions related to such procedures should be made by a judge of the Family Court. Since the initial judgment, the parameters of a 'special medical procedure' have been broadened specifically to encompass gender reassignment in minors, and otherwise uncontroversial medical treatments where parental consent has been refused. The result has been that a person under 18 in Australia who wishes to undergo hormone treatment in anticipation of gender reassignment must seek consent through the Family Court (Cregan 2013).

Hence, in instances where the treatment teams, the parents and the child concerned have all wished to proceed with medical treatment to avoid the onset of puberty of the repudiated sex and instead hormonally induce the physical characteristics of the sex with which the child identifies, a judge of the Family Court has the final say. With all parties in agreement such treatment is likely to be approved once the child has reached 15 or 16. That is, if the family has the financial resources to cover the expenses involved in seeking the required consent through the court, which in 2012 was estimated to cost between AU\$20,000 and AU\$35,000 (Robotham, 2012). So, in most states of Australia, a person under the age of 18 may be considered able to consent to sexual activity but incapable of determining their gender identity (Cregan 2013).

The specific case of *Re Jamie* [2011] FamCA 248[3] is more challenging than the general case discussed so far as Jamie, born genetically male but socially female since she was a toddler, was not yet 13 at the time the case was heard (Robotham, 2012). In the first stage of this case, in line with the precedent that treatment for GID is a special medical procedure, Dessau J. and the parents assumed that the proposed treatment was within the definition of such procedures and required a determination by the court to proceed with the first stage of gender reassignment (Stewart et al., 2012: 235). The judge supported puberty-suppressing treatment but rejected a request to begin oestrogen therapy, leaving that decision until Jamie reached the age of 15 or 16, the accepted age for beginning such treatment. As Cameron Stewart notes (Stewart et al., 2012: 235), an important aspect of this case is that the parents subsequently appealed the status of the treatment as a special medical procedure. They were successful and obtained an outcome that supports the parents' right to give informed consent and they, rather than a judge, will be able to make the decision to begin stage one of the treatment regime (to suppress puberty), on the basis that it was a reversible treatment (*Re Jamie* [2013] FamCAFC 110). Decisions about whether, when and how to proceed with reversible hormone therapies for children with GID have, thus, reverted to the families and the doctors of the young person concerned. Stage two of treatment, which is irreversible, remains an issue in which the competence of the child to consent (even with medical and parental consent) remains a matter to be determined by the courts (Cregan 2013, 2014).

There has therefore been a perceptible change in the legal, social and cultural recognition of the ability of a young person to make informed decisions about re-forming his or her identity. That recognition is both overtly grounded in developmental assumptions of cognitive capacities, but also implies an acceptance of the kind of child agency supported by socialization theorists. In public reporting of this and other similar cases both in Australia and elsewhere there have been dissenting viewpoints on proceeding with such treatments, aside from contesting the legal restrictions on who may consent to treatment. It is known that there are long-term health risks implicit in the relevant hormone treatments, such as osteoporosis, and irreversible effects, such as diminished fertility, which may adversely affect the individual should there be a reversal in identity later in adolescence or adulthood. Weighted against these potential risks is the real anguish that a child with GID feels, that may lead to suicidal or self-injuring behaviour. At a social level, gender theorists question whether GID itself is at least in part a response to the power and rigidity of gender norms. What remains is the fact that, despite the recognition of the heightened capacity of the child to assert his or her identity, the ultimate decisions affecting the child's identity are still being made on his or her behalf by adults (parents, guardians, doctors, judges) (Cregan 2013).

Here we see the effects of the prevalence of rights discourse in legal and medical debates around 'the best interests of the child' as set out in the UNCRC. Jamie's case is premised on her 'right' to determine her own identity: to be an agent of her own embodied being. At the same time, the medical treatment that effects the desired gender change is deeply imbricated in her 'becoming': her developmental (biological) status is being reshaped by the recalibration of embodied hormonal levels, a process that will need to be maintained over a lifetime. Gender theorists are more likely to raise the issue of socialization; that the individual's identity is subject to and unable to accommodate the pressures inherent in social phenomena (rigid gender norms). In other words, that what the individual perceives as a problem of personal identity is the result of restrictive social processes rather than a bodily 'problem' that can be 'perfected' by medical intervention (Fausto-Sterling, 1993). There are certainly cross-cultural examples that demonstrate that there are ways to negate the need for the physical reshaping of the body in order to accommodate non-stereotypical gender identities: the Native American *berdache* or 'Two Spirit', the *hijra* of India, the *kathoeys* or ladyboys of Thailand and the *fa'afafines* of Samoa (Blackwood, 1984). Jamie's case, on the one hand, holds promise for the recognition of children's agency in determining their own future lives but, at the same time, also suggests the potential confirmation of rights-based decision-making in relation to children as residing in 'the family' as supported and facilitated by medical opinion (adult experts), based on a biomedical and developmental notion of the body of the child.

FUTURE IDENTITY: A CHILD'S RIGHT TO KNOW?

This issue of parents making biomedical decisions about children's futures leads us directly into the discussion of our second example, where the intersection of identity, children and medicine is imbricated in the complex history of social and medical responses to fertility and infertility. Like other developed countries which experienced the wave of social change that flowed through the 1960s, Australia took part in the sexual revolution largely made possible by the wider availability of the contraceptive pill. Prior to the pill, which made it possible to have sex without a high likelihood of bearing a child as a consequence, the overwhelming social stigma attached to unmarried pregnant women ensured that it was only the strongest personalities, or those with families prepared to weather the stigma to support them, who kept their children (Cregan 2013).

The only alternative to carrying an unwanted pregnancy to term, abortion, was illegal across Australian jurisdictions until interpretation of the relevant criminal law shifted, in the late 1960s and early 1970s. Up until that time abortion was also prohibitively expensive, from the few doctors who would chance prosecution, and a high-risk procedure when undertaken by a 'backyard abortionist'. With the introduction of the single mothers' pension in 1972, unmarried women who wanted to have their babies and keep them were afforded a financial avenue that allowed them to and the statistics incontrovertibly prove that they chose to do so (Cregan 2013). The numbers of babies available for adoption dropped from nearly 10,000 in 1971–72 to fewer than 700 by 1995–96 (Broadbent and Bentley, 1997). This number has continued to fall and in the most recent data, for 2010–11, there were 384 finalized adoptions in Australia (AIHW, 2011).

Until the development of IVF and its flow-on technologies, which did not become viable alternatives until the mid-1980s, the only recourse for infertile couples who wanted to parent children was to foster, to adopt, or if the cause was male infertility, insemination with donated sperm. While human tissues (gametes) and reproductive experimentation are subject to Federal law, each Australian state has its own infertility authority which is also subject to state legislation. Until 1988 in the state of Victoria, medically assisted sperm donation remained an anonymous procedure and any details recorded about the donors were subject to medical confidentiality. The resultant children of these anonymous sperm donors were, and indeed still are, subject to fundamentally life-shaping decisions made for them. The ethical arguments and implications surrounding the current calls for the opening of these records repeat the debates held in the early 1980s discussed in earlier chapters over unsealing closed adoption records (Cuthbert and Quartly, 2012).[4]

Although sperm donation had been available as a medical option for decades prior to the dramatic drop in the availability of babies for adoption in the mid-1970s, its importance rose as an option of last resort for male infertility and because it also became an essential adjunct to IVF experimentation. In Australia, the sale of human gametes is prohibited but donors are (and were) compensated for their time and expenses in providing their donation. In the late 1970s the payment was AU$20. With more stringent requirements on donations (and inflation) the payment has risen by 1,500 per cent, to AU$300 per donation.[5] As we noted above, prior to 1988 sperm donors were guaranteed anonymity. In the state of Victoria, those offspring born between 1988 and the end of 1997 may seek information if the donor consents to making the information available (Hagan, 2012). For any child born as a result of sperm donation since 1998, non-identifying details and a medical history of the donor are provided to the recipient(s) prior to fertilization, and any sperm donor enters into the process on the understanding of the possibility that they will be sought out by their genetic offspring (Cregan 2013).

Offspring of anonymous donation, that is adults who are now at least 25, have no access to the records of their genetic fathers. There is an issue of contention here in that there is significant lobbying and pressure being put on governments – each state having its own regulations – to make available the identities of donor fathers, whether they desire it or not. One of the most prominent advocates for opening the records, on sperm donors prior to 1988, was Melbourne woman Narelle Grech (1980–2013) who had aggressive bowel cancer with a possible genetic link. She wanted to meet her biological parent and to warn her eight half-siblings of their potential risk of developing the disease (Hagan, 2012), but she was also determined to ensure that full medical histories are available not only to those who have been conceived and born since 1998 but to all donor offspring for whom such records exist. Although the opening of anonymous sperm donor records to all those affected remains unresolved throughout Australia, reform has moved one step closer in Victoria, at least in part due to Narelle Grech's activism. In August 2013 the state government tabled its response to the recommendations of the Victorian Parliament's Law Reform Committee

(Law Reform Committee, 2012), that included the opening of existing records of anonymous donors prior to 1989, the facilitation of contact between donor children and their biological fathers, and the counselling of donors and offspring prior to contact (Cregan 2014).[6]

The health professionals who perform AI have publicly resisted calls to facilitate identification of donors on the basis of the original assurance of confidentiality and the potential for undermining of trust in the profession if that assurance is reneged upon (see transcripts at http://www.parliament.vic.gov.au/lawreform/article/1465). This is certainly an issue, but it is also precisely the same set of arguments raised in the 1970s and 1980s when adoption lobbyists fought to revoke the anonymity of the files of adopted children, many of whom were in their sixties and had had happy relationships with their adoptive parents, yet remained deeply concerned to uncover their identity.[7] Those laws were changed and the attitude to adoption itself has radically altered in the decades since. Not only has this led to repeated formal apologies being made for decades of past adoption practices by federal and state governments, state and federal authorities, hospitals and religious institutions, nationally and internationally (Cuthbert and Quartly, 2012), it has also changed approaches towards favouring 'open' adoptions, where all parties remain aware of the child's genetic, cultural and social heritage.

THE 'MATTER' OF CHILDREN

Sperm donation became more valued and important in the context of more effective contraception and lower adoption rates, which meant fewer children were available to infertile couples. As already mentioned in passing, liberalized abortion practices also had an effect on the reduction of available infants: liberalized, but only very recently (and unevenly) de-criminalized in Australia. Around the globe, abortion has been practised and in many instances culturally sanctioned for millennia, but it remains an ethically contested practice. The base matter from which future children are shaped continues to be a source of enormous social, cultural and religious contention.[8]

As exemplified in the British act against infanticide touched upon in Chapter 2, the point at which a human life begins has been taken to be of great importance. The act attempted to exert protection over infants (and warrant the prosecution of errant mothers), and in doing so implicitly took birth as the beginning of a defensible life.[9] Until at least the late eighteenth century, pregnancy was not considered certain until the 'quickening' (movement) was felt, at around five months' gestation (Duden, 1991). Conversely, by the late twentieth century the assessment of foetal viability and the survival rates of pre-term births were lowered into the second trimester of pregnancy.

While birth as the point at which a foetus becomes an infant is an intuitively appealing demarcation, a number of factors complicate matters. These include the survival of increasingly pre-term births, the personal and emotional investment in the foetus in the first trimester of pregnancy with the availability of sophisticated ultrasonography, and even the psychological attachment to blastocysts (five- or six-day-old embryos) of those undertaking IVF. When a child's life begins is no longer necessarily as clear cut as the moment at which it takes its first breath (if it ever was). This inevitably leads us back to our first question – what is a child? When does a child's life begin?

The majority of the bioethical debate around abortion is centred on just this point. There are philosophical bioethicists who take sentience (the capacity for thought) as the basis of personhood and argue that an embryo, foetus or even a newborn infant does not yet have that capacity and so does not have the same rights as sentient beings. The logical, if highly contentious, extension of this argument is that infanticide is therefore as rational and supportable as abortion (Singer, 1993, 1995). In polar opposition to such a view some religious authorities, most notably in the Catechism of the Catholic Church, take the moment of conception as the point at which personhood obtains and define the embryo in terms of its status as a potential human being (Paragraph 2270). Clearly these positions are irreconcilable, and in many ways unhelpful in attempting to address issues related to future children. What they do have in common is that each pits the interests and rights of the mother against those of the future child, in contrast to debates we have seen in earlier chapters that conflate the interests of mothers and children.

In drawing, to some extent, on current issues in healthcare ethics we are examining the changes underway in how *children as the intended outcome* of technologies of reproduction are being spoken of and imagined, rather than debating personhood prior to birth. Moreover, we are also concerned to raise the matter of just *whose* future children these technologies are likely to be reproducing. However, we recognize that there is a lack of consensus about the point at which a child is accorded the status of real or potential human person. Indeed, the UNCRC does not define when childhood (or more properly a child) begins, thereby avoiding becoming mired in debates on the beginning of personhood that are entailed in debates on abortion. At the same time, the UNCRC allows individual signatories to define the point at which they take childhood to begin, much as other exceptions are accommodated in practice in individual nation-states. Thus the UK, in common with other states that allow or have decriminalized abortion, upholds the UNCRC specifically in relation to infants who have been born, whereas other signatories (particularly where religious objections to abortion are strong) extend the UNCRC's mantle to the unborn. While it is beyond the scope of this chapter to debate the status of the foetus or embryo in any depth, when we refer to future children we do so in the knowledge that the UNCRC leaves the legal definition of the genesis of a child (and ultimately of personhood) to the discretion of signatory countries.

GESTATIONAL SURROGACY IN INDIA

That plurality in practice is exemplified in differing approaches to the regulation of reproductive technologies and the research practices that flow from it. Where there has been a lack of regulation but high standards in medical technology (e.g. Singapore in the 1990s), or where the state provides liberal regulatory support in combination with venture capital, as in the state of California in the USA, reproductive biotechnological research has flourished. Such supportive (or lack of) regulation of reproductive practices is also advantageous in the pursuit of gestational surrogacy. Many countries in the world ban gestational surrogacy outright within their own borders, some extend that ban to their citizens travelling to access it, some allow regulated and restricted surrogacy arrangements (often requiring it be altruistic): and a few countries, like India, are unregulated (Teman, 2010).

California is a prominent destination for those seeking commercial arrangements with gestational surrogates, and can accommodate those who require not only a surrogate to carry the infant to term but also the gametes to create the embryo, whether these are required for medical or social infertility. As a state in a highly technologized developed country with liberal laws but a medical system founded on private insurance, pursuing gestational surrogacy in California is out of the reach of many infertile couples, including US citizens. In India, which is only just approaching legal regulation of gestational surrogacy in the proposed Assisted Reproductive Technologies (Regulation) Bill (2013) (*The Hindu*, 2013b), the costs are a fraction of those in the USA, and surrogacy is run on a commercial model. It has therefore become an increasingly popular destination for medical tourists in search of reproductive services.

There has been considerable debate amongst feminists, ethicists, anthropologists and sociologists on the meaning of reproductive transactions between the Global North and the Global South. There is almost invariably an imbalance, much as in the international trade in organs for transplantation, between those with the capacity to contract a gestational surrogate and the woman who will carry a child to term. Even where the outcomes and the surrogate's own reports of her participation in the arrangement are positive (Pande, 2009, 2010, 2011) the women carrying the children are doing so out of personal financial need, as a 'survival strategy and a temporary occupation' (Pande, 2010: 293). In terms of Global Northern ethical norms that relate to the mother, there are issues of coercion and informed consent at stake. In other words, women enter into the process to relieve debt or improve their family's living standard by undertaking procedures (such as hyper-ovulation) the full risks of which they may not be aware of or in which their consent is not wholly un-coerced (Gupta and Richters, 2008). Birth itself is known to carry risks, even when prior pregnancies have been untroubled and the birth is monitored in a well-equipped hospital. What little research has been conducted on the practices and experiences of the Indian participants focuses firmly on the position of the gestating mother. Similarly, the debate around the proposed Bill is firmly centred on the protection of the rights of the commercial surrogates from exploitation. What of the status of the intended children involved?

In reading Amrita Pande's reports of qualitative interviews with commercial surrogates in India, one of the few sustained researchers in the field, it becomes clear that the women who carry the babies see their reproductive labour as entailing kinship relations. The reported comments of the women, who in this case were housed together in hostels and separated from their own families until after the birth, show they believe even when they are implanted with a genetically non-related embryo that they are contributing to the ongoing life of that child. Pande notes that in some instances this may involve a degree of hopeful fantasy on the part of the women, but they nevertheless understand their experience as one of creating kinship ties (Pande, 2009). This offers a distinct challenge to normative kinship ties, particularly those of the Global North.

As Palattiyil et al. (2010) have noted, those who undertake to commission a commercial surrogate do so for a number of reasons. Of the eight they list (Palattiyil et al., 2010: 689–90), we take three for further discussion that relate most clearly to Global Northerners undertaking international medical tourism (the remainder relate more closely to domestic surrogacy arrangements). Each of these stem from restrictive conditions in their home country: 'exclusion … on the basis of age, marital status or sexual orientation', 'lower costs' and 'a desire to protect their privacy'. As already noted, costs in California are prohibitive for most international medical tourists, which immediately makes India a more attractive prospect for those seeking commercial surrogacy arrangements from the Global North. The medical system, at least where surrogates are cared for, is sophisticated and the medical staff highly trained. The other two reasons mesh more closely with other concerns we have already raised in relation to the child born of such arrangements.

Where couples have been excluded from services otherwise available in their country of origin, international commercial surrogacy makes possible the acquisition of a child. The Bill currently being debated may close one door in this regard: as currently framed, it defines commissioning couples in heteronormative terms (*The Hindu*, 2013b). This closely follows similar dynamics to those that occur in relation to ICA, where in many countries children are only made available to heterosexual married couples. Commercial surrogacy therefore challenges heteronormative family structures.

Finally, while the surrogates Pande interviewed may express a kinship relationship with the infant they carry, one of the key reasons for Global Northerners seeking surrogacy internationally is to access the kind of 'privacy' such as that afforded to sperm donors in Victoria prior to 1989. Some prospective parents may want to uphold the fictive kinship relationships claimed by the surrogates: others prefer to maintain a commercial relationship that ends when the child is delivered. In such circumstances, the child is at the centre of a commercial transaction – indeed, is the 'matter' transacted. Further, the future child will be subject to the same issues of identity-formation entailed in any closed system, whether of assisted reproduction, adoption or surrogate gestation. While there is considerable debate around the appropriate inclusion of surrogates in the lives of future children in the Global North (Laufer-Ukeles, 2013) the lack of regulation in India means that it is entirely reliant on the goodwill of the commissioning couple whether any such relationship continues either for domestically or internationally relocated infants.

The history of practices of secrecy, the inability to access identifying files and the obstinacy on the part of bureaucracies which were characteristic of prior adoption practices are being replayed in relation to calls to rescind the anonymity of sperm donors, as we have seen they continue to be in relation to international adoptions and also in commercial surrogacy arrangements. It is not clear that the opening of adoption files undermined trust in the institutions that fought that openness. It was equally possible that the reluctance of those institutions to be open and their resistance to change had a far greater effect in undermining the public's perceptions of them and fostering negative views of their actions. What has drawn wider approval is the ability of the parties involved to realize that an earlier practice was unjustifiable, open to harming those involved by not being sufficiently thought through, and manifestly not 'in the best interests of the child'.

In the preceding discussion of AI, the rational capacities of adult children born of anonymous sperm donations who seek access to records about their biological fathers are not in question. They are searching for the unknown half of their genetic identity, which has been denied them since conception. Many of them are concerned about the potential health risks to which they may be prone or the possibility of unwittingly entering into incestuous relationships, playing out the same arguments we saw mounted in the debates around adoption. In all our case study examples thus far, decisions over how (or whether) these individuals may proceed are issues in which socially, historically and politically contingent ideas of childhood, and what it is to be a child, prevail.

With regard to anonymous sperm donation, in the middle are the children who could not be asked if they wanted to be conceived and who may live to develop medical problems of which they have been denied forewarning and/or who, as a result of secrecy, lack the capacity to take precautions to avoid developing conditions of which they are at risk. The 'best interests of the child' who would result from a sperm donation, now adult, were considered in a manner subordinate to the wishes of adults. The adult children of sperm donors, like adult children of closed adoptions, were conceived in an act that failed to foresee or fully appreciate the consequences for the child once they are adult. Like children with GID, their interests remain subordinated *into adulthood* because of decisions made by adults on their behalf, 'in the best interests of the child'. The case of unregulated international commercial surrogacy replays the same debates and the same prospects for future children.

The debates around sperm donation and past adoption practices also bring into focus the potential consequences of other means of conceiving and reproducing children that entail similar concerns around identity and the impact of decisions being made on behalf of future children. The fact that decisions made in the relatively recent past about future children continue to have ramifications in the lives of those children–now–adults should give us pause for thought in relation to current or future decisions about the creation of future children, particularly when we can see history so obviously repeating itself in the debates and issues that attend the lobbying of the children affected.

FUTURE PERFECTIBILITY

Conservative political scientist, Francis Fukuyama, prominently, publicly and emotively questioned the effects of enhanced reproductive techniques and biotechnologies in 2002 in his book, *Our Post-Human Future*. His negative response to the ability to manipulate reproduction and the effects that might have for the future of humanity were focused on the future of liberal democracy, but in essence his arguments were based around the possible effects of biotechnologies on the creation of future children (as potential future citizens). He was writing, primarily, in reaction to the first successful cloning of a mammal – Dolly the sheep (1996–2003) – and from concerns that cloning would be applied in human reproduction.

Fukuyama's reactionary response led to a repeat of the all-too-common (and unhelpful) polarization of ethical debate around medical advances – science versus religion – that also characterizes related debates on abortion and women's reproductive rights. However, the central point raised by one social and political critic of Fukuyama remains pertinent and largely unanswered. Simon Cooper (2002) argued that Fukuyama never dealt with the larger question of addressing 'the *meanings* of biotechnological change from a cultural perspective' (2002: 36); that '[b]ecause biotechnology cuts across many of our assumptions about embodied life and social being it must also change our relation to the world' (ibid.: 38). Cooper is suggesting that the biotechnologies under debate do so by challenging our assumptions about embodied life and social being, in and through reproduction. They must therefore also challenge and change our relation to ourselves and by extension to our children and to childhood in general. And they do so by projecting a notion of children as 'perfectible'.

What, then, do biotechnological attempts at creating perfectible children mean? In a deeply material sense, future children are already being shaped, in the range of increasingly sophisticated reproductive technologies that are emerging. Different countries have reacted in disparate ways to the regulation or openness to the biotechnological possibilities for creating future humans, in ways that are rooted in the accepted understandings of when human life begins of the respective society. Further, there are clear divisions in who is able to access such biotechnologies that extend beyond the borders of individual nations, as we saw in relation to surrogacy in India. In this final section of the chapter we look to some of the more contentious propositions around reproduction, and therefore those obvious signs of change already underway, that are related to future children and the future of childhood.

Over more than 50 years of concerted research, assisted reproductive technologies (ARTs) – such as the *in vitro* fertilization and implantation of viable human embryos (IVF) – have gone from being science fantasies, to experimental possibilities, to institutionalized medical realities. In the space of a generation, from the birth of Louise Brown in 1978, IVF became a normalized part of the suite of reproductive interventions. In developed Global Northern nations, IVF is now almost as uncontroversial as the regular ultrasound imaging of foetal development, another bio-technology that has revolutionized parental perceptions of pregnancy and psychological attachment to the infant-yet-to-be born over much the same timeframe. Even though assisted conception remains the exception – even in countries such as the UK, where fertility treatments are well-established, expertly performed and readily available, 98 per cent of pregnancies remain naturally achieved (2010 data, HFEA, 2012: 39) – it is central to the possibilities around the creation of future children, and the techniques involved enable the idealization of a 'perfectible' child.

The initial conditions of possibility that paved the way for IVF and reproductive biotechnologies to affect understandings of children lie in the achievement of effective contraception. It is widely acknowledged that the public release of the contraceptive pill, first trialled in Puerto Rico in 1956 and first distributed for contraceptive use in the USA in 1961, made for a massive difference in the capacity of human beings to monitor and order the number of children they brought into the world (Martin, 1992). Contraception has been available for centuries — if not millennia — in a variety of forms, from douches, barrier methods and abortifacients, to non-vaginal sexual activity and periodic abstinence (Duden, 1999). Apart from the latter two, such methods were not wholly reliable and (hetero-)sexual activity was highly likely to eventuate in pregnancy. From the seventeenth century the likelihood of pregnancy became significantly more manageable, at least for the rich, who were more likely to have access to the latest scientific explanations of the means of conception thanks to microscopy, and to new-fangled and expensive (reusable) sheep-gut condoms (Collier, 2007). Until at least the end of the nineteenth century, for the vast majority of the population in the middle classes and below, children were considered a natural (almost inevitable) consequence of sex. That situation began to change early in the twentieth century with the increasing move towards 'marital' education and making available more reliable contraceptive measures (Rose, 1992). This was as a result of the activism of women like Dr Marie Stopes in the UK (see www.drmarie.org).[10] Although most of the contraceptive methods remained far from foolproof and in some instances difficult to obtain, wider access to the Dutch cap and the rubber condom meant a notion of greater choice came into discussions around childbearing. As a result, children could be 'planned'.

The phenomenon of the child or family-planning accelerated rapidly after the introduction of the contraceptive pill, with its low failure rate.[11] By the late twentieth century, children were no longer an expected consequence of heteronormative sexual activity throughout the Global North and increasingly in the Global South; rather children became a matter of 'choice'. This in itself has affected the perception of children, as discussed in relation to the 'valuable' child. Reproductive medicine is a very particular process of rationalization and anatomization of the human body in which post-modern bodies become 'organs without bodies' (Braidotti, 1989) and women are constructed 'as wombs and childbearing machines, instead of whole persons' (Gupta and Richters, 2008), in which the child is the ultimate product.

Pregnancy can now be avoided indefinitely: however, delayed reproduction is not without cost. At the same time that the physical limits of fertility in females continue to be tested, with IVF now regularly being attempted over the age of 50, the reality remains that conception and child-bearing become more difficult beyond the age of 32, accelerating from the age of 35 onwards. This has, in turn, already influenced the meaning of children and of childhood beyond the notion of a choice that can be planned. Since the increase in the effectiveness of assisted reproductive techniques, for which reliable statistics give a success rate of close to a 25 per cent live birth rate (HFEA, 2012: 4), there has been a shift in the discourse around human reproduction in the developed world. Child-bearing is increasingly spoken of in terms of 'rights' (of parents to have and bear children), a phenomenon in which we have already seen that children, in many ways, are confirmed as parental chattels. Further, the relatively straightforward enhancement and extension of the capacity to bear children is already altering notions of children as objects of value (see Nauck, 2007) and altering the lived experience of childhood by extending the age gap between child, parent and grandparent. Those enhanced capacities have also raised the possibility of further 'choices' and 'rights' that are not so straightforward, which relate back to the known long-term effects on offspring of AI.

It seems unlikely that Fukuyama's fears of human cloning for the creation of fully formed infants is a viable prospect, at least for the foreseeable future, both on practical and ethical grounds. It is strongly opposed at the UN on the basis that it contravenes human dignity.[12] However, there are a number of reproductive practices either possible or in restricted application that do challenge our current relation to children and our notions of childhood. Amongst these are included techniques that stem from IVF technologies and procedures, including the ability to perform pre-implantation diagnostic (PID) screening and/or selectively implant embryos on the basis of choices that go beyond issues critical to the prospective child's health.

PID screening can encompass searching for all manner of genetic markers, which may or may not involve diseases or syndromes, but which are thereby identified. Selection of embryos (for implantation and gestation, or rejection) is already practised on the basis of a range of heritable conditions (Pilnick, 2002). Depending on the legislation of the country in which one lives that might include selecting on the basis of gender, where the condition is chromosomally linked, but gender selection of embryos might also be practised for 'family balance' or on the basis of parental preference (Ettorre, 2002). Screening for chromosomal abnormalities *in vitro* is promoted as a means of avoiding the termination of pregnancy, particularly in cases where there is a known incidence of a condition within a family history. There have also been bioethical debates mounted around allowing screening and selection for virtually any trait that a prospective parent might prefer, such as eye colour, hair colour or 'intelligence'. This has sometimes overtly appealed to the parents' liberal rights to choose 'in the best interests of the child' as formulated by the UNCRC (Robertson and Savulescu, 2001: 39, 49). We also know that children have been brought into being as a result of embryonic selection, specifically to be able to become compatible tissue donors for pre-existing siblings (Ettorre, 2002). In all of these instances, it is the parents' rights that appear paramount, and the implicit outcome of parental decision-making is both a 'perfectible' and an economically or pragmatically 'valuable' child.

If we take a future child to be a potentially real (rather than a hypothetical) being, when someone argues in favour of parents being able to use pre-implantation IVF techniques to determine facets of that future child's physical and mental characteristics the future child that is the product of such a procedure is at stake. To conceive a child expressly to harvest biological materials to assist in the medical treatment of a sibling or other relative, similarly and demonstrably has resultant effects for the lived reality of that child. That child may feel privileged to have been born in such circumstances, but he or she may equally feel they are not valued for themselves but for their biomedical usefulness. If we can extrapolate nothing else from the histories of adoption and of AI, it is that in making decisions on behalf of future children what we choose will have consequences for that child, some of them undoubtedly unforeseeable. What we can foresee from adoption and AI is that as the future child grows his or her identity is bound up in the processes of his or her conception. That identity is affected by any decision made consciously on his or her behalf.

Further, the promises offered by biomedical technologies of the perfect or the perfectible child cannot be confined to the individual couple or their direct offspring. The legitimation in law or policy of the capacity to choose traits or conditions has demonstrable effects on the make-up of a culture or society made possible through the biomedical management of children. Disability activists, amongst others, have understandably been concerned at the denigration of actual people in the selection against (or aborting of pregnancies involving) the more common genetic conditions such as Down's syndrome and achondroplasia and at the potential for anyone with a genetically identifiable condition to be 'selected out' of the population (Shakespeare, 1998).

Debates from bioethics and medical ethics that are based around the bringing into being of children rarely go beyond the hypothetical consideration of a future child, often in terms of its future rights but usually in order to place someone else's rights in competition with or ahead of that possible child; parents, siblings, doctors, society, government. Our aim, here, is not to propose answers but to provoke the rethinking of some of the issues that arise in those debates in the light of the discussions and analyses canvassed in the preceding chapters. Given that the majority of the case studies have centred on developing or under-developed countries, one of the most obvious comments to make is that the kinds of debates around choice and rights that pervade the Global Northern discussion of reproductive technologies simply do not obtain in conditions where the basic means of sustaining life (water, shelter, food) may be uncertain or unmet. And yet, the fact that these debates occur in countries that adhere to and have the power to shape dominant understandings of children and childhood, and the international protocols on reproductive technologies, almost inevitably will have flow on effects for children and childhood of the Global South. We have already seen that women of the Global South are variously providing gametes, gestating and giving birth to children for parents of the Global North (Gupta and Richters, 2008). What remains unexplored is the effect this is having on the existing and future children of the Global Southern women who perform the reproductive labour that makes other people's babies possible. Is the discourse around children and childhood of late modernity, in some odd inverted way, returning to early-modern ideas of child ownership, whereby the child is seen as an economic unit and valued as a commodity?

What matters most in these debates are the ways in which children are conceived of and the disparity between these visions for 'our' children and 'other' children. Even the least reproductive technological intervention, AI to rectify male infertility, has had demonstrable effects on the lived identity of the children born as a result that repeat the lived experiences of adoptees. This observation leads us to the question with which we would like to leave the reader of *Global Childhoods*. Is it not at least equally conceivable that efforts at creating perfectible children, attempts to shape ideal and idealized children, contain within them similar potential outcomes for the identities of the future children who will 'be' and 'become'?

NOTES

1 The first two case studies are an extended and refined reworking of material that has appeared in the *Cambridge Quarterly for Healthcare Ethics*. The authors and publishers would like to express their thanks for the following permissions:

Cregan, K. (2013) 'Who Do You Think You Are?': Childhood and Identity in Australian Healthcare Ethics', *Cambridge Quarterly of Healthcare Ethics*, 22 (3): 232–7. Copyright © 2013 Cambridge University Press. Reprinted with permission.

Cregan, K. (2014) 'Sex Definitions and Gender Practices: An Update from Australia', *Cambridge Quarterly of Healthcare Ethics*, 23 (3): in press. Copyright © 2014 Cambridge University Press. Reprinted with permission.

2 Laws vary from state to state on the age for consensual sexual activity from 16, to 17 and 18, although the last only applies in Queensland, and specifically for anal sex. Defences may also be made for consensual sex at younger ages for a range of reasons. See http://www.aifs.gov.au/cfca/pubs/factsheets/a142090/index.html, accessed 13 October 2013.

3 With thanks to Dr John Waugh of the University of Melbourne for clarifying the legal issues around *Re: Jamie* for me.

4 For more general information and a list of publications arising from the ARC funded History of Adoption Project, see http://www.arts.monash.edu.au/historyofadoption/index.php.

5 In 1978, the boyfriend of one of the authors considered donating and was offered this sum. A raft of tests is required to identify and exclude donations infected with transmissible diseases and some genetic conditions. This payment is based on one clinic that accepts up to five donations, so the total reimbursement can be AU$1500: http://www.spermdonorsaustralia.com.au/how-start, Accessed 13 October 2013.

6 At the time of writing, legal mechanisms to enable the identification of donors prior to 1988 are being enacted, but identification will be at the discretion of the donor: in other words, it is a voluntary register.

7 Again, the dates of legislation vary from state to state, but formal adoption was not possible until the late 1920s. The adoption in Victoria of the father of one of the authors (Kate Cregan) was not formalized until 1930 when he was ten, under the Adoptions of Children Act 1928, although he had been with the people he believed to be his parents from the age of three. See also the History of Adoption Project, http://www.arts.monash.edu.au/historyofadoption/index.php.

8 With thanks to the anonymous reviewer for the suggestion to include both the discussion of abortion and the case of commercial surrogacy in India.

9 For further examples of prosecutions under this act of what appear to have been still-births, see Cregan (2009).

10 And Margaret Sanger in the US, whose programme was tinged with a eugenic enthusiasm.

11   Its prescription was restricted to married women at first, but generally made available to single women from late 1960s onwards.
12   Therapeutic cloning is in use in laboratories, subject to research regulation and compliance with national ethical standards (e.g. in the UK and Australia): that is, the cloning of human embryos for experimental research up to a multicellular stage, *in vitro*, whereby implantation and gestation remains illegal.

Further reading

Ettorre, E. (2002) *Reproductive Genetics, Gender and the Body*. London: Routledge.

Fukuyama, F. (2002) *Our Post-Human Future: Consequences of the Biotechnology Revolution*. London: Profile Books.

Laufer-Ukeles, P. (2013) 'Mothering for money: Regulating commercial intimacy', *Indiana Law Journal*, 88: 1223–79.

Pilnick, A. (2002) *Genetics and Society: An Introduction*. Buckingham: Open University Press.

Singer, P. (1995) *Rethinking Life and Death: The Collapse of our Traditional Ethics*. Oxford: Oxford University Press.

REFERENCES

Abuelas de Plaza de Mayo, n.d. *History of Abuelas de Plaza de Mayo: Children Who Disappeared or Who Were Born in Captivity.* (Website of the Abuelas de Plaza de Mayo) (http://www.abuelas.org.ar/english/history.htm).

Achebe, C. (1985 [1958]) *Things Fall Apart.* London: Heinemann Educational Books.

African Committee of Experts on the Rights and Welfare of the Child (1990) African Charter on the Rights and Welfare of the Child (http://acerwc.org/the-african-charter-on-the-rights-and-welfare-of-the-child-acrwc/).

Ahmad, Y. (2013) 'Understanding target audiences for social marketing programs to prevent child abuse in a Malaysian context'. PhD thesis, Monash University, Melbourne.

Ainsworth, R. (1698) *The Most Natural and Easy Way of Institution.* London: Christopher Hussey.

Alam, E. (2010) 'Cyclone disaster vulnerability and response experiences in coastal Bangladesh', *Disasters*, 34.(4): 931–54.

Alanen, L. (1988) 'Rethinking childhood', *Acta Sociologica*, 31 (1): 53–67.

Alexander, S., Baur, L., Magnusson, R. and Tobin, B. (2009) 'When does severe childhood obesity become a child protection issue?', *Medical Journal of Australia*, 190 (3): 136–9.

Allard, T. (2011) 'Christmas fear: Prosecutors seek three-month term for Bali drug boy', *Sydney Morning Herald*, 11 November (http://www.smh.com.au/world/christmas-fear-prosecutors-seek-threemonth-term-for-bali-drug-boy-20111111–1naq6.html#ixzz1ob8zE1TL).

Altman, V. (2012) 'Globesity: Fat's New Frontier'. *Foreign Correspondent*, ABC TV, 24 July. Transcript at http://www.abc.net.au/foreign/content/2012/s3547707.htm.

Anderson, B. (1983, rev. 1991). *Imagined Communities: Reflections on the Origins and Spread of Nationalism.* London: Verso.

Anderson, G. and Leo, T.W. (2009) 'Child poverty, investment in children and generational mobility: The short and long term well-being of children in urban China after the one child policy', *Review of Income and Wealth*, 55 (Special Issue): 607–29.

Angucia, M., Zeelen, J. and de Jong, G. (2010) 'Researching the reintegration of formerly abducted children in Northern Uganda through Action Research: Experiences and reflections', *Journal of Community and Applied Social Psychology*, 20 (3): 217–31.

Annan, J., Brier, M. and Aryemo, F. (2009) 'From "Rebel" to "Returnee"', *Journal of Adolescent Research*, 24 (6): 639–67.

Anno vicesimo primo Jacobi Regis, 43 &c. *an act to prevent the destroying and murthering of bastard children* (London: printed by Samuel Roycroft, 1680).

Appadurai, A. (2006) *Fear of Small Numbers: An Essay on the Geography of Anger.* Durham, NC: Duke University Press.

Apple, R.D. (1995) 'Constructing mothers: Scientific motherhood in the nineteenth and twentieth centuries', *Social History of Medicine*, 8 (2): 161–78.

Apple, R.D. (2006) *Perfect Motherhood: Science and Childrearing in America*. New Brunswick, NJ: Rutgers University Press.

Archard, D.W. (2011) 'Children's Rights', in E.N. Zalta (ed.), *The Stanford Encyclopedia of Philosophy* (Summer 2011 edition) (http://plato.stanford.edu/archives/sum2011/entries/rights-children/).

Arditti, R. (2007) "'Do you know who you are?" The grandmothers of the Plaza De Mayo', *The Women's Review of Books*, 24 (5): 12.

Ariès, P. (1962) *Centuries of Childhood: A Social History of Family Life*. Tr. Robert Baldick. New York: Alfred A. Knopf.

Ariffin, J. (1995) 'At the crossroads of rapid development: Malaysian society and anomie', *The International Journal of Sociology and Social Policy*, 15 (8–10): 343–71.

Arnold, F. and Fawcett, J.T. (1975) *The Value of Children. A Cross-National Study*. Honolulu: East-West-Center.

Arnold, F., Bulatao, R.A., Buripakdi, C., Chung, B.J., Fawcett, J.T., Iritani, T., Lee, S. J. and Wu, T.S. (1975) *The Value of Children. A Cross-National Study*. Honolulu: East-West-Center.

Arnup, K. (1994) *Education for Motherhood: Advice for Mothers in Twentieth-Century Canada*. Toronto: University of Toronto Press.

Astell, M. (1694) *A Serious Proposal to the Ladies for the Advancement of Their True and Greatest Interest*. London: Wilkin.

Astell, M. (1697) *A Serious Proposal*: Part II. London: Wilkin.

Australian Broadcasting Corporation (2011) 'Post-war effort needed to rebuild Queensland', 13 January (http://www.abc.net.au/news/stories/2011/01/13/3112015.htm).

Australian Broadcasting Corporation (ABC) and British Broadcasting Corporation (BBC) (1992/93) *The Leaving of Liverpool*. Television mini-series.

Australian Electoral Commission (AEC). (2006) *History of the Indigenous Vote*. Canberra: Commonwealth of Australia.

Australian Institute of Health and Welfare (AIHW) (2011) *Adoptions Australia 2010–11*. Canberra: AIHW (http://www.aihw.gov.au/WorkArea/DownloadAsset.aspx?id=10737420773).

Australian Law Reform Commission (ALRC) (2008, rev. 2013) *For Your Information: Australian Privacy Law and Practice*. Canberra: ALRC. (http://www.alrc.gov.au/publications/report-108).

Australian Senate. Legal and Constitutional Affairs References Committee (2012) Detention of Indonesian minors in Australia (http://www.aph.gov.au/Parliamentary_Business/Committees/Senate/Legal_and_Constitutional_Affairs/Completed_inquiries/2010–13/indonesianminors/report/~/media/wopapub/senate/committee/legcon_ctte/completed_inquiries/2010–13/indonesian_minors/report/a01.ashx).

Barns, G. (2011) 'There's a whiff of hypocrisy when it comes to the Bali teen', *Sydney Morning Herald*, 11 October (http://www.smh.com.au/federal-politics/political-opinion/theres-a-whiff-of-hypocrisy-when-it-comes-to-the-bali-teen-20111011–1lhy9.html).

Bar-On, A. (1996) 'Criminalising survival: Images and reality of street children', *Journal of Social Policy*, 26: 63–78.

Barta, T. (1985) 'After the Holocaust: Consciousness of genocide in Australia', *Australian Journal of Politics and History*, 31 (1): 154–61.

Bean, P. and Melville, J. (1989) *Lost Children of the Empire*. London and Sydney: Unwin.

Ben-Arieh, A. (2005) 'Where are the children? Children's role in measuring and monitoring their well-being', *Social Indicators Research*, 74: 573–96.

Beretbitsky, J. (2001) *Like Our Very Own: Adoption and the Changing Culture of Motherhood, 1851–1950*. Kansas City: University of Kansas Press.

Bergquist, K.J.S. (2009) 'Operation Babylift or Babyabduction? Implications of the Hague Convention on the humanitarian evacuation and "rescue" of children', *International Social Work*, 52 (5): 621–33.

Berman, N. (2012) 'Victims of mass rape in the Bosnian genocide'. Photos and Testimonies posted on the website 'We Remember the Bosnian Genocide, 1992–95' (http://bosniangenocide.wordpress.com/2012/05/17/victims-of-mass-rape-in-the-bosnian-genocide-photos-and-testimonies/).

Betancourt, T.S., Brennan, T., Whitfield, T., de la Soudiere, M., Williamson, J. and Gilman, S. (2010a) 'Sierra Leone's former child soldiers: A follow-up study of psychological adjustment and community reintegration', *Child Development*, 81 (4): 1077–95.

Betancourt, T.S., Agnew-Blais, J., Gilman, S., Williams, D.R. and Ellis, B.H. (2010b) 'Past horrors, present struggles: The role of stigma in the association between war experiences and psychosocial adjustment among former child soldiers in Sierra Leone', *Social Science & Medicine*, 70: 17–26.

Betancourt, T.S., Borisova, I., de la Soudière, M. and Williamson, J. (2011) 'Sierra Leone's child soldiers: War exposures and mental health problems by gender', *Journal of Adolescent Health*, 49 (1): 21–8.

Betancourt, T.S., Newnham, E.A., Brennan, R.T., Verdeli, H., Borisova, I., Neugebauer, R., Bass, J. and Bolton, P. (2012) 'Moderators of treatment effectiveness for war-affected youth with depression in Northern Uganda', *Journal of Adolescent Health*, 51 (6): 544–50.

Bhabha, J. (2006) 'The child: What sort of human?' *PMLA*, 121 (5): 1526–35.

bin Mohamad, Mahathir (1991a) *Vision2020* (http://www.isis.org.my/attachments/Vision%202020%20complete.pdf).

bin Mohamad, Mahathir (1991b) 'Malaysia: The way forward' (Vision2020). Text of speech (http://unpan1.un.org/intradoc/groups/public/documents/apcity/unpan003223.pdf).

Bishop, E.C. (1982) *Ponies, Patriots and Powder Monkeys: A History of Children in America's Armed Forces, 1776–1916*. Del Mar, CA: Bishop Press.

Blackwood, E. (1984) 'Sexuality and gender in certain Native American tribes: The case of cross-gender females', *Signs: Journal of Women in Culture and Society*, 10: 27–42.

Bluebond-Langer, M. (1978) *Private Worlds of Dying Children*. Princeton, NJ: Princeton University Press.

Book of Common Prayer, The, ... of the Church of England (1662) London: Collins.

Bordo. S. (2005) 'Adoption', *Hypatia*, 20 (1): 230–6.

Bourdieu, P. (1977 [1972]) *Outline of a Theory of Practice*. Tr. Richard Nice. Cambridge: Cambridge University Press.

Bourdieu, P. (1984 [1979]) *Distinction: A Social Critique of the Judgment of Taste*. Tr. Richard Nice. Cambridge, MA: Harvard University Press.

Bourdieu, P. and Wacquant, L.J.D. (1992) *An Invitation to Reflexive Sociology*. Chicago: University of Chicago Press.

Bowlby, J. (1951) *Maternal Care and Mental Health*. New York and Geneva: WHO.

Bowlby, J. (1953) *Child Care and the Growth of Love*. Harmondsworth: Penguin.

Braidotti, R. (1989) 'Organs without bodies', *Differences: A Journal of Feminist Cultural Studies*, 1: 147–61.

Brandenburg, M.A., Watkins, S.M., Brandenburg, K.L. and Schieche, C. (2007) 'Operation Child-ID: Reunifying children with their legal guardians after Hurricane Katrina', *Disaster*, 31 (3): 277–87.

Brett, R. and Specht, I. (2004) *Young Soldiers: Why They Choose to Fight*. London: Lynne Rienner Publishers.

Briggs, L. (2003) 'Mother, child, race, nation: The visual iconography of rescue and the politics of transnational and transracial adoption', *Gender & History*, 15,(2): 179–200.

Broadbent, A. and Bentley, R. (1997) *Adoptions Australia 1995–96*, Child Welfare Series No. 19. Canberra: AIHW (Cat. No. CWS 3).

Brookfield, T. (2009) 'Maverick mothers and mercy flights: Canada's controversial introduction to international adoption', *Journal of the Canadian Historical Association*, 19 (1): 307–30.

Brooklyn, B. (2012) 'The 1920s: A good decade for women in politics', in R. Francis, P. Grimshaw and A. Standish (eds), *Seizing the Initiative: Australian Women Leaders in Politics, Workplaces and Communities*. Parkville: eScholarship Research Centre, University of Melbourne, pp. 156–70.

Buckingham, D. (2000) *After the Death of Childhood: Growing up in the Age of Electronic Media*. Cambridge: Polity Press.

Bulatao, R.A. (1979) 'On the nature of the transition in the value of children', in J.T. Fawcett (ed.), *Papers of the East-West Population Institute No. 60-A* (March). Honolulu: The East-West Population Institute.

Burton, A. (1991) 'The Feminist quest for identity: British imperial suffragism and "global sisterhood" 1900–1915', *Journal of Women's History*, 3 (2): 46–81.

BWHO (2012) 'Caring after conflict', BWHO 90: 486–7.

Carrington, K. and Pereira, M. (2009) *Offending Youth: Sex, Crime and Justice*. Leichardt, NSW: Federation Press.

Castiglione, B. (2004 [1528]) *The Book of the Courtier*. Tr. G. Bull. Harmondsworth: Penguin.

Catechism of the Catholic Church (http://www.vatican.va/archive/ENG0015/_INDEX.HTM). Accessed 19 December 2013.

Centre for Global Development (2010) Millennial development goals: Progress index scorecard, Malaysia. From the website Millennial Development Index: Gauging Country-Level Achievement (http://www.cgdev.org/userfiles/cms_iframes/mdg_map/scorecards/MY.pdf).

Chadderton, C. and Colley, H. (2012) 'School-to-work transition services: Marginalising "disposable" youth in a state of exception?', *Discourse: Studies in the Cultural Politics of Education*, 33 (3): 329–43.

Chiang-Cruise, R. (2011) 'Surrogacy for Gay Men Forum: Report', 6 November (http://www.gaydadsaustralia.blogspot.com.au/2011_11_01_archive.html).

Child Migrant Trust (2012) (http://www.childmigrantstrust.com/our-work/child-migration-history).

Child Rights Coalition Malaysia (2012) *Status Report on Children's Rights in Malaysia*. Kuala Lumpur: Child Rights Coalition Malaysia (http://www.unicef.org/eapro/Report_on_Childrens_Rights_.pdf).

Children's Defense Fund (2012) (http://www.childrensdefense.org/policy-priorities/ending-child-poverty/president-obama-fy2011-budget-analysis.html).

Choo, C. (1997) 'The role of the Catholic missionaries at Beagle Bay in the removal of Aboriginal children from their families in the Kimberley region from the 1890s', *Aboriginal History*, 21: 14–29.

Choy, C.C. (2007) 'Institutionalizing international adoption: The historical origins of Korean adoption in the United States', in K.J.S. Bergquist, M.E. Vonk and M.D. Feit (eds), *International Korean Adoption: A Fifty-year History of Policy and Practice*. New York: The Haworth Press, pp. 25–42.

Cody, L.F. (2005) *Birthing the Nation: Sex, Science and the Conception of Eighteenth Century Britons*. Oxford: Oxford University Press.

Cohen, H. (1980) *Equal Rights for Children*. Totowa, NJ: Littlefield, Adams, & Co.

Cole, A. and Kmietowicz, Z. (2007) 'BMA rejects call for parents of obese children to be charged with neglect', *British Medical Journal*, 334: 1343.8.

Collier, A. (2007) *The Humble Little Condom: A History*. Amherst, NY: Prometheus Books.

Comacchio, C.R. (1983) *Nations Are Built of Babies: Saving Ontario's Mothers and Children, 1900–1940*. Montreal: McGill-Queen's University Press.

Commission of Inquiry into Abuse of Children in Queensland Institutions (2001) *The Report of the Commission of Inquiry into Abuse of Children in Queensland Institutions* (the Forde Inquiry). Brisbane: Queensland Government Printer.

Commission to Inquire into Child Abuse (2009) Commission Report [Ryan Commission]. Accessed on 28 October 2013 at (http://www.childabusecommission.ie/rpt/pdfs/).

Cooley, C. (1902) *Human Nature and the Social Order*. New York: Scribner.

Cooper, S. (2002) 'The small matter of our humanity', *Arena Magazine*, 59: 34–8.

Crawley, H. (2010) '"No one gives you a chance to say what you are thinking": Finding space for children's agency in the UK asylum system', *Area*, 42 (2): 162–9.

Cregan, K. (2009) *The Theatre of the Body: Staging Death and Embodying Life in Early-Modern England*. Tournhout, Belgium: Brepols.

Cregan, K. (2013) '"Who do you think you are?": Childhood and identity in Australian healthcare ethics', *Cambridge Quarterly of Healthcare Ethics*, 22 (3): 232–7.

Cregan, K. (2014) 'Sex definitions and gender practices: An update from Australia', *Cambridge Quarterly of Healthcare Ethics*, 23 (3): in press.

Cressy, D. (1997) *Birth, Marriage and Death: Ritual, Religion and the Life Cycle in Tudor and Stuart England*. Oxford: Oxford University Press.

Cuthbert, D., Murphy, K. and Quartly, M. (2009) 'Adoption and feminism: Towards framing a feminist response to contemporary developments in adoption', *Australian Feminist Studies*, 24 (62): 395–419.

Cuthbert, D., Spark, C. and Murphy, K. (2009) '"That was then, but this is now": Historical perspectives on intercountry adoption and domestic child adoption in Australian public policy', *Journal of Historical Sociology* 23(3): 427–52.

Cuthbert, D. and Quartly, M. (2012) 'Forced adoption in the national story of apology and regret', *Australian Journal of Politics and History*, 58 (1): 82–96.

Cuthbert, D. and Quartly, M. (2013) 'Forced child removal and the politics of national apologies in Australia', *American Indian Quarterly*, 37 (1–2): 178–202.

Cuthbert, D and Fronek, P. (2014) 'Perfecting adoption: Reflections on the rise of commercial offshore surrogacy and family formation in Australia', in A. Hayes and D. Higgins (eds), *Families, Policy and the Law: Selected Essays on Contemporary Issues for Australia*. Melbourne: Australian Institute of Family Studies.

Daiute, C. (2008) 'The rights of children, the rights of nations: Developmental theory and the politics of children's rights', *Journal of Social Issues*, 64 (4): 701–23.

Dambach, M. and Baglietto, C. (2010) 'Haiti: "Expediting" intercountry adoptions in the aftermath of a natural disaster … preventing future harm.' International Social Services (http://www.iss-ssi.org/2009/assets/files/Haiti%20ISS%20final-%20foreword.pdf).

Daniell, James (2013) 'Sichuan 2008: A disaster on an immense scale', BBC News (Science and Environment) 9 May (http://www.bbc.co.uk/news/science-environment-22398684).

Darroch, R.K., Meyer, P.A. and Singarimbun, M. (1981) 'Two are not enough: The value of children to Javanese and Sudanese parents', *Papers of the East-West Population Institute No. 60-D*. Honolulu: East-West Population Institute.

Davin, D. (1992) 'British women missionaries in nineteenth-century China', *Women's History Review*, 1 (2): 257–71.

de Montesquiou, A. (2007) 'Darfur women describe gang-rape horror', *The Washington Post*, 28 May (http://www.washingtonpost.com/wp-dyn/content/article/2007/05/27/AR2007052700634_pf.html).

Descartes, R. (1641) *Meditations on First Philosophy*. Paris.

Dever, M. (2005) 'Baby talk: the Howard government, families, and the politics of difference', *Hecate*, 31 (2) 45–61.

Dickens, C. (1838) *Oliver Twist*. London: Richard Bentley.

Dickens, C. (1850) *David Copperfield*. London: Bradbury and Evans.

Dickens, C. (1860) *Great Expectations*. London: Chapman and Hall.

Dixit, R.K. (2001) 'Special protection of children during armed conflicts under the Geneva Conventions regime', ISIL Yearbook of International Humanitarian and Refugee Law (http://www.worldlii.org/int/journals/ISILYBIHRL/2001/2.html).

Doyle, J. (2010) *Misguided Kindness: Making the Right Decisions for Children in Emergencies*. London: Save the Children Fund (http://www.crin.org/docs/Misguided_Kindness.pdf).

Dubinsky, K. (2010) *Babies without Borders: Adoption and Migration Across the Americas*. New York: New York Press.

Duden, B. (1991) *The Woman Beneath the Skin*. Tr. T. Dunlap. Cambridge, MA: Harvard University Press.

Duden, B. (1999) 'The fetus on the "farther shore": Toward a history of the unborn', in L.M. Morgan and M.W. Michaels (eds), *Fetal Subject: Feminist Positions*. Philadelphia: University of Pennsylvania, pp. 13–25.

Dumais, S. (2002) 'Cultural capital, gender and school success: the role of habitus', *Sociology of Education*, 75(1): 44–68.

Early Childhood Australia (n.d.) (http://www.earlychildhoodaustralia.org.au/early_childhood_news/submissions/young_children_are our future.html).

Economic Planning Unit, Prime Minister's Department, Malaysia and UN Country Team Malaysia (2010) *Malaysia: The Millennial Development Goals at 2010* (http://www.undp.org.my/files/editor_files/files/Malaysia%20MDGs%20report%20clean%200419.pdf).

Ekirch, A.R. (1990) *Bound for America: The Transportation of British Convicts to the Colonies, 1718–1775*. New York: Oxford University Press.

Elias, N. (2000) *The Civilizing Process: Sociogenetic and Psychogenetic Investigations*. Oxford: Blackwell Publishers.

Elkind, D. (1981) *The Hurried Child: Growing Up Too Fast Too Soon*. Reading, MA: Perseus Publishing.

Enarson, E. and Phillips, B. (2008) 'Invitation to a new feminist disaster sociology: Integrating feminist theory and methods', in B. Phillips and B.H. Morrow (eds), *Women and Disasters: From Theory to Practice*. Bloomington, IL: International Research Committee on Disasters, pp. 41–74.

Ennew, J. (2000) 'Why the Convention is not about street children. Revisiting children's rights: 10 years of the UN Convention on the Rights of the Child', in D. Fottrell (ed.), *Revisiting Children's Rights: 10 Years of the UN Convention on the Rights of the Child*. Dordrecht: Kluwer, pp. 169–82.

Erasmus, D. (1509) *The Praise of Folly*. Tr. John Wilson 1668. Facsimile edition 1958. Ann Arbor, MI: University of Michigan Press.

Erasmus, D. (1517) *The Complaint of Peace*. Basel. J. Froben.

Erasmus, D. (1530) *De civilitate morum puerilium* (A Handbook for Good Manners for Children). Basel: J. Froben.

Ettorre, E. (2002) *Reproductive Genetics, Gender and the Body*. London: Routledge.

Family and Community Development Committee. 2013. *Betrayal of Trust: Inquiry Into The Handling Of Child Abuse By Religious And Other Non-Government Organisations*. 2 Vols. Parliament of Victoria. Melbourne. Accessed at (http://www.parliament.vic.gov.au/images/stories/committees/fcdc/inquiries/57th/Child_Abuse_Inquiry/Report/Inquiry_into_Handling_of_Abuse_Volume_1_FINAL_web.pdf and http://www.parliament.vic.gov.au/images/stories/committees/fcdc/inquiries/57th/Child_Abuse_Inquiry/Report/Inquiry_into_Handling_of_Abuse_Volume_2_FINAL_web.pdf).

Family Court of Australia (1998) *A Question of Right Treatment: The Family Court and Special Medical Procedures for Children, An Introductory Guide for Use in Victoria*. With a foreword by Chief Justice Alastair Nicholson. Melbourne: Family Court of Australia Publications Unit.

Family Court of Australia (2011) Re: Jamie (Special medical procedure) [2011] FamCA 248 (http://www.austlii.edu.au/au/cases/cth/FamCA/2011/248.html).

Family Court of Australia (2013) *Re Jamie* [2013] FamCAFC 110 (http://www.familycourt.gov.au/wps/wcm/connect/FCOA/home/).

Fass, P. (2007) *Children of a New World: Essays in Society, Culture and the World*. New York: New York University Press.

Fausto-Sterling, A. (1993) 'The five sexes: Why male and female are not enough', *The Sciences*, April/May: 20–24.

Federle, K. (1994) 'Rights flow downhill', *International Journal of Children's Rights*, 2: 343–68.

Fitzgerald, H. and Kirk, D. (2009) 'Identity work: Young disabled people, family and sport', *Leisure Studies*, 28 (4): 469–88.

Fitzpatrick. C. (2013) 'The High Court and wrongful conception: Reflections on Melchior', *Hearsay: The Journal of the Bar Association of Queensland*, 64, September (http://www.hearsay.org.au/index.php?option=com_content&task=view&id=415 &Itemid=48).

Folbre, N. (1983) 'Of patriarchy born: The political economy of fertility', *Feminist Studies*, 9 (2): 261–84.

Foucault, M. (1975) *The Birth of the Clinic: An Archaeology of Medical Perception*. Tr. A.M. Sheridan Smith. New York: Random House.

Foucault, M. (1988) *Madness and Civilization: A History of Insanity in the Age of Reason*. Tr. R. Howard. New York: Vintage Books.

Foucault, M. (1991) *Discipline and Punish: The Birth of the Prison*. Tr. A. Sheridan. London: Penguin.

Fraser, A. (1984) *The Weaker Vessel*. London: Methuen.

Freeman, M. (1992) 'Introduction: Rights, Ideology and Children', in M. Freeman and P.E. Veerman (eds), *The Ideologies of Children's Rights*. Dordrecht: Martinus Nijhoff, pp. 3–6.

Fronek, P. (2009) 'Understanding the emergence, diffusion and continuance of inter-country adoption from South Korea to Queensland, Australia'. PhD thesis. University of Queensland.

Fronek, P. (2012) 'Operation Babylift: Advancing intercountry adoption into Australia', *Journal of Australian Studies*, 36 (4): 445–8.

Fronek, P. and Cuthbert, D. (2012a) 'The future of inter-country adoption: A paradigm shift for this century', *International Journal of Social Welfare*, 21 (2): 215–24.

Fronek, P. and Cuthbert, D. (2012b) 'History repeating: Disaster-related intercountry adoption and the psychosocial care of children', *Social Policy and Society*, 11 (3): 429–47.

Fukuyama, F. (2002) *Our Post-Human Future: Consequences of the Biotechnology Revolution*. London: Profile Books.

Furedi, F. (2001) *Paranoid Parenting*. London: Allen Lane.

Furness, D.-L. (2008) 'Australia's poor adoption record', *The Drum,* 14 January (http://www.abc.net.au/unleashed/36942.html).

Furness D.-L. (2013) National Press Club: Adoption Crisis Forum (Speakers Deborra-Lee Furness, Dr Jane Aronson, Dr Karyn Purvis and Louise Voigt), 13 November 2013 (http://www.abc.net.au/news/2013–11–13/national-press-club-adoption-crisis-forum/5089322).

Geyer, M. and Paulmann, J. (2001) *The Mechanics of Internationalism: Culture, Society, and Politics from the 1840s to the First World War*. Oxford: Oxford University Press.

Giddens, A. (1991) *Modernity and Self-Identity: Self and Society in the Late Modern Age*. Cambridge: Polity.

Gill, A. (1998) *Orphans of the Empire: The Shocking Story of Child Migration to Australia*. Milsons Point, NSW: Random House Australia.

Gillard, J. (2013) 'National apology for forced adoptions'. Text of speech delivered in the Australian Parliament on 21 March (http://www.ag.gov.au/About/Forced-AdoptionsApology/Documents/Nationalapologyforforcedadoptions.pdf).

Gillen, J. and Hancock, R. (2006) '"A day in the life": Exploring eating events involving two-year-old girls and their families in diverse communities', *Australian Journal of Early Childhood*, 31 (4): 23–9.

Gillespie, J. (2013) 'Being and becoming: Writing children into planning theory', *Planning Theory*, 12 (1): 64–80.

Goldman, F. (2012) 'Children of the dirty war: A reporter at large', *The New Yorker* 88 (19 March): 5.

Government of India, Ministry of Women and Child Development (2013) National Policy for Children (http://wcd.nic.in/childwelfare/npc2013dtd29042013.pdf).

Grady, H. (2012) 'Should extremely obese children be taken into care?', *The Report*, BBC Radio 4, 16 August (http://www.bbc.co.uk/news/health-19267308).

Greer, F.R. and Apple, R.D. (1991) 'Physicians, formula companies, and advertising: A historical perspective', *American Journal of Diseases of Childhood*, 145 (3): 282–6.

Gupta, J.A. and Richters, A. (2008) 'Embodied subjects and fragmented objects: Women's bodies, assisted reproduction and the right to self-determination', *Journal of Bioethical Inquiry*, 5 (4): 239–49.

Gurr, A. (1987) *Playgoing in Shakespeare's London*. Cambridge: Cambridge University Press.

Gurr, A. (2009) *The Shakespearean Stage: 1574–1642*. Cambridge: Cambridge University Press.

Hagan, K. (2012) 'More time needed for egg, sperm donor decision', *The Age*, October 12 (http://www.theage.com.au/victoria/more-time-needed-for-egg-sperm-donor-decision-20121011–27fp8.html).

Hague Conference on Private International Law (1980) Convention on the Civil Aspects of International Child Abduction (http://www.hcch.net/index_en.php?act=conventions.text&cid=24).

Hague Conference on Private International Law (1993) Convention on Protection of Children and Co-Operation in Respect of Intercountry Adoption (http://www.hcch.net/index_en.php?act=conventions.text&cid=69).

Hague Justice Portal (2010) Haiti earthquake and intercountry adoption of children (http://www.haguejusticeportal.net/index.php?id=11382).

Hailey, J. (1999) 'Ladybirds, missionaries and NGOs. Voluntary organizations and co-operatives in 50 years of development: A historical perspective on future challenges', *Public Administration and Development*, 19: 467–85.

Hallden, G. (2005) 'The metaphors of childhood in preschool context'. Paper presented at Australian Association for Research in Education (AARE) conference, Sydney, 27 November–1 December.

Hammarberg, T. (1990) 'The UN Convention on the Rights of the Child – and how to make it work', *Human Rights Quarterly*, 12: 97–105.

Hamnett, R. (2008) 'Child protection: Child soldiers and the International Criminal Court', *Alternative Law Journal (AltLJ)*, 33 (3): 175–6.

Harris-Short, S. (2001) 'Listening to "the other"? The Convention on the Rights of the Child', *Melbourne Journal of International Law*, 2 (2): 304–47.

Harris-Short, S. (2003) 'International human rights law: Imperialist, inept and ineffective? Cultural relativism and the UN Convention on the Rights of the Child', *Human Rights Quarterly*, 25 (1): 130–81.

Heywood, C. (2001) *A History of Childhood: Children and Childhood in the West from Medieval to Modern Times*. Cambridge: Polity.

Hill, D. (2001) *The Forgotten Children: Fairbridge Farm School and its Betrayal of Australia's Child Migrants*. Sydney: Random House.

Hobbes, T. (1981 [1651]) *Leviathan*. London: Penguin.

Hoffman, L.W. and Hoffman, M.L. (1973) 'The value of children to parents', in J.T. Fawcett (ed.), *Psychological Perspectives on Population*. New York: Basic Books, pp. 19–76.

Hogarth, W. (1968) *Hogarth: The Complete Engravings*. London: Thames & Hudson.

Holland, P. (1985) *What is a Child? Popular Images of Childhood*. London: Virago Press.

Hübinette, T. (2005) *Comforting an Orphaned Nation: Representations of International Adoption and Adopted Koreans in Korean Popular Culture*. PhD thesis, University of Stockholm (http://www.diva-portal.org/smash/record.jsf?pid=diva2:197367).

Hübinette, T. (2006) 'From orphan trains to babylifts: Colonial trafficking, empire building, and social engineering', in J.J. Trenka, C. Oparah and S.Y. Shin (eds), *Outsiders Within: Writing on Transracial Adoption*. Cambridge, MA: South End Press, pp. 139–50.

Hughes, R. (1987) *The Fatal Shore: A History of the Transportation of Convicts to Australia, 1787–1868*. London: Collins Harvill.

Human Fertilisation and Embryology Authority (HFEA) (2012) *Fertility Treatment in 2011*. London: HFEA(http://www.hfea.gov.uk/104.html).

Human Rights and Equal Opportunity Commission (HREOC) (1997) Bringing them Home: Report of the National Inquiry into the Separation of Aboriginal and Torres Strait Islander Children from Their Families 1997. Canberra: HREOC. Commonwealth of Australia (http://www.humanrights.gov.au/publications/bringing-them-home-stolen-children-report-1997).

Innes, M.A. (2001) 'Genocide, ethnocide or hyperbole? Australia's Stolen Generation and Canada's hidden holocaust', *Cultural Survival Quarterly*, 25,(4) (http://www.culturalsurvival.org/publications/cultural-survival-quarterly/genocide-ethnocide-or-hyperbole-australias-stolen).

International Committee of the Red Cross (ICRC) (1977) *Protocol Additional to the Geneva Conventions of 12 August 1949, and relating to the Protection of Victims of International Armed Conflicts (Protocol I)*, 8 June 1977 (http://www.icrc.org/applic/ihl/ihl.nsf/Treaty.xsp?documentId=AA0C5BCBAB5C4A85C12563CD002D6D09&action=openDocument).

International Committee of the Red Cross (ICRC) (2004) *Inter-agency Guiding Principles on Unaccompanied and Separated Children*. Geneva: Central Tracing Agency and Protection Division, International Committee of the Red Cross (http://www.unicef.org/violencestudy/pdf/IAG_UASCs.pdf).

International Labour Organization (ILO) (1973) *Minimum Age Convention* (http://www.ilo.org/dyn/normlex/en/f?p=NORMLEXPUB:12100:0::NO::P12100_ILO_CODE:C138).

International Labour Organization (ILO) (1999) Convention No. 182 on the Worst Forms of Child Labour (http://www.ilo.org/dyn/normlex/en/f?p=NORMLEXPUB:12100:0::NO::P12100_ILO_CODE:C182).

International Social Service and the International Reference Centre for the Rights of Children Deprived of their Family (2009) Earthquake in Haiti: Intercountry Adoption Cases (http://www.iss-ssi.org/2009/assets/files/news/haiti_position%20CIR_ENG.pdf).

International Social Services (ISS) (2010) 'The grey zones of intercountry adoption', Hague Conference on Private International Law, The Hague, The Netherlands.

Iritani, T. (1977) *The Value of Children: Japan*. Honolulu: East-West-Center.

Jacobs, M.D. (2009) *White Mother to a Dark Race: Settler Colonialism, Maternalism, and the Removal of Indigenous Children in the American West and Australia, 1880–1940*. Lincoln: University of Nebraska Press.

James, W. (1983 [1890]) *The Principles of Psychology*. Cambridge, MA: Harvard University Press.

James, A., Jenks, C. and Prout, A. (1998) *Theorizing Childhood*. Cambridge: Polity.

James, A. and Prout, A. (eds) (1990) *Constructing and Reconstructing Childhood: Contemporary Issues in the Sociological Study of Childhood*. London: Falmer Press.

Jenks, C. (1982) *The Sociology of Childhood*. London: Batsford Academic and Educational.

Jenks. C. (1996) *Childhood*. London: Routledge.

Ji, C., Chen, T. and the Working Group on Obesity in China (WGOC) (2013) 'Empirical changes in the prevalence of overweight and obesity among Chinese students from 1985 to 2010 and corresponding preventive strategies', *Biomedical Environmental Science*, 26 (1): 1–12.

Jones, G. (2013) 'The population of Southeast Asia'. Singapore: National University of Singapore, Asia Research Institute Working Paper Series No. 196.

Jones, G.A. (2005) 'Children and development: rights, globalization and poverty', *Progress in Development Studies*, 5 (4): 336–42.

Jonson, B. (1975) *The Complete Poems*. Ed. G. Parfitt. London: Penguin.

Jordans, M., Komproe, I., Tol, W., Ndayisaba, A., Nisabwe, T. and Khort, B. (2012) 'Reintegration of child soldiers in Burundi: A tracer study', *BMC Public Health*, 12: 905–27.

Kanagaratnam, P., Raundalen, M. and Asbjornsen, A. (2005) 'Ideological commitment and posttraumatic stress in former Tamil child soldiers', *Scandinavian Journal of Psychology*, 46: 511–20.

Kashi. J. (1976) 'The Case of the unwanted blessing: Wrongful life', *University of Miami Law Review*, 31: 1409–31.

Kehily, M.J. (2010) 'Childhood in crisis? Tracing the contours of "crisis" and its impact upon contemporary parenting practices', *Media, Culture & Society*, 32 (2): 171–85.

Kempe, C.H., Silverman, F.N., Steele, B.F., Droegemueller, W. and Silver, H.K. (1962) 'The battered-child syndrome', *Journal of American Medical Association*, 18 (1): 17–24.

Kempe, R. and Kempe, C. (1978) *Child Abuse*. Boston, MA: Harvard University Press.

Kershaw, R. and Sacks. J. (2008) *New Lives for Old: The Story of Britain's Child Migrants.* Kew: The National Archives.

Key, E. (1909 [1900]) *The Century of the Child [Barnets århundrade].* Tr. Marian Franzos. London: G.P. Putnam and Sons.

Kidd, R. (2006) *Trustees on Trial: Recovering the Stolen Wages.* Canberra: Aboriginal Studies Press.

King, M.L. (2007) 'Concepts of childhood: What we know and where we might go', *Renaissance Quarterly,* 60: 371–407.

Kjørholt, A.T. (2013) 'Childhood as social investment, rights and the valuing of education', *Children and Society,* 27: 245–57.

Klasen, F., Oettingen, G., Daniels, J., Post, M., Hoyer, C. and Hubertus, A. (2010) 'Posttraumatic resilience in former Ugandan child soldiers', *Child Development,* 81 (4): 1096–114.

Kligman, G. (1998) *The Politics of Duplicity: Controlling Reproduction in Ceauşescu's Romania.* Berkeley, CA: University of California Press.

Korbin, J. (2003) 'Children, childhoods and violence', *Annual Review of Anthropology,* 32: 431–46.

Koven. S. and Michel, S. (eds) (1993) *Mothers of a New World: Maternalist Politics and the Origins of Welfare States.* New York and London: Routledge.

Kunzel, R. (1993) *Fallen Women, Problem Girls: Unmarried Mothers and the Professionalization of Social Work, 1890–1945.* New Haven, CT and London: Yale University Press.

Ladd-Taylor. M. (1994) *Mother-Work: Women, Child Welfare and the State, 1890–1930.* Urbana: University of Illinois Press.

Lancy, D.F. (2008) *The Anthropology of Childhood: Cherubs, Chattels, Changelings.* Cambridge: Cambridge University Press.

Lansdown, G. (1994) 'Children's Rights', in B. Mayall (ed.), *Children's Childhoods: Observed and Experienced.* London: Falmer Press, pp. 33–44.

Larson, E.A. (2004) 'Children's work: The less-considered childhood occupation', *The American Journal of Occupation Therapy,* 58 (4): 369–79.

Laufer-Ukeles, P. (2013) 'Mothering for money: Regulating commercial intimacy', *Indiana Law Journal,* 88: 1223–79.

Laurence, A. (1994) *Women in England, 1500–1760: A Social History.* London: Phoenix.

Law Reform Committee (2012) *Inquiry into Access by Donor-Conceived People to Information about Donors.* Melbourne: Victorian Government Printer.

League of Nations (1924) *Geneva Declaration of the Rights of the Child* (http://www.un-documents.net/gdrc1924.htm).

Lee-Koo, K. (2011) 'Horror and hope: (Re)presenting militarised children in global North-South relations', *Third World Quarterly,* 32 (4): 725–42.

Lengborn, T. (1993) 'Ellen Key (1849–1926)', *Prospects: The Quarterly Review of Comparative Education,* XXIII (3/4): 825–37.

Lewis, J. (1980) *The Politics of Motherhood: Child and Maternal Welfare in England, 1900–1939.* London: Croom Helm.

Lewis, N. (1998) 'Human rights, law and democracy in an unfree world', in T. Evans (ed.), *Human Rights, Fifty Years On: A Reappraisal.* Manchester: Manchester University Press, pp. 77–103.

Linebaugh, P. (1975) 'The Tyburn riot against the surgeons', in D. Hay et al. (eds), *Albion's Fatal Tree: Crime and Society in Eighteenth-Century England*. London: Allen Lane.

Linebaugh, P. (1992) *The London Hanged*. Cambridge: Cambridge University Press.

Lloyd, G. (1984) *The Man of Reason: 'Male' and 'Female' in Western Philosophy*. London: Methuen.

Lloyd, P. (2011) 'Call for judicial inquiry into detention of Indonesian teenagers', 'PM', ABC radio, 15 November (http://www.abc.net.au/pm/content/2011/s3367274.htm).

Loach, J. (Director) (2010) *Oranges and Sunshine*. Written by R., Munro. See Saw Films in conjunction with Sixteen Films.

Locke, J. (1690) *An Essay Concerning Human Understanding*. London.

Locke, J. (1693) *Some Thoughts on Education*. London: A. and J. Churchill.

Lowe, A. (2012) 'Is this child abuse? The courts think so', *The Age,* 12 July (http://www.theage.com.au/victoria/is-this-child-abuse-the-courts-think-so-20120711-21wdb.html#ixzz2aPUQO93T).

Luke, C. (1989) *Pedagogy, Printing, and Protestantism: The Discourse on Childhood*. New York: State University of New York Press.

Lynott, P. and Logue, B. (1993) 'The "Hurried Child": The myth of lost childhood in contemporary American Society', *Sociological Forum*, 8 (3): 471–91.

Macfarlane, A. (1970) *The Family Life of Ralph Josselin, a Seventeenth Century Clergyman*. Cambridge: Cambridge University Press.

Macfarlane, A. (1985) *Marriage and Love in England: Modes of Reproduction: 1300–1840*. Oxford: Blackwell.

Mackenzie, C.G. (1993) 'Demythologising the missionaries: A reassessment of the functions and relationships of Christian missionary education under colonialism', *Comparative Education*, 29 (1): 45–66.

MacKinnon, C.A. (2006) 'Genocide's Sexuality', in *Are Women Human? And Other International Dialogues*. Cambridge, MA: The Belknap Press of Harvard University Press, pp. 209–33.

McCory. S. (2006) 'The International Convention for the Protection of all Persons from Enforced Disappearance', *Human Rights Review*, 7 (3): 545–64.

McMullin, J. (2011) 'Reintegrating young combatants: Do child-centred approaches leave children – and adults – behind?', *Third World Quarterly*, 32,(4): 743–64.

Machel, G. (1996) *Promotion and Protection of the Rights of Children: Impact of Armed Conflict on Children (Machel Report)*. United Nations Department for Policy Coordination and Sustainable Development (DPCSD) (http://srsg.violenceagainstchildren.org/sites/default/files/documents/UN%20Resolutions/A-51–306_Machelstudy.pdf).

Mæland, B. (2010) *Culture, Religion, and the Reintegration of Female Child Soldiers in Northern Uganda*. New York: Peter Lang.

Mail Online (2013) 'Mother wins damages after baby's death' (http://www.dailymail.co.uk/news/article-150538/Mother-wins-damages-babys-death.html).

Makin, B. (1673) *An Essay to Revive the Antient Education of Gentlewomen*. London: J. D.

Malthus, T. (1798) *An Essay on the Principle of Population*. London: J. M. Dent (first Everyman edition 1914, this edition 1973).

Markus, A. (2001) 'Genocide in Australia', *Aboriginal History*, 25: 57–69.

Marshall. A. and McDonald. M. (2001) *The Many-Sided Triangle: Adoption in Australia*. Carlton, Melbourne: Melbourne University Press.

Marten, J. (ed.) (2002) *Children and War: A Historical Anthology*. New York: New York University Press.

Martin, E. (1992) *The Woman in the Body: A Cultural Analysis of Reproduction*. Boston, MA: Beacon Press.

Mead, G.H. (1934) *Mind, Self and Society*. Chicago: University of Chicago Press.

Mekonen, Y. (2010) 'Measuring government performance in realising child rights and child wellbeing: The approach and indicators', *Child Indicators Research*, 3: 205–41.

Merleau-Ponty, M. (2001 [1962]) *Phenomenology of Perception*. Tr. C. Smith. London: Routledge.

Mezmur, B.D. (2009) 'Intercountry adoption as a measure of last resort in Africa: Advancing the rights of a child rather than a right to a child', *International Journal of Human Rights*, 6 (10): 82–103.

Molla, T. (2013) 'Higher education policy reform in Ethiopia: The representation of the problem of gender inequality', *Higher Education Policy*, 26: 193–215.

Montgomery, H. (2009) *An Introduction to Childhood: Anthropological Perspectives on Children's Lives*. Oxford: Wiley-Blackwell.

Morris, M. (2013) 'Cost of raising children jumps by more than 50 per cent since 2007', ABC News, 23 May (http://www.abc.net.au/news/2013–05–23/kids-eat-into-family-budget-like-never-before/4708076).

Murdoch, L. (2011) 'Australia imprisons Indonesian boys', *The Age*, 14 June (http://www.theage.com.au/national/australia-imprisons-indonesian-boys-20110613-1g0il.html).

Murphy, K., Pinto, S. and Cuthbert, D. (2010) '"These infants are future Australians": Making the nation through intercountry adoption', *Journal of Australian Studies*, 34 (2): 141–61.

Muteshi, J. and Sass, J. (2005) *Female Genital Mutilation in Africa: An Analysis of Current Abandonment Approaches*. Nairobi: PATH.

Nag, M., White, B. and Peet, R.C. (1978) 'An anthropological approach to the study of the economic value of children in Java and Nepal', *Current Anthropology*, 19: 293–306.

Nauck, B. (2000) 'The changing value of children – A special action theory of fertility behavior and intergenerational relationships in cross-cultural comparison'. Paper presented at the seminar 'Low fertility, families and public policies', The European Observatory on Family Matters, Seville, September 15–16 (http://www.google.com.au/url?sa=t&rct=j&q=&esrc=s&source=web&cd=1&ved=0CCsQFjAA&url=http%3A%2F%2Fwww.unav.es%2Ficf%2Fmain%2Fdocumentos%2FNauck_Value-of-children.pdf&ei=OOlpUrrIC42hiAeD7YCoBA&usg=AFQjCNHfpFaORG46ylS_c1vR_kYRuI9ScA&bvm=bv.55123115,d.aGc).

Nauck, B. (2007) 'Value of children and the framing of fertility: Results from a cross-cultural comparative survey in 10 societies', *European Sociological Review*, 23 (5): 615–29.

New York Society for the Prevention of Cruelty to Children (2000) New York Society for the Prevention of Cruelty to Children 125 Anniversary, 1975–2000 (http://www.nyspcc.org/nyspcc/history/attachment:en-us.pdf).

Nicolas, G., Schwartz, B. and Pierre, E. (2009) 'Weathering the storms like bamboo: The strengths of Haitians in coping with natural disasters', in A. Kalayjian, D. Eugene and G. Reyes (eds), *International Handbook of Emotional Healing: Ritual and Practices for Resilience After Mass Trauma*. Westport, CT: Greenwood Publishing, pp. 93–106.

Nieuwenhuys, O. (1998) 'Global childhood and the politics of contempt', *Alternatives*, 23: 267–89.

Niner, S., Ahmad, Y. and Cuthbert. D. (2013) 'The "social tsunami": Media coverage of child abuse in Malaysia's English-language newspapers in 2010', *Media, Culture & Society*, 35 (4): 435–53.

Niner, S., Cuthbert, D. and Ahmad, Y. (forthcoming, 2014) 'Good mothers, bad mothers: motherhood, modernity and politics in representations of child abuse in Malaysia's English-language newspapers', *Feminist Media Studies*, 14 (6).

Ozment, S. (1999) *Flesh and Spirit: Private Life in Early Modern Germany*. New York: Penguin.

Pal, S. (2004) 'Do children act as old age security in rural India? Evidence from an analysis of elderly living arrangements', EconWPA: Labor and Demography Working Paper Series No. 0405002 (http://ideas.repec.org/p/wpa/wuwpla/0405002.html).

Palattiyil, G., Blyth, E., Dishva, D. and Balakrishnan, G. (2010) 'Globalization and cross-border reproductive services: Ethical implications of surrogacy in India for social work', *International Social Work*, 53 (5): 686–700.

Palmer, S. (2006) *Toxic Childhood: How Modern Life is Damaging our Children and What We Can Do About It*. London: Orion Publishing Group Limited.

Pande, A. (2009) '"It may be her eggs but it's my blood": Surrogates and everyday forms of kinship in India', *Qualitative Sociology*, 32: 379–97.

Pande, A. (2010) '"At least I am not sleeping with anyone": Resisting the stigma of commercial surrogacy in India', *Feminist Studies*, 36 (2): 292–312.

Pande, A. (2011) 'Transnational commercial surrogacy in India: Gifts for global sisters?', *Reproductive Biomedicine Online*, 23: 618–25.

Paris, M. (2000) *Warrior Nation: Images of War in British Popular Culture, 1850–2000*. London: Reaktion Books.

Parliament of Australia, Senate Community Affairs References Committee (2001) *Lost Innocents: Righting the Record. Report on Child Migration, 30 August 2001*. Canberra: Senate Community Affairs References Committee Secretariat, Commonwealth of Australia.

Parliament of Australia, Senate Community Affairs References Committee (2004) *Forgotten Australians: A Report on Australians Who Experienced Institutional or Out-of-Home Care as Children, 30 August 2004*. Canberra: Community Affairs References Committee, Commonwealth of Australia.

Parliament of Australia, Senate Community Affairs References Committee (2012) *Commonwealth Contribution to Past Forced Adoption Practices* (http://www.aph.gov.au/Parliamentary_Business/Committees/Senate_Committees?url=clac_ctte/comm_contrib_former_forced_adoption/report/index.html).

Parliament of New South Wales, Legislative Council, Standing Committee on Social Issues. (2000) *Releasing the Past: Adoption Practices 1950–1998*. Sydney.

Parliament of Tasmania (1999) *Past Adoption Practices*. Hobart.

Passi, S. (2013) 'Children in Malaysia have been labelled the fattest in the region, but their weight carries a greater burden than just their size', *Southeast Asia Globe*, 11 April (http://sea-globe.com/obese-children-malaysia/).

Payne, R. (2012) '"Extraordinary survivors" or "ordinary lives"? Embracing "everyday agency" in social interventions with child-headed households in Zambia', *Children's Geographies*, 10 (4): 399–411.

Pedersen, J. and Sommerfelt, T. (2007) 'Studying children in armed conflict: Data production, social indicators and analysis', *Social Indicators Research*, 84,(3): 251–69.

Piaget, J. (1972) *Psychology and Epistemology* (1927). Tr. P. Wells. Harmondsworth: Penguin.

Pienaar, K. (2013) 'The making of HIV/AIDS in South Africa: An ontological politics of disease'. PhD thesis, Monash University.

Pilnick, A. (2002) *Genetics and Society: An Introduction*. Buckingham: Open University Press.

Pimlott-Wilson, H. (2011) 'The role of familial habitus in shaping children's views of their future employment', *Children's Geographies*, 9 (1): 111–18.

Poe, A. (2010) 'UNICEF's effective attack on intercountry adoption', *Washington Post*, 30 November (http:// communities.washingtontimes.com/neighborhood/red-thread-adoptive- family-forum/2010/nov/30/unicefs-effective-attack-inter-country-adoption/).

Pollock, L. (1983) *Forgotten Children: Parent-Child Relations from 1500–1900*. Cambridge: Cambridge University Press.

Pollock, L. (1987) *Lasting Relationships: Parents and Children over Three Centuries*. Hanover, NH: University Press of New England.

Postman, N. (1982) *The Disappearance of Childhood*. New York: Delacorte Press.

Pringle, R. (2004) 'Adoption in Britain: Reflexive modernity?', *Australian Feminist Studies*, 19 (44): 225–40.

Pupavac, V. (1998) 'The infantilisation of the south and the UN Convention on the Rights of the Child', *Human Rights Law Review*, 3 (2): 3–8.

Pupavac, V. (2001) 'Misanthropy without borders: The international children's rights regime', *Disasters*, 25 (2): 95–112.

Quartly. M. (2010) 'The rights of the child in global perspective', *Children Australia*, 35 (2): 38–42.

Quartly, M., Swain, S. and Cuthbert, C. (2013) *The Market in Babies: Stories of Australian Adoption*. Clayton, Victoria: Monash University Publishing.

Queensland Law Reform Commission (2003) *Damages in an Action for Wrongful Death*. Brisbane: Queensland Law Reform Commission.

Qvortrup, J. (1991) *Childhood as a Special Phenomenon: An Introduction to a Series of National Reports*. Vienna: European Centre.

Qvortrup, J., Bardy, M., Sgritta, G. and Wintersberger, H. (eds) (1994) *Childhood Matters: Social Theory, Practice and Politics*. Aldershot: Avebury. Press.

Radio Free Asia (2011) 'Quake parent protest in Sichuan', 1 January (http://www.rfa.org./english/news/china/parents-0111201215185.html).

Ramesh, A. (2001) 'UN Convention on Rights of the Child: Inherent weaknesses', *Economic and Political Weekly*, 36 (22), June 2–8: 1948–50.

Ramusack, B. (1990) 'Cultural missionaries, maternal imperialists, feminist allies: British women activists in India, 1865–1945', *Women's Studies International Forum*, 13 (4): 309–21.

Riggs, D.W. and Due, C. (2010) 'Gay men, race privilege and surrogacy in India', *Outskirts: Feminisms Along the Edge 22* (http://www.outskirts.arts.uwa.edu.au/volumes/volume-22/riggs).

Robertson, S. and Savulescu, J. (2001) 'Is there a case in favour of predictive genetic testing in young children?' *Bioethics*, 15 (1): 26–49.

Roberts, Elizabeth (1985) *A Woman's Place: An Oral History of Working Class Women 1890–1940*. Oxford: Blackwell.

Robinson, M.J. (2007) 'The News Interest Index, 1986–2007: Two decades of American news preferences. Part 1: Analyzing what news the public follows – and doesn't follow', Pew Research Center (http://pewresearch.org/files/old-assets/pdf/NewsInterest1986–2007.pdf).

Robotham, J. (2012) 'Child sex-change ruling fails to solve the confusion', *The Age*, 11 February (http://www.theage.com.au/national/child-sexchange-ruling-fails-to-solve-the-confusion-20120210–1sjt6.html?skin=text-only).

Roose, R. and Bouverne-De Bie, M. (2007) 'Do children have rights or do their rights have to be realised? The United Nations Convention on the Rights of the Child as a frame of reference for pedagogical action', *Journal of Philosophy of Education*, 41 (3): 431–43.

Rose, J. (1992) *Marie Stopes and the Sexual Revolution*. London: Faber and Faber.

Rotabi, K.S. and Bergquist, K.J.S. (2010) 'Vulnerable children in the aftermath of Haiti's earthquake of 2010: A call for sound policy and processes to prevent international child sales and theft', *Journal of Global Social Work Practice*, 3 (1) (http://www.globalsocialwork.org/vol3no1/Rotabi.html).

Rousseau, J.J. (1762) *Emile*. Paris: S.I.

Rudd, K. (2008) Text of the Apology to the Stolen Generations (http://www.dfat.gov.au/indigenous/apology-to-stolen-enerations/national_apology.html).

Rudd, K. (2009) Transcript of Apology to the Forgotten Australians and former child migrants, Great Hall, Parliament House, 16 November (http://pandora.nla.gov.au/pan/110625/20091116–1801/www.pm.gov.au/node/6321.html).

Rush, E and La Nauze, A. (2006) *Corporate Paedophilia: Sexualisation of Children in Australia*. The Australia Institute, Discussion Paper 60 (http://www.tai.org.au/documents/dp_fulltext/DP90.pdf).

Russel, R. (1698) *A Little Book for Children*. London: J. Blare.

Ryan, P.J. (2008) 'How new is the "new" social study of childhood? The myth of a paradigm shift', *Journal of Interdisciplinary History*. XXXVIII, (4): 553–76.

Said, E. (1978) *Orientalism*. New York: Pantheon Books.

Sam, D.L. (2001) 'Value of children: Effects of globalization on fertility behavior and child-rearing practices in Ghana', *Institute of African Studies Research Review*, 17 (2): 5–16.

Schabas, W.A. (1996) 'Reservations to the Convention on the Rights of the Child', *Human Rights Quarterly*, 18 (2): 472–91.

Schabas, W.A. (2000) *Genocide in International Law: The Crime of Crimes.* Cambridge: Cambridge University Press.

Schiebinger, L. (1993) *Nature's Body: Sexual Politics and the Making of Modern Science.* London: Pandora.

Scholtz, C. (2006) *Negotiating Claims: The Emergence of Indigenous Land Claim Negotiation Policies in Australia, Canada, New Zealand, and the United States.* New York and London: Routledge.

Scott, D. and Swain, S. (2002) *Confronting Cruelty: Historical Perspectives on Child Protection.* Melbourne: Melbourne University Press.

Sellick, P. (2001) 'Responding to children affected by armed conflict: A case study of Save the Children Fund (1919–1999).' PhD thesis, Bradford University.

Selman, P. (2011) 'Intercountry adoption after the Haiti earthquake: Rescue or robbery?' *Adoption and Fostering*, 35 (4): 41–9.

Selman, P. (2012) 'The global decline of intercountry adoption. What lies ahead?' *Social Policy and Society*, 11 (3): 381–97.

Serrallier, I. (1956) *The Silver Sword.* London: Jonathan Cape.

Shakespeare, T. (ed.) (1998) *The Disability Studies Reader: Social Sciences Perspectives.* London: Cassell.

Shakespeare, W. ([c. 1599] 2009) *As You Like It.* Cambridge: Cambridge University Press.

Shepler, S. (2005) 'The rites of the child: Global discourses of youth and reintegrating child soldiers in Sierra Leone', *Journal of Human Rights*, 4 (2): 197–211.

Shorter, E. (1975) *The Making of the Modern Family.* New York: Basic Books.

Sikkink, K. (2008) 'From pariah state to global protagonist: Argentina and the struggle for international human rights', *Latin American Politics*, 7 (3): 545–66.

Sim, C. (2013) 'Childhood obesity cause for concern', *New Straits Times*, 11 April. (http://www.nst.com.my/opinion/columnist/childhood-obesity-cause-for-concern-1.252814#ixzz2ZmAM31Mm).

Singer, P. (1993) *Practical Ethics* (2nd edn). Cambridge: Cambridge University Press.

Singer, P. (1995) *Rethinking Life and Death: The Collapse of our Traditional Ethics.* Oxford: Oxford University Press.

Smart, C. (1989) *Feminism and the Power of Law.* London: Routledge.

Smolin, D.M. (2007) 'Intercountry adoption and poverty: A human rights analysis', *Capital University Law Review*, 36: 413–53.

Smolin, D.M. (2012) 'Of orphans and adoption, parents and the poor, exploitation and rescue: A scriptural and theological critique of the evangelical Christian adoption and orphan care movement', *Regent Journal of International Law*, 8 (2): 267–324.

Stanley, F. (2005) 'Future human capital', *Australian Life Scientist*, March–April: 24.

Stephens, S. (1995) 'Introduction: Children and the politics of culture in "late capitalism"', in S. Stephens (ed.), *Children and the Politics of Culture.* Princeton, NJ: Princeton University Press, pp. 3–48.

Stern, D., Smith, S. and Doolittle, F. (1975) 'How children used to work', *Law and Contemporary Problems*, 39 (3): 93–117.

Stewart, C., Cockburn, T., Madden, B., Callaghan S. and Ryan, C.J. (2012) 'Leave to intervene in cases of gender identity disorder; normative causation; financial harms and involuntary treatment; and the right to be protected from suicide', *Journal of Bioethical Inquiry*, 9: 235–42.

Stivens, M. (1998a) 'Theorising gender, power and modernity in affluent Asia', in K. Sen and M. Stivens (eds), *Gender and Power in Affluent Asia*. London: Routledge, pp. 1–34.

Stivens, M. (1998b) 'Sex, gender and the making of the new Malay middle-classes', in K. Sen and M. Stivens (eds), *Gender and Power in Affluent Asia*. London: Routledge, pp. 87–126.

Stivens, M. (1998c) 'Modernising the Malay mother', in K. Ram and M. Jolly (eds), *Maternities and Modernities: Colonial and Postcolonial Experiences in Asia and the Pacific*. Cambridge: Cambridge University Press, pp. 50–80.

Stone, L. (1979) *The Family, Sex and Marriage in England, 1500–1800* (abridged edition). Harmondsworth: Penguin.

Strasser, M. (1999) 'Wrongful life, wrongful birth, wrongful death, and the right to refuse treatment: Can reasonable jurisdictions recognize all but one?' *Missouri Law Review*, 64: 29–75.

Sudworth, J. (2013) 'Questions linger after deadly Sichuan quake', BBC News, 10 May (http://www.bbc.co.uk/news/world-asia-china-22476977).

Swain, S. (2012) 'Market forces: Defining the adoptable child, 1860–1940', *Social Policy and Society*, 11 (3): 399–414.

Sydney Morning Herald (SMH) (2011) 'Sexual abuse claim on boat boy', 14 November (http://www.smh.com.au/national/sexual-abuse-claim-on-boat-boy-20111113–1ndw8.html).

Taylor, K.H. (2008) 'Hawaiian history revisited: Illuminating silenced perspectives and Hawaiian resistance in the writings of American missionaries', *Swedish Missiological Themes [Svensk Missions Tidskrift]*, 96 (2): 105–26.

Teman, E. (2010) *Birthing a Mother: The Surrogate Body and the Pregnant Self*. Berkeley, CA: University of California Press.

The Hindu (2011) 'Compensation for death of child in accidents should not be a pittance: Tribunals must determine the sum rationally and judiciously', 26 August (http://www.thehindu.com/news/national/compensation-for-death-of-child-in-accidents-should-not-be-a-pittance/article2397558.ece).

The Hindu (2013a) 'Tribunal awards compensation for child's death', 2 September (http://www.thehindu.com/news/cities/Kochi/tribunal-awards-compensation-for-childs-death/article5083024.ece).

The Hindu (2013b) 'Gaps in surrogacy bill', 27 October (http://www.thehindu.com/features/metroplus/society/gaps-in-surrogacy-bill/article5276062.ece). Accessed 20 December 2013.

The Orphan Foundation (2008) Website (http://www.theorphanfoundation.org/about_the_foundation.htm).

Thoilliez, B. (2011) 'How to grow up happy: An exploratory study on the meaning of happiness from children's voices', *Child Indicators Research*, 4: 323–51.

Thorne, B. (2003) 'Editorial: Children and the 2003 war in Iraq', *Childhood*, 10: 259–63.

Threadgold, S. and Nilan, P. (2009) 'Reflexivity of contemporary youth, risk and cultural capital', *Current Sociology*, 57: 47–68.

Threadgold, T. (2002) *Feminist Poetics: Histories, Performances*. London: Routledge.

Tomanovic, S. (2004) 'Family habitus as the cultural context for childhood', *Childhood*, 11 (3): 339–60.

UN (1948) *Universal Declaration of Human Rights* (UNUDHR). (http://www.un.org/en/documents/udhr/).

UN (1959) *Declaration of the Rights of the Child* (UNDRC) (http://www.unicef.org/lac/spbarbados/Legal/global/General/declaration_child1959.pdf).

UN (1989) *Convention on the Rights of the Child* (UNCRC) (http://www2.ohchr.org/english/law/crc.htm).

UN (2000a) *Millennial Development Goals* (http://www.un.org/en/events/pastevents/millennium_summit.shtml).

UN (2000b) *Optional Protocols to the Convention on the Rights of the Child on the Sale of Children, Child Prostitution and Child Pornography* (http://www.ohchr.org/EN/ProfessionalInterest/Pages/OPSCCRC.aspx).

UN (2000c) *Optional Protocol on the Involvement of Children in Armed Conflict* (http://www.ohchr.org/EN/ProfessionalInterest/Pages/OPACCRC.aspx).

UN (n.d.) *Briefing Paper: Ending Violence Against Women and Girls* (http://www.un.org/en/globalissues/briefingpapers/endviol/index.shtml).

UNHCR (1994) *Joint Statement on the Evacuation of Unaccompanied Children from Rwanda* (http://www.refworld.org/docid/3ae6b31ef.html).

UNICEF (2003) *Our History* (http://www.unicef.org/about/who/index_history.html).

UNICEF (2006) *Saving Children from the Tragedy of Landmines* (http://www.unicef.org/media/media_32034.html).

UNICEF (2007a) *Child Poverty in Perspective: An Overview of Child Well-Being in Rich Countries* (http://www.unicef-irc.org/publications/pdf/rc7_eng.pdf).

UNICEF (2007b) *Paris Principles and Guidelines on Children Associated with Armed Forces or Armed Groups 2007* (http://www.unicef.org/protection/files/Paris_Principles_EN.pdf).

UNICEF (2007c) *Protecting the World's Children: Impact of the Convention on the Rights of the Child in Diverse Legal Systems*. Cambridge and New York: Cambridge University Press and UNICEF.

UNICEF (2010) *Country Office Annual Report for Malaysia (EAPRO)* (http://www.unicef.org/malaysia/Malaysia_Annual_Report_2010_Final_Edit_260811.pdf).

UNICEF (2012a) *Australian Government Reports to the UN* (http://www.unicef.org.au/Discover/Australia-s-children/Child-Rights-Taskforce/Australian-Government-reports-to-UN.aspx).

UNICEF (2012b) *Orphans* (http://www.unicef.org/media/media_45279.html).

UNICEF (2013) *International Day of the Girl Child* (http://www.unicef.org/gender/gender_66021.html).

Uppard, S. (2003) 'Child soldiers and children associated with fighting forces', *Medicine, Conflict and Survival*, 19 (2): 121–7.

Uprichard, E. (2008) 'Children as "being and becomings": Children, childhood and temporality', *Children & Society*, 22: 303–13.

Van Emden, R. (2005) *Boy Soldiers of the Great War*. London: Headline Books.

Varness, T., Allen, D., Carrel, A. and Fost, N. (2009) 'Childhood obesity and medical neglect', *Pediatrics*, 123: 399.

Vicedo, M. (2011) 'The social nature of the mother's tie to her child: John Bowlby's theory of attachment in post-war America', *British Journal for the History of Science*, 44 (3): 401–26.

Vindevogel, S., De Schryver, M., Broekaert, E. and Derluyn, I. (2013) 'Challenges faced by former child soldiers in the aftermath of war in Uganda', *Journal of Adolescent Health*, 52: 757–64.

Vitus, K. (2010) 'Waiting time: The de-subjectification of children in Danish asylum centres', *Childhood*, 17 (1): 26–42.

Voigt, K. (2012) 'Childhood obesity and restrictions of parental liberty: A response to "paternalism, obesity, and tolerable levels of risk"', *Democracy and Education*, 20 (1), Article 8. (http://democracyeducationjournal.org/home/vol20/iss1/8).

Wall to Wall and BBC 1 (2004–present) *Who Do You Think You Are?*

Warren, A. (1998) 'The orphan train', *The Washington Post*, November (http://www.washingtonpost.com/wp-srv/national/horizon/nov98/orphan.htm).

Welch, I. (2005) 'Women's work for women: Women missionaries in 19th century China'. Paper presented to the Eighth Women in Asia Conference, Women's Caucus of the Asian Studies Association of Australia. University of Technology Sydney, 26–28 September.

Whitelaw, A. (2012) 'Hundreds pay for overseas surrogacy', *The Age*, 3 June (http://www.theage.com.au/opinion/political-news/hundreds-pay-for-overseas-surrogacy-20120602–1zp1u.html).

Winn, M. (1983) *Children Without Childhood: Growing Up Too Fast in the World of Sex and Drugs.* New York: Pantheon.

WHO (2012) *Population-based Approaches to Child Obesity Prevention* (http://apps.who.int/iris/bitstream/10665/80149/1/9789241504782_eng.pdf).

WHO (2013) *Media Notes: WHO Issues Guidance on Emerging Double Threat of Childhood Obesity and Under Nutrition in Low- and Middle-income Countries* (http://www.who.int/mediacentre/news/notes/2013/obesity_undernutrition_20130605/en/).

Wyness, M. (2006) *Childhood and Society: An Introduction to the Sociology of Childhood.* New York: Palgrave.

Yu, Z., Han, S., Chu, J., Xu, Z., Zhu, C. and Guo, X. (2012) 'Trends in overweight and obesity among children and adolescents in China from 1981 to 2010: A meta-analysis', *PLoS One*, 7 (12): e51949.

Zelizer, V. (1985) *Pricing the Priceless Child: The Changing Social Value of Children.* Princeton, NJ: Princeton University Press.

Zigler, E. (1975) 'The Vietnamese children's airlift: Too little and too late' (http://eric.ed.gov/ERICWebPortal/custom/portlets/recordDetails/detailmini.jsp?_nfpb=true&ERICExtSearch_SearchValue_0=ED119827&ERICExtSearch_SearchType_0=no&accno=ED119827). Accessed 13 March 2010.

Zucker, K.J. (2005) 'Gender Identity Disorder in children and adolescents', *Annual Review of Clinical Psychology*, 1: 467–92.

INDEX

A

abolition of slavery, 123, 126
Abolition of Slavery Act (1833), 123
abortion, 152, 154–5, 159
Abuelas de Plaza de Mayo (grandmothers of the Plaza de Mayo) (Argentina), 120–21
abuse of children, 37, 40, 48, 49, 57, 77, 80, 84, 105, 107, 113, 115, 144
  and obesity, 51
  and the modern State, 115–19, 123, 125–6, 144
  see also child soldiers; First International Congress on Child Abuse and Neglect (1976); forced child migration; government inquiries and reports; institutionalized children; International Society for the Prevention of Child Abuse and Neglect; Malaysia; NYSPCC; regulation of child abuse; sexual abuse/exploitation of children
Act to prevent the destroying and murthering of bastard children (1680), 24–6
Addams, Jane, 41
adoption, 6, 83, 95, 96, 122, 123, 139–43, 161–2, 163*n*. 7
  as child rescue, 93, 95–102 *passim*
  'closed', 141, 153–4, 157–8
  and family formation, 99, 101, 139–43, 153, 154
  forced, 115, 120, 121–2
  as ideocide, 120–22
  infant and child, 120, 140–43, 152, 154
  inter-country (ICA), 16, 36, 57, 93, 95–6, 97, 99–102, 111, 115, 126, 143
  'open', 154, 157
  see also Argentina; Australia; Conventions; government inquiries and reports: Australia; orphans/unaccompanied children
affective attachment to children/infants, 22, 23, 24–27, 95, 96, 129, 133, 141, 142, 143
  see also child and parent bonding
Africa
  forced child migration, 122, 124
  children in war zones, 94, 106, 118
  as colonies, 8, 44, 122
  FGM, 71–2
  habitus, 92*n*. 1
  HIV/AIDS, 95, 97
  missionary activity, 16, 43
  and slavery, 122
  and UNCRC, 69–71

Africa *cont.*
  see also ACRWC; child soldiers; children and HIV/AIDS; Darfur; Democratic Republic of Congo; FGM; Northern Uganda; Rwanda; Sierra Leone; South Africa
African Charter on the Rights and Welfare of the Child (ACRWC) (1990), 56, 57, 69–71
African Committee of Experts on the Rights and Welfare of the Child (ACERWC), 70
African Union, 56
age of consent, 6, 13, 18*nn*. 3, 4, 25, 45, 103, 104, 149–52; *see also* Re Jamie
agentic child, *see* child agency
'ages of man', 21–2; *see also* developmentalism; life stages; Shakespeare
Ainsworth, Robert, 27, 28, 29, 31; *The Most Natural and Easy Way of Institution* (1698), 27, 28–9
Alanen, Leena, 12, 14, 23, 78, 80; 'Rethinking Childhood' (1988), 12
American Society for the Prevention of Cruelty to Animals (ASPCA), 40
Andersen, Hans Christian, 58; *Little Match Girl* (1845), 58
Anderson, Benedict, 116; *Imagined Communities* (1983), 116
Angucia, Margaret, et al., 107
Annales School, 15; *see also* Ariès, Philippe
Annan, Jeannie, et al., 107, 108
Anne of Green Gables (1908), 140
Appadurai, Arjun, 117, 120
Argentina, 114, 119–22, 125
  see also Abuelas de Plaza de Mayo; disappeared children (Argentina); ideocide
Ariès, Philippe, 15, 20–21, 22, 24, 32, 139
  Centuries of Childhood: A Social History of Family Life (1962), 20–21
artificial insemination (AI), 148, 149, 153–4, 161–2
  see also sperm donation
Asia, 8, 16, 43, 49, 94, 132
  see also South Asia, South-East Asia, individual countries by name
Assisted Reproductive Technologies (ARTs), 143, 157, 159, 160
  see also artificial insemination; surrogacy (gestational); IVF; sperm donation
Assisted Reproductive Technologies (Regulation) Bill (2013) (India), 156
Astell, Mary, 29